A HISTORY OF THE MARRANOS

HARPER TORCHBOOKS ❦ The Temple Library

Published in association with
The Jewish Publication Society of America

A HISTORY OF THE MARRANOS

Cecil Roth

HARPER TORCHBOOKS ⧫ The Temple Library
Harper & Row, Publishers
New York

CECIL ROTH

Born in England in 1899, Cecil Roth has been reader in Jewish studies at Oxford University since 1939. Among Professor Roth's numerous works are: HISTORY OF THE JEWS IN ENGLAND, HISTORY OF THE JEWS OF ITALY, A SHORT HISTORY OF THE JEWISH PEOPLE, THE HOUSE OF NASI, A LIFE OF MENASSEH BEN ISRAEL, THE JEWS IN THE RENAISSANCE (TB/834), *and many monographs on the history of the Jews of England, Italy, and Spain.*

FOR

IRENE

6. VI. 31

TABLE OF CONTENTS

LIST OF ILLUSTRATIONS

FOREWORD

I have the great honor to present to the Reader, in the following pages, what may fairly be described as the most romantic episode in all history. As long ago as 1894, Joseph Jacobs indicated "one of the great desiderata of Jewish literature — a . . . history of the Marranos or secret Jews of the Peninsula." That lacuna is here filled, for the first time.

It is hoped that the interest in it will not be confined to the Jew. The record of the "New Christians" is an inseparable part of the stories of Spain and Portugal, at the period of their greatest brilliance. It constitutes a fundamental, though tragic, chapter of ecclesiastical history. It touches on the life of every country of Western Europe in the seventeenth and eighteenth centuries, at crucial points. It is the background to the biography of countless persons of the highest eminence, both in the Peninsula and abroad. It had important reactions in politics, literature, science, and commerce. Throughout, it received lurid illumination from the flares of the autos-da-fè. Each of these aspects deserves a whole volume. I stand astonished at my own moderation in having compressed them into chapters, or even paragraphs.

It is not, however, its importance which gives the history of the Marranos its appeal, but its incredible romance. The submerged life which blossomed out at intervals into such exotic flowers; the unique devotion which could transmit the ancestral ideals unsullied, from generation to generation, despite the Inquisition and its horrors; the figures of rare heroism which every now and again emerged to burst upon the world; the extraordinary climax in our own days—all combine to make a story unparalleled in history for sheer dramatic appeal. If the volume does not live up to the expectations which this description may have aroused, it is the fault of the author, and not of his subject.

London, June 1931.

FOREWORD TO THE THIRD EDITION

The events that have taken place since this work was first published have changed the entire perspective of Jewish history. Pathetic parallels to Marrano history were known in Europe during the tragic period of Nazi oppression. Moreover, very important research has been done recently on the early days of crypto-Judaism in Spain, on the origins of the Inquisition, and on various aspects of the history of the Marrano Diaspora. Years have diminished, though it is to be hoped not entirely obliterated, the author's high romanticism of a quarter-century ago. Nevertheless, in this new edition it has been thought best to leave this work basically as it first emerged, with the correction only of major errors of fact.

Oxford, July 1958

"Contra la verdad no ay fuerça."

Isaac Aboab, 1605–1693

First Rabbi in America: Pernambuco, Brazil, 1642–1654.

Haham of Sephardic Community of Amsterdam, 1626–1642; 1654–1693.

INTRODUCTORY

The Antecedents of Crypto-Judaism

CRYPTO-JUDAISM, in one form or another, is as old as
the Jew himself. In Hellenistic days, some weaklings
endeavored to conceal their origin in order to escape
ridicule when participating in the athletic exercises.
Under the Roman rule, there was wide-spread subterfuge
to avoid the payment of the special Jewish tax, the *Fiscus
Judaicus*, which had been instituted after the fall of
Jerusalem; and the historian Suetonius gives a vivid
account of the indignities inflicted upon an old man of
ninety in order to discover whether or no he was a Jew.

The official attitude, as crystallized in the dicta of the
Rabbis, was plain. A man might, and should, save his
life if the occasion demanded it, by any means—murder,
incest, or idolatry alone excepted. Only when the alternative was to commit one of these three offences against
divine and human law was death to be preferred. However, this aphorism applied exclusively to cases where
positive action was demanded: the concealment of
Judaism, unaccompanied by any formality, was another
matter. Rigorists indeed insisted that a man should
refuse even to make a change in his garments, if it were
demanded as a measure of religious oppression. Yet
such stern devotion to principle could not be expected
from all persons. Traditional Jewish law, in fact, made
special provision for cases when observance of ceremonial
practices became impossible because of compulsion

1

(*Ones*), or in time of persecution (*She'at ha-Shemad*). The theory was put to the test in late Talmudic times, in the fifth century, during the Zoroastrian persecution in Persia. This consisted, however, in enforced neglect of traditional observance rather than positive conformity to the dominant religion. Judaism was thus driven to some extent underground, regaining complete freedom only some years later.

A fresh phase in Jewish life had been entered with the growth of Christianity, which became supreme in Europe in the fourth century. The new faith, which claimed exclusive possession of religious truth, inevitably regarded proselytization as one of the greatest of moral obligations. The Church, indeed, officially condemned conversion by forcible means. It specifically disapproved of the application of such methods even to the laudable object of saving the souls of Jews. Baptisms so effected were generally held to be invalid. Thus Pope Gregory the Great (590–604), who set the example subsequently followed by the Catholic Church in its policy towards the stubborn adherents of the older faith, repeatedly condemned forcible conversions, although he eagerly welcomed proselytes secured by any other means. In this attitude, he was faithfully imitated by the majority of his successors. However, the papal injunctions were not infrequently disregarded. The theory, that conversion by force was uncanonical, was not indeed disputed. Instead, the Jews would be threatened with death or with expulsion, it being clearly understood that baptism would save them. It occasionally happened that they bowed to necessity, their acceptance of Christianity under such circumstances being regarded as spontaneous. There had been a famous case of mass forced conversion at Magona (Mahon) in the island of Minorca, under the auspices of Bishop Severus, in 418. A similar episode took place at Clermont, in Auvergne, on the morrow of Ascension Day, 576; and, notwithstanding the intense disapproval of Pope Gregory, the example was followed elsewhere in France in the ensuing period. Fired by this example, in 629 King Dagobert ordered all the Jews of the country to accept baptism under pain of banishment. Almost immediately afterwards, his measure was imitated in the kingdom of Lombardy.

It is self-evident that conversions effected by such means must be insincere. Inevitably, the victims continued wherever possible to practice Judaism in secret, and took the first opportunity of reverting to their ancestral faith; there was a notable instance at the time of the persecutions in the Byzantine Empire, under Leo the Isaurian, in 723. The Church itself was fully conscious of this, doing all it could to prevent the continuance of relations between professing Jews and their renegade brethren, by whatever means their conversion had been secured. The Rabbis on their side were not behind-hand in recognizing the fact. They called these reluctant apostates *anusim* ("forced ones"), treating them very differently from deliberate renegades. One of the earliest utterances of rabbinic scholarship in Europe is a regulation of Gershom of Mayence, "The Light of the Exile" (c. 1000), prohibiting unkind treatment of forced converts who returned to the Jewish fold. His own son, indeed, had been among the victims of persecution; and, though he died a professing Christian, was mourned by his father just as if he had remained a steadfast Jew. In the service of the Synagogue a special prayer found its way imploring the divine protection for all the House of Israel and the "Forced Ones" of Israel who were in peril by land and sea, not differentiating between the two categories. When the age of martyrdom began for medieval Jewry, with the Rhineland massacres at the period of the first Crusade (1096), many persons saved their lives by accepting baptism. Subsequently, with the sedulous encouragement and protection of Solomon ben Isaac of Troyes ("Rashi"), the great Franco-Jewish scholar, many of them returned to Judaism; though the ecclesiastical authorities looked black at the loss of these precious souls which had been won for the Church.[1]

The phenomenon of Marranism is more, however, than the commonplace occurrence of forcible conversion, followed frequently by the practice of Judaism in secret. Its essential element is that this clandestine religion is passed on from generation to generation. This is by no means a unique occurrence. Among the reasons given for the expulsion of the Jews from England in 1290 was that they persisted in seducing recent converts to return to the "vomit of Judaism." Ancient Jewish authorities add that many children were kidnaped and sent to the northern part of the country, where they long continued their ancestral religious practices. To this fact, reports one chronicler, was due the readiness of the English to accept the Reformation, as well as their predilection for biblical names and certain dietetic peculiarities obtaining in Scotland. The tale is not quite so improbable as might appear on the surface: and it is interesting as an indication of how the phenomenon of the crypto-Jew may sometimes appear in the most unlikely places. Similarly, for two hundred years at least after the expulsion of the Jews from the South of France, spiteful antiquaries were able to trace, in some outstanding noble families (which, they said, still practiced Judaism in the privacy of their homes), the blood of those who had preferred to remain in the country as professing Catholics.[2]

There are other parallels to the phenomenon of the Marrano which are even closer. The most remarkable of all is the story of the *neofiti* (neophytes) of Apulia, only recently brought to light after many centuries of oblivion. At the close of the thirteenth century, the Angevin rulers of the kingdom of Naples brought about a general conversion of the Jews in their dominions, centered about the city of Trani. Under the name of *neofiti*, these continued a crypto-Jewish existence for three centuries or more afterwards. Their secret fidelity to Judaism was one of the problems which led to the activity of the Inquisition in the kingdom of Naples in the sixteenth century. In February 1572, several were burned at the stake in Rome, including Teofilo Panarelli, a savant of some reputation. Others succeeded in escaping to the Balkans, where they joined the existing Jewish communities. Certain vague recollections of Judaism persist amongst their descendants in southern Italy down to the present day.

The phenomenon was by no means confined to the Christian world. Even now, there are communities of crypto-Jews of many centuries' standing to be found in several parts of the Moslem world. The Daggatun of the Sahara continued Jewish practices long after their formal conversion to Islam, and traces of this have not entirely died out among their offspring. The Donmeh of Salonica[3] were the descendants of those adherents of the pseudo-Messiah, Sabbatai Zevi, who followed him into apostasy; and, while ostensibly conforming Moslems, they practice a Messianic Judaism in their homes. Further East, there are yet closer parallels. The religious persecutions in Persia in the seventeenth century and after left in the country, particularly at Meshed, many families who are punctiliously scrupulous in Jewish observance in private while outwardly devout adherents to the dominant faith. Many have fled to Afghanistan, Turkestan, and especially to Palestine: but a remnant still remains, numbering some hundreds of families, and known as *Jedidim*. Although they bear Moslem names, their real identity is an open secret. Regular bribery of the officials secures them freedom from molestation. Marriages before the *Kadi* according to Mohammedan law are repeated according to the Jewish ceremonial at home. Similarly, there are double funeral rites. Since they cannot maintain their own butchers, all of them are familiar with the method of slaughtering animals according to the traditional Jewish rite. They have underground prayer-houses, the entrances to which are guarded by women to prevent disturbance. They have no alternative but to keep their shops open on the Sabbath: but they avoid doing business by putting in charge a small child, who will say that his father is away, or else by asking such exorbitant prices that the purchaser will be discouraged. Near Khorasan there is another body of *Jedid al-Islam*, whose history is identical. Similar to them are the Tschola of Bokhara, officially converted to

Mohammedanism in the last century, but still largely Jewish in practice, and wholly so by descent.

The classical land of crypto-Judaism, however, is Spain. Here, the tradition was so protracted, and so general, that one almost suspects some predisposition to it in the very atmosphere of the country. As far back as the Roman period, the Jews of the Peninsula had been numerous and influential. Many of them, indeed, claimed to trace their descent from the aristocracy of Jerusalem, who had been carried into exile by Titus, or even by earlier conquerors. After the Barbarian invasions, in the fifth century, their position at first ameliorated; for the Visigoths embraced the Arian form of Christianity, and tended to favor the Jews both as strict monotheists and as an influential minority, whose support was worth conciliating. However, upon their conversion to Catholicism, they began to show the traditional zeal of the neophyte. The Jews were the first to suffer. In 589, with the accession of Reccared to the throne, the current ecclesiastical legislation began to be rigorously enforced against them in every detail. His immediate successors were not so intolerant; but from the accession of King Sisebut (612–620), a spirit of the utmost fanaticism prevailed. In 616, possibly at the instigation of the Byzantine Emperor Heraclius, he issued an edict ordering the baptism of all the Jews of his kingdom, under the pain of banishment and the loss of all their property. According to Catholic authorities, ninety thousand embraced Christianity at this time. This cataclysm, known to the Jewish chroniclers of a later period as the "First Evil," was the earliest of the great disasters which punctuated the history of the Jews of Spain.

Down to the reign of Roderic, "the last of the Visigoths," the tradition of persecution continued consistently, save for brief intermissions. Over a large part of the period, the practice of Judaism was utterly proscribed. Nevertheless, the moment governmental vigilance was relaxed, the recent converts seized the opportunity to revert to their ancestral religion. Successive Councils of Toledo, from the fourth to the eighteenth, devoted their energies to devising fresh methods to prevent backsliding. The association of neophytes with their former coreligionists was prohibited. The children of suspects were to be seized, to be brought up in an uncontaminated Christian atmosphere. The recent converts were forced to sign a declaration binding themselves to observe no Jewish rite in future; though they made an exception with respect to eating the flesh of the pig, which, they said, it was physically impossible for them to touch. In spite of all these provisions, the notorious infidelity of the recent converts and their descendants remained one of the great problems of Visigothic statesmanship down to the period of the Arab invasion in 711. The number of the Jews found in the country by the latter proves the utter failure of the conversionist attempts. The tradition of Marranism in the Peninsula had already emerged.[4]

With the coming of the Arabs, a Golden Age was initiated for the Jews of Spain; first in the Caliphate of Cordova, and after its fall (1012) in the minor kingdoms which sprang up on its ruins. The strength of Judaism in the Peninsula became immensely reinforced.

Its communities exceeded in numbers, in culture, and in wealth, those of any other country in the whole of the western world. The long tradition of tolerance was interrupted with the invasion of the Almoravides, at the beginning of the twelfth century. When the puritan Almohades, a North African sect, were summoned to the Peninsula in 1148 to check the threatening advance of the Christian powers, the reaction became drastic.[5] The new rulers introduced to Spain the intolerance which they had already shown in Africa. The practice of Judaism or of Christianity was proscribed throughout those provinces which were still subject to Moslem rule. Most of the Jews fled to the Christian kingdoms of the north: and it is from this period that the hegemony of the communities of Christian Spain may be said to date. Large numbers were put to the sword or sold into slavery. A minority, however, followed the example set a few years previously by their brethren in northern Africa, outwardly embracing the religion of Islam. Yet in their hearts they remained steadfast. Once more, large parts of the Peninsula knew the phenomenon of insincere proselytes, paying lip service to the dominant faith, but in the privacy of their homes faithful to the traditions of Judaism. Their infidelity was notorious. In the African possessions at least of the Almohades, the recent converts were compelled to wear a distinguishing sign. One of the most distinguished Arab poets of the period, Abu-Ishak Ibrahim ibn Sahl of Seville, was of Jewish extraction, and returned to the religion of his fathers when his native city was recaptured by the Christians.[6]

Among the victims of the Almohadan persecution was Rabbi Maimon, son of Joseph, who left Cordova with his family and, after a considerable period of wandering, found refuge in Fez. Here, Maimon wrote his famous Letter of Consolation to comfort his coreligionists in this time of affliction. However, it was possible to live in Morocco at this time only under the outward guise of Moslems; and it would appear that Maimon ben Joseph's family, under the stress of circumstances, had to bow to necessity and do likewise. When, some little time later, a foreign rabbi replied in the negative to the inquiry of some Moroccan Jews as to whether it was permissible for them assume Islam in order to save their lives, he was rebuffed in a lengthy epistle by Maimon's famous son, Moses.[7] In a closely reasoned torrent of invective, the latter demonstrated not only that such procedure was permissible, but also that for a man to imperil his life by acting otherwise would be a grievous sin; for the Moslems, unlike the Christians, required in such cases merely a formal declaration of conformity, without insisting upon the neglect of Jewish practices or the performance of any idolatrous act. This is not the place to discuss the ethical or the legal aspect of the problem. So much, however, may perhaps be said. A contemporary French or German Jew would not have spoken in this fashion. To the north of the Pyrenees, a spirit of greater fortitude prevailed. The Jews of the Rhineland, who "sanctified the name of God" to a man rather than abjure their faith, were more heroic, if less picturesque, than their Andalusian brethren.

CHAPTER I

THE BEGINNINGS OF MARRANISM

THE beginnings of the Reconquest, or *Reconquista*, in Spain had involved obvious danger for the Jews. The rude Christian warriors could not easily distinguish between one sort of unbeliever and another; and the Jews, dressed in the same fashion as the Moslems, speaking their language, and belonging in essence to the same culture, inevitably shared their fate. When any place was captured, the synagogue, like the mosque, was piously burned, and the Jewish population put to the sword.

From the tenth century, however, a different spirit began to show itself. The initial religious fanaticism commenced to wane. It was realized that the Jews constituted an important minority, whose support should be conciliated if the Christian position in the Peninsula were to be maintained. Moreover, it was clear that the Jews could be of great utility to the Court, whether as physicians, as financiers, as interpreters, or as diplomats. Accordingly, notwithstanding occasional legislative manifestations of religious bias, the favorable policy of the Moslem states with regard to the Jews was adopted in its entirety. With the reign of Alfonso X of Castile (1065–1109), and the capture of Toledo, in 1085, the Christian states became dominant in the Peninsula. Jewish life and Jewish scholarship continued to flourish under the Cross as they had done under the Crescent.

11

After the Almohadan invasion, when the practice of any religion other than Islam was proscribed in Andalusia, Christian tolerance compared most favorably with Moslem persecution; and the center of Spanish Jewry was definitely transferred to the northern states.

The gradual conquest of the Moorish territories progressively diminished the necessity of conciliating the minority. Hence, from this period, there was a gradual deterioration in the position of the Jews. In 1212, a Christian coalition defeated the Moslems at the decisive battle of Las Navas de Tolosa, and their power was finally crushed. Before many years had passed, they were driven back into the kingdom of Granada, and the exiguous frontier, which was to remain with few changes until the close of the fifteenth century, had been established. This epoch synchronized with the promulgation of the anti-Jewish policy which had been enunciated by the Lateran Councils of 1179 and 1215. In Spain, this was embodied in the famous Code of Alfonso the Wise of Castile (1252–1282), known as the *Siete Partidas* (Seven Sections). This was, however, enforced only locally and sporadically. The social and economic degradation of the Jew was never completed in the Peninsula, as it was in other parts of Europe. Cultural activities continued undisturbed: and, in spite of occasional local outbreaks, life and property were generally safe.

Nevertheless, the tide of hostility against the Jews gradually rose. The Crusaders from across the Alps had attacked the community of Toledo, in the approved Rhineland fashion, as they set out on the campaign which was to culminate in the battle at Las Navas de Tolosa. On that occasion, indeed, the Christian inhabitants came

to the rescue. But before long, foreign example became
unnecessary. There were sporadic popular outbreaks,
especially in the north of the country, where the French
example was potent. Thus, in 1328, the communities
of Navarre were almost exterminated in a series of
massacres. At the time of the Black Death, the attacks
upon the Jews in Savoy and Germany were anticipated
in Catalonia, though they remained localized. The turn-
ing-point came a few years later. The favor shown by
Pedro the Cruel of Castile to the Jews, and their enthusi-
astic espousal of his cause, resulted in much suffering
for them at the time of the struggle for the throne which
ensued between him and Henry of Trastamara, his
half-brother. One prosperous *judería* (Jewry) after
another was sacked during the course of the civil war.
When finally Pedro was overthrown, the Jews suffered
for their attachment to his cause. To the prejudices of
the Church and the antipathies of the people was now
added the resentment of the sovereign. The new king,
Henry II, made no secret of his feelings. For the first
time, the repressive ecclesiastical policy, including even
the wearing of the Jewish badge of shame, was more or
less consistently enforced.

In the financial administration of the country, individual Jews continued to enjoy considerable influence.
The most notable instance was Don Joseph Pichon, who
occupied the position of *almoxarifo* and *contador mayor* —
important posts in the financial administration of the
kingdom. In 1379, certain private enemies among his
own coreligionists procured his judicial murder. The
sovereign, Juan I (1379–1390), beside himself with passion at the loss of his minister, was still further antago-

nized; and amongst the population of Pichon's native city of Seville, where he had been surprisingly popular, feeling against the Jews rose alarmingly.

In October 1390, Juan I of Castile died, being succeeded by his infant son, Henry III (1390–1406). During the minority, great authority was enjoyed by the Queen Mother, Leonora, whose confessor, Ferrand Martinez, Archdeacon of Ecija, immediately became a power in the state. The latter was a man of little learning, but noteworthy for his indomitable spirit, and a sworn enemy of the Jews. For the past twelve years, he had been inveighing against them from the pulpit and endeavoring to procure their expulsion from the various towns of the region. Injunctions from the king, and even from the Pope, had been quite ineffectual to silence him. He asserted roundly that the twenty-three synagogues in the diocese of Seville had been constructed in defiance of the laws, and should be torn down. Now, with the death of the king, and almost simultaneously that of the Archbishop Barroso, who had previously been able to check his activities to some extent, Martinez was freed from all restraint, and procured, by letters to the local clergy, the partial destruction of some of the unauthorized Jewish places of worship. Half-hearted instructions addressed to him from the Court, to desist from his activities and make good the damage, only served to enlist the sympathy of the populace on his side. A feeling of unrest spread throughout the country. The advent of Lent, with its reminders of the Passion, served as the pretext for a fresh series of inflammatory sermons which keyed the popular passions to the highest pitch.

On Ash Wednesday (March 15, 1391), a turbulent

crowd broke into the Jewish quarter of Seville, which was in imminent danger of sack. The civic authorities had a couple of the ringleaders seized and scourged, but this served only to exasperate the feelings of the rest. After some further disturbances, order was outwardly restored; but the spirit of unrest still simmered, while Martinez continued his unbridled invective from the pulpit. At length, on June 4, 1391, the mob could no longer be restrained. An orgy of carnage raged in the city. The *Judería* was pitilessly sacked. As many as four thousand persons, it was estimated, were killed; while those who did not succeed in making good their escape were able to save their lives only by accepting baptism. The fury spread during that summer and autumn through the whole of the Peninsula, from the Pyrenees to the straits of Gibraltar. At Ecija and at Carmona, the whole community was exterminated. At Cordova, the entire *Judería* was reduced to ashes: Toledo was the scene of a frightful massacre on the fast-day of the seventeenth of Tammuz. Similar outbreaks took place in seventy other towns in Castile. In Aragon, despite the severe measures taken by King Juan I to suppress the disorders, the example was followed. In the kingdom of Valencia (in the capital city of which the lead had been given on July 9 by a crowd of hysterical boys) not a single professing Jew was left alive. At Barcelona, in spite of the protection of the authorities, the whole community was wiped out. From Catalonia, the frenzy spread to the Balearic Islands, where on August 2 an exterminatory massacre took place at Palma. The total number of victims was said to have amounted to as many as fifty thousand in all. There were some important communities — as, for example, that of Barcelona, which had maintained an unbroken existence from the eighth century at least — which henceforth were never reëstablished. Outbreaks were avoided only in Moslem Granada and, thanks to the vigorous measures of protection taken by the Crown, in Portugal. In Aragon, those responsible for the disorders were punished, though in most cases not too severely. In Castile, however, the passivity of the authorities showed that they condoned the outrages which had been committed.

A wave of massacres of this description was not by any means new in Jewish history. Something of the sort had taken place on the Rhineland during the Crusades, in England in 1189–90, and throughout Germany at the period of the Black Death. The consequences of this occasion, however, were unique. Elsewhere, it had been only a weak remnant which had accepted baptism as the alternative to death. The vast majority had unquestioningly preferred martyrdom "for the Sanctification of the Name" rather than abjure their faith. But in Spain conditions were different. The morale of the people had been undermined by centuries of well-being. Their social assimilation to the general population had progressed so far as to make the change seem perhaps less drastic. The expulsions throughout Europe — from England in 1290, from France in 1306 and 1394, from the majority of the cities of Germany at the time of the Black Death — had cut off most avenues of escape. Possibly, the recent disasters had made them feel that there was, after all, no hope for their religious and national future. But, above all, there was a moral difference, which had been shown in the long tradition of crypto-Judaism in the

Peninsula. It was not difficult for insincere, temporizing Jews to become insincere, temporizing Christians. Whatever the reason, throughout the Peninsula, large bodies of Jews accepted baptism *en masse* in order to escape death. At Toledo, the example was set by the aged Samuel Abrabanel, formerly the confidential adviser of Henry of Trastamara; and a majority of the community followed his example. At Barcelona, those who saved their lives by the same means are said to have been numbered in thousands. In Valencia, the wealthy and influential Joseph Abarim and Samuel Abravalla led the way; and they were followed by all of their surviving coreligionists, except a few who remained in hiding. So many came forward for baptism, it was said, that the holy chrism in the churches was exhausted, and it was regarded as miraculous that the supply held out. The number of converts here alone was stated, with palpable exaggeration, to amount to eleven thousand. In some places, the Jews did not wait for the application of compulsion, but anticipated the popular attack by coming forward spontaneously, clamoring for admission to the Church. All told, the total number of conversions in the kingdoms of Aragon and Castile was reckoned at the improbable figure of two hundred thousand. It was a phenomenon unique in the whole of Jewish history.

The movement did not stop with the restoration of order. Fray Vincent Ferrer, to whose fiery eloquence the outbreak at Valencia had been due, continued to travel about preaching to the Jews and endeavoring to secure their conversion. In 1411 he traversed Castile from end to end, in pursuance of what he had come to regard as his mission. In one place after another, he appeared in the synagogue bearing a scroll of the Law in one arm and a crucifix in the other, while an unruly mob at his heels added force to his arguments. Everywhere, many persons allowed themselves to be won over by his impassioned appeals. On a single day, in Toledo, he is said to have gained four thousand converts. Some whole communities gave way in a body. In the Bishopric of Segovia, the remnants of Judaism were almost entirely destroyed. Subsequently, the self-appointed missionary returned to Aragon, where he followed a similar course. Here he was assisted by the apostate Mestre Gerónimo de Santa Fé (*Megadef*—"the blasphemer"—as he was acrostically called by his former coreligionists). The latter had succeeded in inducing the anti-Pope, Benedict XIII, whose body-physician he was, to stage a disputation on the merits of the two religions at Tortosa (1413–1414). During its course and after its conclusion, the labors for the faith continued. Converts were secured in large numbers at Saragossa, Calatayud, Daroca, Fraga, and Barbastro. The entire communities of Alcañiz, Caspe, Maella, Lérida, Tamarit, and Alcolea followed the lead. Thirty-five thousand additional converts are said to have been secured in the two kingdoms during the course of a few years.

Of the neophytes, some returned to Judaism when the immediate danger was past, fleeing for the purpose to parts of the country where they were unknown, or else to Moslem Africa. The vast majority, however, remained in their former places of residence as conforming Christians. Although the canons of the Church condemned conversion by force (as we have seen), baptism secured even by such means was generally, though not

invariably, regarded as an irrevocable sacrament, from
which there was no escape. Even had the Church condoned backsliding, the popular fury would indubitably
have punished it. Moreover, large numbers had accepted
Christianity under only a remote threat of violence, the
canonical force of their conversion being unquestionable.
In any case, however doubtful their sincerity might be,
their condition as titular Christians became permanent.

Thus, from the close of the fourteenth century, a
completely new state of affairs existed in Spain. By the
side of those, now sadly decreased in wealth and
numbers, who still openly professed their Judaism, there
were vast numbers of *conversos* (converts); totaling,
according to report, some hundreds of thousands in all.
Some of them, perhaps, were sincere enough. It is sufficient to mention Pablo de Santa Maria, who, as
Solomon ha-Levi, had at one time been a rabbi, but
subsequently rose to the dignity of Bishop of his native
Burgos, and member of the Council of Regency of
Castile. There were many others, who had not been
over-sincere in their attachment to Judaism, and did not
find much difficulty in accommodating themselves
equally well to their new religion. But the vast majority
had accepted Christianity only to escape death, and
remained at heart as completely Jewish as they had ever
been. Outwardly, they lived as Christians. They took
their children to church to be baptized, though they
hastened to wash off the traces of the ceremony as soon
as they returned home. They would go to the priest to
be married, though they were not content with the ceremony and, in the privacy of their houses, performed
another to implement it. Occasionally, they would come

to be shriven; but their confessions were so unreal that
one priest is said to have begged a piece of the garment
of one of them as a relic of so blameless a soul!

Behind this outward sham they remained at heart as
they had always been. Their disbelief in the dogmas of
the Church was notorious, and was not always concealed. They kept all the traditional ceremonies, in
some instances down to the least details. They observed
the Sabbath so far as lay in their power; and it was
possible to see, from a height overlooking any city, how
many chimneys were smokeless on that day. The more
punctilious would eat only meat prepared in the Jewish
fashion and supplied by a Jewish butcher.[1] Some even
went so far as to circumcise their children. In most cases,
they married exclusively amongst themselves. They con-
sorted familiarly with their old coreligionists, often continuing to live in the same quarter. On occasion, they
furtively frequented the synagogues, for the illumination
of which they regularly sent gifts of oil. Alternatively,
they would form religious associations with titularly
Catholic objects and under the patronage of some
Christian saint, using this as a cover for observing
their ancestral rites.[2] In race,[3] in belief, and largely in
practice, they remained as they had been before the
conversion. They were Jews in all but name, and
Christians in nothing but form. They were moreover
able to transmit their disbelief to their children, who,
though born in the dominant faith and baptized at birth,
were as little sincere in their attachment to it as their
fathers.

Nevertheless, with the removal of the religious disabilities from which they had previously suffered, the social

and economic progress of the recent converts and their decendants became phenomenally rapid. However dubious their sincerity, it was now out of the question to exclude them from any walk of life on the ground of their creed. The Law, the administration, the army, the universities, the Church itself,[4] were all overrun by recent converts of more or less questionable sincerity, or by their immediate descendants. They thronged the financial administration, for which they had a natural aptitude, protest being now impossible. They pushed their way into the municipal councils, into the legislatures, into the judiciary. They all but dominated Spanish life. The wealthier amongst them intermarried with the highest nobility of the land, few impoverished counts or hidalgos being able to resist the lure of their gold. Within a couple of generations, there was barely a single aristocratic family in Aragon, from the royal house downwards, which was free from the "taint" of Jewish blood. Many were the offices of importance at Court occupied by *conversos* or their children. In 1480, both the supreme court of justice of that kingdom and the Cortes were presided over by persons of Jewish extraction. A certain jurist of the period amused his leisure during a period of pestilence by drawing up genealogical lists demonstrating the precise Jewish antecedents of a very large proportion of the contemporary notables — the famous *Libro Verde de Aragon* ("Green Book of Aragon"). Conditions in Castile were very similar.[5]

The progress of the Santángel family was characteristic. Noah Chinillo had been a member of an old Saragossan Jewish family established at Calatayud. One of his five sons, Azariah Chinillo, became converted to

Christianity in the early years of the fifteenth century, in consequence of the preaching of Fray Vincent Ferrer. As was usual amongst the renegades, he assumed a saint's name instead of his old Jewish patronymic, becoming known as Luis de Santángel. He removed to Saragossa, studied law, attained high office at court, and was raised to the nobility. His nephew, Pedro de Santángel, was Bishop of Majorca. His son, Martin, was *zalmedina*, or magistrate, at the capital. Other members of the family attained high rank in Church and state. A Luis de Santangel of a later generation, perhaps grandson of the founder of the family, was financial agent in Aragon and in 1473 represented the knights and nobles at a meeting of the Estates of the realm. Another person bearing the same name farmed the taxation and ultimately became *escribano de racion* (Secretary of the Royal Household) and one of the most influential men in the state. Within a very few years of their acceptance of Christianity, the Santángel family was one of the most important in the whole country. As subsequent events were to show, their attachment to Catholicism was lukewarm in the extreme.

More dramatic still was the rise of the De la Caballeria family. It had already been prominent in Catalonia from as early as the thirteenth century, when Don Judah de la Caballeria, ibn Labi, had acted as *baile* (bailiff) for King Jaime I. Many of his descendants attained similarly high position. At the close of the fourteenth or beginning of the fifteenth century, eight out of the nine sons of Don Solomon ibn Labi de la Caballeria, the then head of the family, were baptized. Their lineage was so ancient and so honorable that they did not change their surname — an almost unexampled phenomenon. The eldest brother, Bonafus, who assumed the Christian name of Pedro, was *mestre racional*, or Comptroller General, at the court of Aragon, won the favor of Queen Maria, and was her commissioner at the Cortes convened at Monzon and Alcañiz (1436–7). He was the author of a fiercely anti-Jewish work, *Zelus Christi contra Judaeos et Sarracenos* (Zeal of Christ against the Jews and Saracens), upon which he was engaged for fourteen years, and in which he accused his former coreligionists of all imaginable and some unimaginable crimes. In 1464, he was assassinated — possibly at the instigation of his fellow-Marranos. All his sons subsequently attained high position: Alfonso was appointed Vice-Chancellor of the Kingdom, Luis became Counselor to King Juan, and Jaime was a trusted companion of Ferdinand the Catholic. One of Bonafus's brothers, Samuel, who likewise assumed the name of Pedro, rose to high office in the Church. Another, Isaac (Fernando), was Vice-Principal of the University of Saragossa; and Ahab (Felipe) became a leader in the Cortes. The youngest brother, Luis, who was baptized in infancy, rose to the office of High Treasurer of the kingdom of Navarre. The sons of Isaac de la Caballeria amassed vast fortunes by farming the public taxes, and attained high position in the state by reason of their wealth. One of them, Pedro, was partly responsible for negotiating the epoch-making marriage between Ferdinand of Aragon and Isabella of Castile, which united the Spanish monarchy. Another member of the family, Martin de la Caballeria, was appointed to the command of the fleet at Majorca. The remaining son of Don Solomon ibn Labi, Benveniste, continued faithful to Judaism. However, after his death, his family followed the general tendency of the time. One of his daughters married Don Apres de Paternoy, a wealthy landowner of Jewish extraction, and their descendants were important in Spanish history. His son Vidal, an accomplished Hebrew poet, who assumed the name of Gonzalo, continued his literary interests after his conversion, and translated some of the works of Cicero into Spanish. By marriage, the family became closely allied with all the wealthiest and most influential of the *converso* families in the kingdom. It was an outstanding, but not by any means an exceptional, illustration of the completeness and thoroughness with which the recent converts and their immediate descendants penetrated into every conceivable field of Spanish life.

A few further important figures of the fifteenth century may be mentioned in illustration. We have already seen the high rank attained by Solomon ha-Levi, *alias* Pablo de Santa Maria, Bishop of Burgos. His son, Alfonso, who had been converted to Christianity with him, followed him in that dignity, and was one of the Spanish delegates to the great Church Council of Basle, the anti-Jewish policy of which he advocated. His brother, Gonzalo, was Bishop of Sigüenza, and several other members of the family attained eminence in politics and literature. Juan de Torquemada, Cardinal of San Sisto, was (it was alleged) of immediate Jewish descent, as were also the saintly Hernando de Talavera, Archbishop of Granada, and Alonso de Oropesa, General of the Geronimite Order. The Lunas, Mendozas, Villahermosas, and others of the proudest nobility contracted family alliances with wealthy *conversos*. So did the Henriquez family, to which the mother of Ferdinand the Catholic belonged. The Zaportas of Monzon intermarried with the royal house of Aragon. Ximeno Gordo, a popular idol, lorded it over Saragossa. The Epses, Clementes, Coscons and Villanovas became notorious for their wealth. Sancho de Paternoy filled the post of *mestre racional*, or Comptroller of the Royal Household. The immensely wealthy Gabriel Sanchez, nephew of Alazar Ussuf of Saragossa (Luis Sanchez), was elevated to the office of Treasurer. In Castile, the families of Gonzalez, Chinet, and Coloma attained similar dignities. Hernando de Pulgar, a member of another *converso* house, was Secretary to Queen Isabella. Alonso de Cabrera, who belonged to the same class and was governor of the Alcazar at Segovia, married her favorite, Beatriz de Bobadilla. Don Juan Pacheco, Marquis of Villena and Grand Master of the Order of Santiago (who was king-maker in Castile in the reign of Henry the Impotent and actually aspired to Isabella's hand), was a descendant on both sides of the former Jew, Ruy Capon. His brother, Don Pedro Giron, was Grand Master of the Order of Calatrava; while the Archbishop of Toledo was their uncle. Seven at least of the principal prelates of the kingdom were of Jewish extraction — not to mention the *contador mayor*, or Treasurer. Indeed, there was hardly a single office of importance at either court, especially in the financial administration, which was not occupied by the descendants of some converted Jew, or by members of families closely allied with them.

In intellectual life, conditions were similar. The revival of vernacular literature at the court of Juan II of Aragon was due in considerable measure to the genius of persons of Jewish blood, and was largely inspired by the *converso*,

Alfonso de Santa Maria. The latter's kinsman, Micer Gonzalo de Santa Maria, a great-nephew of the former Bishop of Burgos and assessor to the Governor of Aragon, was virtually Historiographer Royal. Hernando de Pulgar was a notable figure in literature as well as in politics. Andrés Heli, another writer of high eminence, traced his descent to a Jewish family of Saragossa. In a later generation, Pedro Guttierez de Santa Clara, the historian of the conquest of Peru, belonged to the same category. Fernando de Rojas, the father of the Spanish novel and author of *Celestina*, which had an immeasurable influence upon European literature in every country, was similarly of Jewish blood. Juan de España of Toledo, known as *El Viejo*, was a sound Talmudist as well as a poet of note, and introduced rabbinic phrases into his pasquinades against his former coreligionists. In this he was imitated by his rival, Fra Diego de Valencia.[6] Other well-known poets of Jewish blood included Rodrigo Cota da Maguaque (long considered, incorrectly, the author of *Celestina*), Anton de Montoro, Pero Ferrus, and Juan de Valladolid. Francisco Lopez de Villalobos was one of the most famous physicians of his time, and an author of considerable reputation, who is considered one of the classical writers of the Spanish tongue. Even the foremost anti-Jewish writers of the period, such as Pablo de Heredia and Alfonso de Zamora, were *conversos*. In the arts, mention may be made of Juan de Leví, a religious painter highly esteemed at the beginning of the fifteenth century; and of Juan de Altabás, who flourished at its close.[7]

Numerically, the importance of the converts, with their rapidly increasing descendants and their wide-

spread family connections, was very considerable. In the
south of the country, it was said, they numbered something like one third of the population of the larger towns.
If this were the case, there must have been at least
three hundred thousand in all (some authorities suggest
ten times the figure) throughout the Peninsula. This
number would however include all — both those who
were of full Jewish blood and their half-Gentile kinsmen,
the fervent proselytes and their unwilling fellows. Those
who were completely Jewish, by descent and by sympathy, were not by any means so numerous. Nevertheless, they formed in the organism of the state a vast,
incongruous body which it was impossible to assimilate,
and not easy to neglect.

Amongst the Jews, these recent converts to Christianity, or even their remoter descendants, were known
by the name of *Anusim* — the "Forced Ones," who had
adopted the dominant religion under duress. The general
population, on the other hand, used a variety of terms to
describe them. They were called *conversos* — a term
which could properly be applied only to the actual converts themselves. More strictly, they were denominated
New Christians (*Nuevos Christianos*) to distinguish them
from the general population of "Old Christians." Satir-
ically, they were sometimes termed *Alboraycos*, from al-
Burak, the marvelous steed of Mohammed, which was
neither horse nor mule, male nor female — much like the
persons to whom the name was applied, who were neither
Jews nor Christians.[8] However, they were popularly
known, more generally, as *Marranos*. Many origins have
been sought for this word. It has been derived from the
Hebrew *Mar'at 'Ayin*, or Appearance of the Eye, as

referring to the fact that these persons were only ostensibly Christians. Other fanciful derivations are from the word *Mumar*, or apostate, given a Spanish ending (*Mumarano*); *Moḥram Atta*—"Thou art Excommunicated"; or *Mar Anuss*—"Master *Anuss*." However, the fact that the term was practically[9] unknown amongst the Jews indicates that it did not originate amongst them, and that a non-Hebrew origin must be sought for it. One such derivation which has been suggested is from the second word in the ecclesiastical term of execration *Anathema Maranatha*;[10] another is from the Arabic *Mura'in*, signifying hypocrite. However, all this linguistic speculation is needless. The word Marrano is an old Spanish term dating back to the early Middle Ages and meaning swine. Applied to the recent converts in the first place perhaps ironically, with reference to their aversion from the flesh of the animal in question, it ultimately became a general term of execration which spread during the sixteenth century to most of the languages of western Europe. The word expresses succinctly and unmistakably all the depth of hatred and contempt which the ordinary Spaniard felt for the insincere neophytes by whom he was now surrounded. It is the constancy shown by them and their descendants that has redeemed the term from its former insulting connotation, and endowed it with its enduring power of romance.

CHAPTER II

THE ESTABLISHMENT OF THE INQUISITION

As the fifteenth century advanced, it became increasingly obvious that the recent mass-conversions to Christianity had enhanced, rather than solved, the difficulties of the religious position in Spain. Instead of the previous homogeneous body of Jews, there was now in addition a vast number of titular Christians scattered throughout the country, pushing their way into every walk of life, and constituting a problem of their own.

The attitude of the Church in relation to them was easily understandable. As we have seen, Roman Catholicism officially disapproved of the policy of securing conversions by force. It was nevertheless held widely, if not universally, that conversions thus secured were valid. The victims therefore had to be considered in the fullest degree sons of the Church, any reversion to their former beliefs or practice being an heretical action. Much, moreover, depended upon the interpretation of the term "violence." If a man were dragged forcibly to the font and baptized, in spite of his protests, there was no question about the invalidity of the baptism. If on the other hand he consented to the operation in order to save his life, there was an element of spontaneity in the transaction. If he came forward voluntarily, in anticipation of attack, it might be said that he accepted baptism of his own free will. Sometimes, the element of compulsion was even more remote and indirect. More-

over, a fresh generation had by now grown up, born
after their parents' conversion, and baptized in infancy
as a matter of course. As to the canonical status of the
latter, there was no question. They were full Christians;
and the observance of the Catholic religion was as much
incumbent upon them as it was upon any other son or
daughter of the Church.

It was, however, notorious that they were Christians
only in name; observing, in public, a minimum of the
new faith while maintaining, in private, a maximum of
the old one. The position, as far as the Church was
concerned, was more difficult by far than it had been
before the fatal year 1391. Previous to that date, there
had been a considerable body of unbelievers outside the
Church, easily recognizable, and rendered theologically
innocuous by a systematic series of governmental and
clerical regulations. Now, there was a similarly large
body inside the fold, insidiously working its way into
every limb of the body politic and ecclesiastic, openly
contemning in many cases the doctrines of the Church
and contaminating by its influence the whole mass of the
faithful. Baptism had done little more than to convert a
considerable proportion of the Jews from infidels outside
the Church to heretics inside it. The only solution to
the problem would have been to allow the recent converts and their descendants to return openly to Judaism,
and thus restore the position which had obtained previous to 1391. In an age which took religion so seriously,
this was out of the question. It is doubtful, moreover,
whether the populace on the one hand or many of the
conversos themselves on the other would have consented

to it. Inevitably, therefore, the problem of the New Christians claimed more and more attention from the leaders of the Spanish Church. The Provincial Council of Tortosa, in 1429, and the General Council of Basle, in 1434, took the matter into consideration, and urged that measures should be taken to check the blasphemous duplicity of these recent adherents to the Christian faith. It was natural, and indeed pardonable, that all the pulpits resounded to impassioned sermons calling attention to the misconduct of the New Christians and urging that steps should be taken to check them.

The populace, whose feelings thus became more and more inflamed, could not be expected to appreciate the theological subtleties of the matter. In the Marranos it could see only hypocritical Jews, who had lost none of their unpopular characteristics, fighting their way into the highest positions in the state. The change which the formality of baptism had made in their favor was accentuated by the contrast with their unconverted brethren, who since the beginning of the fifteenth century had become utterly humiliated and had by now reached the nadir of their misery. The natural ability and acumen of the *conversos* had attracted them in vast numbers above all to the financial administration, from which, as Jews, they had previously been excluded. Throughout the country, they farmed the taxes. Thus, they inevitably became identified in the popular mind with the royal oppression. The occupation was as remunerative as it was unpopular; and the vast fortunes which were rapidly accumulated added jealousy to the other grounds for dislike. In some parts of the country, further considerations came into question. Thus, in Catalonia, the *conversos* supported the Crown against the populace, earning thereby a further measure of enmity.

The nobility, on their side, scorned and detested the New Christians, partly for the reasons given above, but especially for their enterprise. A hidalgo of ancient lineage could not restrain his jealousy when he saw the scion of a family well-known in the *judería* forcing himself into high office at court, snapping up all the best matrimonial alliances for his daughters, and procuring high advancement in the Church for his sons. The prejudice was most marked in Castile, especially in the southern provinces — Toledo, Murcia, and Andalusia, but it was little less in other parts of the Peninsula. The problem was almost identical with that of the Jews before 1391, accentuated by a blind resentment of the Marrano hypocrisy and of the golden opportunities which it had furnished.

Political conditions enhanced the difficulties of the situation. The real ruler of the kingdom of Castile, after King Juan II attained his majority, was his capable but intensely unpopular favorite, Alvaro de Luna. Seeking his instruments wherever was most convenient, the latter appointed the immensely wealthy Diego Arias Dávila,[1] a New Christian, as treasurer of the kingdom. Through the latter, other Marranos began to rise to similar high positions. Thus they began to share in the unpopularity of the Minister. In 1449, de Luna ordered a forced loan of 1,000,000 *maravedis* to be raised in Toledo for the purpose of defending the frontier. The levy was regarded with abhorrence, and the odium for it fell upon the Marrano tax-gatherers who attempted to collect it. Two Canons, fired with religious ardor, preached resistance. The great bell of the Cathedral tolled to summon the populace. A fierce mob attacked the house of Alonso de Cota, one of the wealthiest of the tax-farmers, sacked it, and set it on fire. Then, rushing to the Barrio de la Magdalena, where many of the rich Marrano merchants lived, they repeated the process. Some of the other party, led by Juan de la Cibdad, sallied out fully armed. They were, nevertheless, forced back, the leaders being killed and their bodies hanged head downwards from the public gallows—the execution traditionally reserved for Jews. All attempts to punish the city were in vain, and the citizens refused to admit the troops sent to chastise the malefactors. An emergency court was organized to discuss whether the *conversos* could hold any public office. In spite of the outspoken clerical opposition, a quasi-judicial pronouncement known as the *Sentencia Estatuto* was passed. The bitterness of its language reveals the extreme tension which existed between the two sections of the population. The *conversos* were declared incapable of holding office or of bearing testimony against Christians; and twelve judges, notaries, and civic counselors of Jewish extraction, as well as one presbyter, were immediately deposed. From Toledo, the disorders spread to Ciudad Real. Here, the knights of the Order of Calatrava headed the Old Christian faction. There was much fighting in the streets; and for five days the quarter occupied by the *conversos* was sacked.

Appeal against the *Sentencia Estatuto* was made to the Pope, Nicholas V. It was obviously uncanonical, in that it deprived converts to the faith of the full privileges of

Christians. He condemned it therefore repeatedly, in Bulls of 1449 and 1451, besides excommunicating those responsible for promulgating it. Its real importance, however, lay in the attitude of mind which it expressed; and this could not be so easily eradicated.

In proceeding against the leaders of the Toledo outbreak, Alvaro de Luna had been lukewarm; for he suspected that the New Christians were implicated in the intrigues against himself. This was in part true; and some influential members of the class sat in the court which condemned him to death in 1453. Nevertheless, his fall was generally regarded as a triumph for the old nobility and a severe blow against the Marranos. In the following year, the king died, and was succeeded by his elder son, Henry the Impotent (1454–1474). Among the favorites by whom he allowed himself to be guided in the early part of his reign were several persons of Jewish extraction. His misgovernment led to his temporary deposition; and his reinstatement on the throne was effected only upon the understanding that he would take serious action in the problem which was perturbing the realm. His confessor was Fray Alonso de Spina, rector of the University of Salamanca, who (though reportedly of Jewish origin) sedulously endeavored to stir up the general feeling against the insincere New Christians. His *Fortalicium Fidei* (Stronghold of the Faith), composed about 1460, raked up all the old charges against the Jews and their baptized brethren, who were asserted to be the worst of all. Meanwhile, stories of their enormities were circulating in increasing numbers. It was alleged, for example, that very many had recently circumcised their children — one friar asserted that he

had tangible proof of the truth of the story. In one
house in Medina del Campo, it was said, thirty men
were laid up at one time in consequence of having
undergone the operation.

Toledo continued to remain the hot-bed of disturbance,
in spite of the attempts of the Archbishop to conduct an
inquiry into the causes of the dissension and to bring
about an understanding. Both sides armed themselves;
Fernando de la Torre, a leader of the New Christians,
boasted that he had four thousand men ready for any
emergency. A conference held in the Cathedral on
July 21, 1467, failed to restore peace. Swords were
drawn, and one man was killed. Fierce fighting continued
in the streets for nine days. In the end, the *conversos*
were worsted, de la Torre and his brother being captured
and hanged. Meanwhile, eight streets in the mercantile
center of the town were laid in ashes. The victorious
faction removed all of their opponents from office, and
reënacted the *Sentencia Estatuto* of eighteen years before.
Since the pretender to the throne, Alfonso XII, refused
to confirm what they had done, they transferred the
allegiance of the city back to Henry the Impotent, who
thus had an additional reason to throw his influence
against the *conversos*.

Similar occurrences took place elsewhere throughout
Castile. In 1468, as the price of the adherence of Ciudad
Real to his cause, Henry decreed that henceforth no
converso should hold office in the city. At Cordova, the
bishop Pedro de Córdova y Solier formed a religious
confraternity, known as the Christian Brotherhood,
membership of which was confined to Old Christians.
On March 14, 1473, during the procession which was to

inaugurate the new body, the cry was raised that the image of the Virgin had been bespattered with foul water thrown from a window by a little Marrano girl. With fierce shouts of *Viva la Fé de Dios* ("Long live the faith of God"), the mob broke loose and attacked the houses occupied by the *conversos*. Alonso Fernandez de Aguilar, assisted by his brother Gonsalvo (later, as the *Gran Capitan*, to become one of the most distinguished generals of his age), led a body of troops to suppress the disorder, and killed one of the ringleaders. It happened that Alonso's wife was a New Christian, being a member of the widely-ramified family of Pacheco. His stern action thus served to infuriate the mob, which alleged that he had been bought over by his kinsmen. After a short interval, rioting broke out again, and the Aguilars were driven to take refuge in the Alcazar. A general sack followed, accompanied by murder and rape, which continued for three days, until no further victims were to be found. Order was restored only on the understanding that no *converso* was in the future to be allowed to live in the city.

From Cordova, the wave of disorder spread through the rest of Andalusia. At Jaen, the Constable of Castile, who had endeavored to preserve the peace, was barbarously murdered as he knelt before the altar, the New Christians being subsequently plundered and despatched at leisure. In the following year, there was a similar outbreak in the north of the country, centering at Segovia, where the bodies of the victims were piled in heaps in the streets.[2] Of the important towns, only a few escaped without disturbances but, except at Almodovar del Campo, no attempt was made to punish the culprits.[3]

There was no parallel to this in the whole of Spanish history save for the wave of massacres in 1391. There was, however, one great difference. On that occasion, it had been possible for those attacked to save their lives by accepting baptism. Now, no such avenue of escape lay open. In 1474, when Isabella and her consort, Ferdinand (who was to become king of Aragon five years later), ascended the throne, the *converso* poet, Antón de Montoro, of Cordova, addressed their Majesties a poem in which he painted a terrible picture of the deplorable condition of his brethren. Obviously the problem was an acute one. To the devout Christian mind, only one solution offered itself — the introduction of the Inquisition.

The conception of inflicting punishment for heresy was almost as old as the Church itself. Already in the days of the Roman emperors Theodosius and Justinian, special tribunals existed for the purpose. Under its present title, however, the Inquisition dates back only to the period of the Albigensian heresy, which threatened the existence of the Church in the thirteenth century. It was placed at the outset under the control of the Dominican friars, who stimulated it to ever greater efforts. When the immediate problem was partially solved, attention was turned to Judaizing heretics and to renegades who had lapsed again into Judaism after their conversion; conforming Jews, as such, stood outside the bounds of the Church, and did not come under its scope unless they were guilty of religious interference with Christians or attack on Christianity. About the year 1276, a number of backsliding converts were burned in the south of France; while another person who had

relapsed into Judaism suffered similarly at Paris on
March 31, 1310. The institution had penetrated at an
early date into the kingdom of Aragon, which was always
greatly subject to French influences. Here, in 1233, the
Archbishop of Tarragona had been empowered to appoint
Inquisitors: and, in 1359, a number of fugitives from
France who had relapsed into Judaism were hunted down.
But the Aragonese Inquisition had long been inactive;
while, in Castile, the institution had never hitherto
gained a footing.

Inquisitorial powers for the hunting out and punishment of heresy were vested in the bishops, by virtue
of their office.⁴ A few such cases occurred in Spain from
the middle of the fifteenth century. However, other
problems were more pressing; the bishops were absorbed
in their more worldly interests; and the general condition
of the country was too unruly to allow regular operations
to be initiated. An external impetus was thus essential.

For some time past the idea of introducing an
Inquisition into the country had been mooted. In
1451, indeed, Alvaro de Luna had obtained from Pope
Nicholas V a delegation of the Papal inquisitorial powers
to a couple of high ecclesiastical dignitaries. In their
commission it was specifically stated that they might
proceed even against bishops: a plain indication that the
unpopular minister was mainly desirous of obtaining an
additional weapon to use against the *converso* prelates
who opposed his policy. However, this license was
never acted upon. From 1461 onwards, Fray Alonso
de Spina, inspired by the Observant Franciscans, began
to agitate for the introduction of a special tribunal.
Their extreme violence and lack of moderation defeated

the attempt. The Geronimite Order, under the influence of their saintly General, Fray Alonso de Oropesa, strenuously advocated the use of the existing ecclesiastical machinery, and the opposing side were for the moment silenced. Nevertheless, in the Concordat of Medina del Campo in 1464–5 with his revolted nobles, Henry IV enjoined the bishops throughout the land to establish a searching inquiry into the conduct of the New Christians, and to punish rigorously those found guilty of backsliding. In consequence of this, there were a few victims, at Toledo, Llerena, and elsewhere.

For some time after her accession, the attention of Isabella the Catholic was taken up by the civil war. Alonso de Spina meanwhile continued his agitation without intermission. He now had powerful assistance at Court. Thomás de Torquemada, who had been the queen's confessor while she was still Infanta, was fanatically opposed to the Marranos, in spite of the fact that he himself was reputedly of Jewish extraction on one side. It was said, indeed, that before her brother's death he had made Isabella take a vow that, should she reach the throne, she would devote herself to the extirpation of heresy. He was outdone in virulence by Fray Alonso de Hojeda, Prior of the Dominican Convent of S. Pablo at Seville, who lost no opportunity of urging extreme measures against the enemies of the true faith. The ruling Pope, Sixtus IV, was no less eager, and hopefully invested his Legate to Castile with full Inquisitorial powers. The sovereigns would not permit any outside interference in the affairs of their country, and the Papal attempt ended in failure. An inquiry which was instituted in Seville revealed nevertheless that there were good grounds for suspecting the orthodoxy of a great part of the population of Andalusia, and, indeed, of Castile as a whole.

In 1477, the civil war came to an end. With the restoration of peace, Isabella came to Seville, remaining there for over a year. The sight of the *conversos* who thronged the court, monopolizing many of the highest offices, stimulated Hojeda to fresh efforts. For a long time he had no success; but a chance episode strengthened his case. On the night of Wednesday, March 18, 1478, a number of Jews and Marranos were surprised together, at some mysterious celebration, by a young cavalier who had penetrated into the *Judería* for the purpose of carrying on an intrigue with a fair Jewess who had taken his fancy. As a matter of fact, it was the eve of Passover, and it is obvious that they had come together simply for the purpose of the *Seder* celebration. By an unfortunate but by no means uncommon coincidence, it happened to be Holy Week. Under the circumstances, no explanation commended itself to the general mind except that these miscreants had assembled, at the season of the Passion of Jesus, in order to blaspheme the Christian religion. When the news reached the ears of the Prior of S. Pablo, he immediately hastened to Court and laid the evidence before the sovereigns. This, according to report, finally decided them. The Spanish ambassadors to the Holy See were immediately instructed to obtain a Bull authorizing the establishment of an Inquisition. Sixtus hesitated: prompted not so much by humanity, as by the desire to keep the new body under his own control. Ultimately, however, he complied. On November 1, 1478, a Bull was issued empowering the

Spanish sovereigns to appoint three bishops or other suitable persons above the age of forty, whom they might remove or replace at will, with complete jurisdiction over heretics and their accomplices. In this simple, unostentatious way, the Spanish Inquisition was launched on its career of blood.

Even now, matters did not move too rapidly. It was only on September 17, 1480, that commissions were issued to Miguel de Morillo, Master of Theology, and Juan de San Martin, Bachelor of Theology, both members of the Dominican Order, with instructions to begin their activities forthwith. On October 9, a royal order was published, securing them free transport and provisions on their way to Seville, where they were to begin operations. On their arrival in the city, on Christmas day, they were received at the door of the Chapter House by the municipal council, who conducted them to the City Hall A solemn procession was arranged for the following Sunday so as to inaugurate their activities with due pomp.

The recent developments had come as a great blow to the *conversos* of Seville, who had felt convinced that they would be able to avert the danger which threatened. The city was one of the principal New Christian centers. No serious disturbances had taken place there in recent years: and Marranos played an extremely prominent part in every aspect of local life. They determined therefore to resist with all their might. The lead amongst them was taken by Diego de Susan, an immensely wealthy New Christian merchant, whose fortune was said to amount to ten millions of *maravedis*. He was one of the eight persons who had supported the canopy

a couple of years before on the occasion of the baptism
of the Infant Juan. With him were associated numerous
other influential merchants, including several members
of the Town Council. The conspirators held a meeting
one night in San Salvador; this was the parish church
of the part of the city most favored by the Marranos,
many of them serving on its governing body. A couple
of prominent personalities from the neighboring cities
of Utrera and Carmona were also summoned to attend.
An account of the impassioned harangue which was
delivered by one of the leaders has come down to us.
"How can they come against us?" he cried. "We are the
principal members of the city, and well liked by the
people. Let us assemble our men. If they come to
take us, we will set the city in a turmoil, with our followers and our friends." As his voice died away, an old
man who had been asked to attend was heard to
mutter despairingly out of the shadows: "By my life,
to assemble men and to be prepared seems good to me.
But the hearts, where are they? Find me the hearts!"

In spite of this warning, the conspiracy persisted.
Each man present promised money, arms, or men.
Pedro Fernandez Benedeva, major-domo of the Church,
whose son was a canon, brought together weapons in
his house to arm one hundred men. The plotters only
awaited the conclusion of their preparations to strike
the blow.

Diego de Susan had a daughter, nicknamed *La
Susanna*, whose surprising beauty had earned her the
name *La Hermosa Hembre*.⁵ She was carrying on an
intrigue with a Christian *caballero*, to whom in a moment
of weakness she disclosed the secret. Through his instru-

mentality, it was revealed to the Inquisitors. Nothing could have served their turn better, as all the principal Marranos of the region were placed in their power at a single stroke. A series of arrests was carried out. Many of the richest and most honorable citizens of Seville, including several magistrates and other civic dignitaries, were involved. They were hurriedly tried and condemned to death. The first-fruits were seen on February 6, 1481, when the first Act of Faith[6] was held, six men and women being burned alive. The sermon was preached by Fray Alonso de Hojeda, who was thus enabled to see the triumphant results of the agitation which he had been carrying on for so many years. The spectacle was repeated a little later. Hojeda was not, however, privileged to witness it, since the pestilence which was to carry away fifteen thousand of the people of Seville had just begun, he himself being one of its earliest victims.

Amongst the three who suffered on the second occasion was Diego de Susan himself. He went to the stake quite calm and unmoved. The halter fastened round his neck trailed uncomfortably in the mud. He turned to a bystander. "Be so good as to lift up the end of my scarf," he said courteously. As though to show that the work thus begun was to be permanent, a *quemadero*, or burning place, was constructed in the Campo de Tablada just outside the city walls. At the four corners were erected figures of the four prophets, in plaster of Paris. The cost of this embellishment was defrayed by a burgher named Meza, whose zeal won him the lucrative position of receiver of the property confiscated by the Holy Office. He was however himself subsequently discovered to be a Judaizer, and was burned on the spot which he had helped to adorn.

La Hermosa Hembre, left destitute on her father's death, was befriended by Rainoldo Romero, Bishop of Tiberias, who procured her admission into a convent. The life was naturally irksome to her and she soon escaped. She adopted a life of shame and died in want, leaving directions that her skull should be placed as a warning over the door of the house which had been the scene of her disorderly life, in what was subsequently known as the *Calle de la Muerte* (Street of Death).[7] Here it remained until the building was pulled down during the course of structural alterations in the first half of the nineteenth century; and it was said that strange cries of grief and distress were sometimes heard to issue from the fleshless, grinning jaws.

Meanwhile, the activities of the Inquisition had been extending. On the first news of its establishment, many Marranos had fled to the surrounding territories. Peremptory demands were addressed to the local nobility, ordering them to give up the fugitives. The terror which the tribunal had excited was such that they immediately complied. From the Marquisate of Cadiz alone, eight thousand persons were sent back. So rapidly did the number of prisoners at Seville grow that the Inquisitors were forced to remove their headquarters from the Convent of S. Pablo, where they had first established themselves, to the Castle of Triana, iust outside the city, the dungeons of which soon became overcrowded. *Conversos* of blameless reputation were not allowed to leave the city even during the time of plague save on condition that they left their property behind.

The Inquisitors themselves took up their residence at Aracena, where they managed to find plenty to do; but as soon as the pestilence showed signs of diminishing, they returned to the city. Autos-de-fé continued without intermission, a month seldom elapsing in which none was held. Property to an immense value was confiscated, most of the proceeds going to the Crown. Even the dead were not spared, their bones being exhumed and burned after a mock trial. This was not altogether a pointless formality, since the condemnation automatically led to confiscation. By November 4, no less than 298 persons had been burned, while 98 had been condemned to perpetual imprisonment. Vast numbers of others, who came forward spontaneously to confess their guilt on the understanding that they would be dealt with mercifully, were made to parade as penitents. At one of these solemnities, fully fifteen hundred men and women were exhibited. The severity displayed was so extreme that the *conversos* appealed to the Pope, who, in January 1482, wrote to the Spanish sovereigns expressing his disapproval of the methods employed. A list was drawn up and circulated of thirty seven signs (most of them grotesque) by which a Judaizer could be recognized; from changing linen on the Sabbath to washing the hands before prayer, and from calling children by Old Testament names to turning the face to the wall at the moment of death. The promise of a free pardon in return for full confession within a stipulated time encouraged wholesale denunciations, and placed thousands more in the power of the dreaded Tribunal. The aid of the Jews was called in to help in the work, their rabbis being compelled to enjoin their congregations, under pain of excommunication, to reveal everything in their knowledge concerning Judaizers. Judah ibn Verga, the scholarly head of the community of Seville, who had encouraged many Marranos to revert to their ancestral rites, anticipated arrest by a timely flight to Lisbon. Even thither, the long arm of the Inquisition stretched out after him, and he ultimately died in prison as a result of the tortures which he underwent.[8]

It had soon become manifest that the work was too great for the Tribunal at Seville to cope with alone. By a papal brief of February 11, 1482, seven other Inquisitors were nominated — amongst them Thomás de Torquemada, the Queen's fanatical confessor. Other appointments followed at intervals. Additional tribunals were speedily organized at Jaen, Ciudad Real, Cordova, and probably also at Segovia. At Cordova, among the victims of the earliest auto-de-fé was the mistress of the Treasurer of the Cathedral, who was himself burned in the following year. The tribunal of Ciudad Real was intended for the province of Toledo. In its first auto, on February 6, 1484, four persons figured; at the second, on the 23rd and 24th of the same month, thirty men and women were burned alive, as well as the bones or effigies of forty more who had anticipated proceedings by death or flight. In its two years of existence, the Tribunal burned fifty-two obstinate heretics and condemned 220 fugitives, as well as sentencing 183 persons to perform public penance.

In 1485, the seat of this Tribunal was transferred to Toledo. The *conversos* of that city, who were both numerous and wealthy, followed the example of those of Seville, and formed a plot to prevent it from entering into its functions. It was their intention to raise a tumult during the procession of Corpus Christi (June 2), in the hopes of despatching the Inquisitors during the disorder. Subsequently, they proposed to seize the city gates and the tower of the Cathedral, and to hold the place against the Crown. As at Seville, however, the plot was betrayed. On February 12, 1486, the first auto was held. Seven hundred and fifty persons of both sexes figured in it. They were compelled to march through the city in procession, bareheaded and barefoot, carrying unlighted tapers and surrounded by a howling mob, which had streamed in from the neighboring country-side to witness the spectacle. At the doorway of the sacred edifice, they were marked on the forehead with the symbol of the Christian faith, with the words: "Receive the sign of the Cross which ye have denied and lost." By the sentence which was promulgated over each individual before the High Altar, they were fined one-fifth of their property for the war with the Moors, subjected to a perpetual incapacity to hold honorable office or to wear other than the coarsest garments, and were required to march in procession on six Fridays in succession, flagellating themselves with hempen cords. Any disobedience to these injunctions would be treated and punished as a relapse into heresy. At the second auto, 900 penitents appeared; at the third, a further 750. Before the year had elapsed, the total approached five thousand. Besides those who were thus treated with relative leniency, large numbers were burned, as many as fifty persons sometimes on one day. Among the victims were several friars and ecclesiastical dignitaries, who had hitherto lived in an odor of unblemished sanctity.

In 1483, a supreme council was established to coordinate the work of the various local tribunals of Castile and Leon, under the title *Consejo de la Suprema y General Inquisición* (Counsel of the Supreme and General Inquisition). Thomás de Torquemada, one of the seven Inquisitors designated in the previous year, was appointed at its head. On October 17, 1483, the Pope issued a brief extending his authority also over the kingdom of Aragon, with Catalonia and Valencia. Thus, the Spanish Inquisition became unified under one central control.

Under Torquemada's direction, activities in Castile became more and more severe. Ultimately he went so far as to take proceedings on a charge of protecting their kinsfolk against two Bishops of Jewish descent: the venerable Juan Arias Dávila, Bishop of Segovia, son of the former treasurer of the Kingdom, who had given proof of his zeal for the faith by the ferocity with which he had persecuted the Jews of his diocese; and Pedro de Aranda, Bishop of Calahorra, President of the Council of Castile.[9] Both were sent to Rome for trial. The former died, apparently before sentence could be promulgated; the latter was deposed and degraded from orders, dying in prison in the Castle of St. Angelo. It does not appear that in either case the accusations were based upon anything more than personal enmity.

In the kingdom of Aragon, notwithstanding the fact that the Inquisition had already been at work in the thirteenth century, there was great resistance to the introduction of the institution on the Castilian model. Nevertheless, after violent debates, the Cortes which had assembled at Tarazona gave its assent on April 14, 1484. Activities were not long in commencing; and further tribunals were set up in Valencia and Saragossa in the course of the same year. The New Christians of Aragon were, however, wealthy, influential and well-organized, and determined to take matters into their own hands. Shortly after the first auto held at Saragossa, on May 10, 1484, the Inquisitor Gaspar Juglar was found dead. It was confidently asserted that he had been poisoned; but so unostentatious a mode of satisfying their vengeance does not seem in accordance with the bellicose spirit of the *conversos*. Their attention was concentrated on Pedro Arbues, Canon of the Cathedral of Saragossa, who was the heart and soul of the Tribunal. A conspiracy was formed against him which involved many of the most prominent persons in Aragon: Sancho de Paternoy, the *mestre racional* at court; Gabriel Sanchez, the High Treasurer of the kingdom; Francisco de Santa Fé, assessor to the Governor of Aragon and son of the notorious conversionist, Gerónimo de Santa Fé. It is obvious that amongst these were included some whose sympathy with Judaism must have been of a feeble nature, but who joined in the conspiracy because they knew of the danger which the introduction of the Inquisition involved to all those of Jewish origin, especially if they were possessed of any wealth. Among them they raised a fund and engaged a couple of bravos to assist in carrying out the desperate deed. On the night of September 15, 1485, while Arbues was kneeling in prayer in the Cathedral, between the choir and the High Altar, he was attacked. Notwithstanding the armor which he wore, in anticipation of some such event, he was mortally wounded. Two days later, he died. He was of course revered as a saint. Miracles were reported to be effected by his relics. A splendid tomb was erected over his body. Finally, in 1867, he was formally canonized by the Holy See.

The crime was tactically as well as morally a blunder. When the news of the attack became known in the city, excited crowds gathered together; and only the efforts of the Archbishop averted a murderous attack upon the Jews and *conversos*. The Inquisition soon set about exacting a bloody vengeance. The actual assassins were put to death with a refinement of cruelty. Their accomplices figured in a succession of autos. The total number of persons who suffered for complicity has been reckoned at as many as two hundred, though the figure is possibly exaggerated. Francisco de Santa Fé anticipated his sentence by suicide. Sancho de Paternoy, after long tortures, was condemned to perpetual imprisonment; though, in the end, his wealth and influence secured his release and reinstatement. Luis de Santángel, the *escribano de racion* (Secretary of the Household), escaped; but his cousin and namesake, who had been one of the chief conspirators, was beheaded in the market-place, his head being set on a pole and his body burned; he had stood in high favor at Court, being knighted by Juan II for services in battle. Numbers of others fled to France, and were burned in effigy. Alfonso de la Caballeria, Vice-Chancellor of the kingdom, who had been implicated in the conspiracy against Arbues, appealed to Rome, and was able to have his orthodoxy confirmed. He was however unable to prevent the exhumation and burning of the bones of his grandmother, or his wife's appearance as a penitent in an auto-de-fé. Thus, when his son subsequently married King Ferdinand's granddaughter, the blood of the royal house of Aragon mingled with that of condemned heretics.

In the following years, the tribunal of Saragossa continued its activity. A large number of the *conversos* of the city were virtually in its hands, to condemn when it pleased. The names of the great families of Santángel and Sánchez appear with monotonous regularity in its records. Even the court historian, Micer Gonzalo de Santa Maria, fell into its clutches, and died in prison, after three trials. Within fifteen years, over fifty autos were held in the city. In 1488, in spite of the general opposition, activities began in Barcelona, where the tribunal for Catalonia had been set up at the close of the previous year. Among the earliest victims was another member of the family of Gerónimo de Santa Fé. In the following year, a tribunal for the Balearic Islands was established in Majorca.

Professing Jews meanwhile had continued to live in Spain without serious disturbance. Compared with their ancestors of a century before, they were only a miserable remnant; decimated by massacre and conversion, and broken down by the humiliating legislation which was being enforced against them with ever increasing severity. The recent developments had not affected them to any great extent. So long as they did not meddle in matters of faith, the Inquisition could not interfere with them, as being infidels outside the Church, and not heretics within it. The position was however hopelessly illogical. A Marrano, Christian only in name, would be burned alive for performing in secret only a tithe of what his unconverted brethren were performing every day in public with impunity. It was hopeless to attempt to extirpate the Judaizing heresy from the land while Jews were left in it to teach their kinsmen, by precept and by example, the practices of their ancestral religion. A trumped-up story of the martyrdom at Avila, for ritual purposes, of an unnamed child from La Guardia, by Jews and *conversos* acting in conjunction, was taken as proof of the complicity between the two elements. Recent research has established the fact that the alleged victim never existed outside the frenzied imagination of a few fanatical clerics. Nevertheless, the Inquisition was stimulated to fresh efforts; and, within eight years, seventy persons suffered on the charge. The episode, wholly fictitious though its basis was, provided a fresh weapon against the Jews, which Torquemada did not scruple to use.

The spiritual problem was intensified by other considerations. Spain, after many long centuries of disruption, was at last realizing its national unity. It was inevitable that it should begin to strain, more and more, against the alien element which the Jews presumably constituted. The religious zeal, which expressed the Spanish national genius, was at its acme. This resulted in 1492 in the capture of Granada and the final completion of the work of reconquest which had lasted for seven centuries. There was now not the slightest further reason why the sympathies of the Jewish minority need be conciliated for support against the Moslems. Moreover, the growing degradation and impoverishment of the Jews had rendered nugatory the material advantages which their presence had formerly conferred upon the State. They could be dispensed with without misgiving and without loss. Accordingly, on March 30, 1492, in the captured Alhambra, the Spanish sovereigns decreed the expulsion of the Jews from all their dominions — the crowning disaster in the history of the Jews in medieval Europe. Four months later, by July 31, they had all departed. The history of the Marranos, thus left in isolation, enters upon a new phase.

CHAPTER III

THE GENERAL CONVERSION IN PORTUGAL

THE Jewish exiles who were driven out of Spain in 1492 were scattered to every corner of the Mediterranean world. Large numbers went overseas to Italy and to the Moslem countries, where they could count at least on tolerance. It was thus that the great communities of the old Turkish Empire, which even today still speak the Castilian of their fathers, were formed. But the largest single body unenterprisingly took the obvious course and crossed the frontier into Portugal. Jews had been settled here ever since the birth of the monarchy and generally had been well-treated. The wave of massacres of 1391 had not affected them; and, save for an isolated attack upon the community of Lisbon in 1449, the reaction which had prevailed in the rest of the Peninsula during the fifteenth century had left the country virtually untouched. It offered itself therefore as the natural place of refuge for the less adventurous. Neither the native Jews on the one hand nor the counselors of state on the other were anxious to receive the influx. However, the ruling monarch, João II, was more friendly; though he was plainly actuated by anticipation of profit rather than by a sense of humanity. Thirty important families, headed by Rabbi Isaac Aboab, the last Sage of Castile, were permitted to establish themselves at Oporto. Another six hundred wealthy householders, who could afford to pay a tax of one hundred *cruzados* apiece, were allowed to settle in other parts of the country. Besides these, a number of craftsmen, who might be of assistance in the preparations for the forthcoming African campaign, were allowed to take up their residence on the payment of a nominal sum.

Only these were to be allowed to settle permanently. Others might enter the country on the payment of a poll-tax of eight *cruzados* for each adult, on the understanding that they would not remain for longer than eight months. Within this period the king bound himself to find shipping for their transport wherever they desired. The number of those who crossed the frontier under this agreement is reckoned to have amounted to nearly one hundred thousand souls.

The conditions upon which they entered the country were not fulfilled. Shipping was provided only tardily; and those who ventured on board were treated with the greatest cruelty, being disembarked whether they desired it or no at the nearest point in Africa. All those who remained behind, through no fault of their own, after the prescribed period had lapsed were declared to have forfeited their liberty, and were sold as slaves. A large number of children were ruthlessly torn from their parents' arms, seven hundred being sent to populate the insalubrious island of St. Thomé, off the African coast,[1] where the vast majority inevitably perished.

In the midst of this, João II died. He was succeeded by his cousin, Manoel "the Fortunate" (1495–1521). The latter, on his accession, seemed to deserve the title which posterity bestowed upon him. Recognizing that those Jews who had not left the realm in time were guiltless, he restored them their liberty; and he even went so far as to refuse the gift which was offered to him by the communities of the kingdom in gratitude for his generous action. A contemporary authority indicates that it was hoped to win them over to Christianity by this display of magnanimity. Possibly this was the case; for, shortly afterwards, the young king showed himself in a very different light. Ferdinand and Isabella, who had united Castile and Aragon by marriage, had a daughter, Isabella. If she became Manoel's wife, there was a prospect that their children would ultimately rule over the whole of the Peninsula. However, the Catholic sovereigns, who resented unreasoningly the reception of the Spanish refugees elsewhere, would consent to the match only on condition that the smaller country was "purified" of the Jews as their own dominions had been. The matter was brought up before the Great Council of the realm. Opinions were varied, some members warning the king against strengthening his African enemies by the expulsion of this thrifty and diligent section of the population. It was the Infanta herself who decided matters, writing to Manoel that she would not enter his country until it was cleansed of the presence of all infidels. This was decisive. On November 30, 1496, the marriage treaty was signed. Less than a week later, on December 5, there was issued from Muje a royal decree banishing the Jews and Moslems from the country. They were given ten complete months to wind up their affairs. After the lapse of this period, at the end of October 1497, none was to remain.

Hardly was the ink dry on this edict, when Manoel began to take the other side of the question into consideration. His psychology was curious and warped.

but, in its way, by no means inconsistent. His previous friendliness towards the Jews had been due to his recognition of their value as citizens. He was naturally unwilling to lose their services, though, as long as they remained faithful to their ancestral religion, he could no longer allow them to remain in the realm. Moreover, he appears to have been genuinely anxious to save their souls, whether they were willing or no. The conclusion was obvious. For his own sake, for the sake of his realm, and for the sake of the Jews themselves, they must be driven to accept the Christian faith. If only they did this, the obvious disadvantages of their imminent departure from the country — political, financial, economic — would all be obviated: and into the bargain they would be assured of eternal felicity.

He struck first at the parents through the children: a step advised by an apostate, Levi ben Shem-tob, who displayed in this foul act of treachery perfect familiarity with the Jewish mentality. The Council of State, assembled at Estremoz, disapproved of the plan; especially the clerical party, led by the noble Fernando Coutinho, subsequently Bishop of Silves, who stoutly maintained that the step meditated was uncanonical. The king, more fanatical than the Church, was unmoved, retorting that the action he proposed was for the sake of religion, and that he did not trouble about the law. On Friday, March 19, 1497, orders were issued throughout the country for all children between the ages of four and fourteen years to be presented for baptism on the following Sunday. That day, as it happened, was the beginning of the feast of Passover — the birthday of Hebrew freedom! At the appointed time, those children who were not presented voluntarily were seized by the officials and forced to the font. Scenes of indescribable horror were witnessed as they were torn away by the royal bailiffs. The latter did not obey their instructions too closely, frequently seizing young people of both sexes up to the age of twenty. In many cases, parents smothered their offspring in their farewell embrace. In others, they threw them into wells in order to save them from the disgrace of apostasy, and then killed themselves. Sometimes, even old men were dragged to the churches and forcibly baptized by over-zealous fanatics, who were under the impression that a general conversion of all the Jews had been ordered. The desired effect of forcing the parents to accompany their children into baptism rather than lose them for good was achieved only on exceptionally rare occasions. In all other cases, the unwilling neophytes, some mere babies, were distributed throughout the country, as far as possible from home, to be brought up in Christian surroundings.

No considerations of rank availed. Judah Abrabanel, one of the more eminent physicians of his age, whose father was a familiar figure in half the courts of southern Europe, lost his twelve-year-old son, whom he commemorated in a touching Hebrew elegy. Isaac ben Abraham ibn Zachin, a learned refugee from Spain, killed himself and his children "for the sanctification of the Name." Contemporary opinion was not entirely callous. Some kind-hearted Christians received the children of their Jewish neighbors into their own homes, in order to help them to escape.

More than thirty years later, the terrible scenes still lived in the mind of the old Bishop Coutinho. "I saw many persons dragged by the hair to the font," he wrote. "Sometimes, I saw a father, his head covered in sign of grief and pain, lead his son to the font, protesting and calling God to witness that they wished to die together in the law of Moses. Yet more terrible things that were done with them did I witness, with my own eyes." The children of the Moslems, who were included in the edict of expulsion, were untouched. The authorities cynically confessed the reason. It was that there were lands in which the Crescent was supreme, and in which reprisals might be carried out!

Meanwhile, the final date fixed for the departure of the Jews from the country approached. Originally, three ports of embarkation had been assigned — Lisbon, Algarve, and Oporto. After some vacillation, the king changed his mind and announced that all were to pass through the capital. The Jews assembled there from all parts of the country, to the number of some 20,000 souls. On their arrival here, they were herded successively into the palace known as *Os Estãos*, which was generally utilized for the reception of foreign ambassadors.[2] There they were kept cooped up in vast numbers, without food or drink, in hopes that the deprivation would open their eyes to the true faith. Periodical visits were paid to them by the Queen's apostate physician, Master Nicholas, and his brother, Dom Pedro de Castro, a prominent ecclesiastic, who endeavored to persuade them to adopt Christianity. Under these circumstances, many accepted baptism. Those who still refused were kept closely guarded until the time-limit set for their departure from the country had elapsed. Then they were informed that by their disobedience they had forfeited their liberty, and that in consequence they were now the King's slaves. By this means, the resistance of the majority was broken down, and they went in droves to the churches for baptism. Others were dragged to the font by brute force. The defiant attitude of some won them the martyrdom they craved. The rest, still protesting, had holy water sprinkled over them and were declared to be Christians. Only a few, led by Simon Maimi, the last *Arrabi-Mor*, or Chief Rabbi of Portugal, kept up open opposition. In order to induce these to set an example to the rest, they were half walled-up in a dungeon. They still refused to yield; and after a week Maimi died in consequence of his sufferings. Some of the recent converts, at the peril of their lives, took the body to the Jewish burial-ground for interment. Two more of his companions similarly succumbed; the rest, not more than seven or eight in all, were transported to Africa. This pathetic relic was all that was left of the ancient and once renowned Portuguese Jewry.

The expulsion from Portugal is thus, as a matter of fact, a misnomer. The number of those who were able to emigrate was so exiguous as to be negligible. What put an end to the residence of the Jews in the country was a General Conversion of unexampled comprehensiveness, knowing almost no exceptions and carried out by means of an unbridled exercise of force.

There was thus a vast difference between the mass conversions in Spain and in Portugal. In the former country, it was only the weaker who had yielded — sometimes, indeed, in order to save their lives, but frequently even when immediate danger was absent. In the latter case, matters were entirely dissimilar. Those who submitted to baptism with any show of willingness, however remote, were few in the extreme. In most instances, they were not even afforded the alternative of martyrdom. They were literally forced to the font and, after the merest parody of the baptismal ceremony, were declared to be Christians. Those who were thus treated comprised all elements in the Jewish population — the rich as well as the poor, the learned, the pious, the indifferent. Included with them moreover were many of the recent exiles from Castile, amongst whom were some of the noblest and most stalwart scions of Spanish Jewry. Thus, even the family of the last Sage of Castile, who had died but a few months after he had reached Oporto, were forced to give in; though their descendants afterwards returned to great prominence in Jewish life. Eminent scholars and rabbis, like Solomon ibn Verga, the chronicler, or Levi ben Habib, subsequently spiritual leader of the community of Jerusalem, were among those who were compelled by sheer force to accept Catholicism. It was thus inevitable that the Portuguese New Christians were stauncher than those of Spain. The latter all but died out in the course of the sixteenth century. The former displayed more vitality, showing themselves able to maintain their resistance in spite of centuries of persecution and (as we shall see) providing the Inquisition of Spain with an ample field of activity long after the native Judaizers had been exterminated.

There was a further factor, which made for the greater tenacity of Marranism in Portugal. In Spain, from the moment of the expulsion of the Jews in 1492 and the violent breach of the direct Jewish tradition in the country, the Inquisition had existed, grimly determined to do its utmost to stamp out all traces of Judaizing. Its task was relatively simple. In Portugal, in this respect, conditions were entirely different. There, no Inquisition existed until nearly half a century after the Edict of Expulsion. In the intervening period, the emigration of New Christians was generally forbidden; while on the other hand some of the more steadfast of the Spanish Judaizers crossed the frontier into the land of greater security. During this period, the Portuguese Marranos had ample opportunity to accommodate themselves to the possibilities of crypto-Judaism, that acquired in the process a strength and tenacity which, in the event, proved almost invincible.

It had been impossible to expect immediate religious conformity from the bewildered Portuguese *conversos*, who had suddenly been declared to be Christians but were absolutely ignorant of the religion to which they now officially belonged. Though they were driven to the churches at regular intervals, fathers and sons together, in order to have the rudiments of Catholicism flogged into them, it was obvious that their knowledge of their new faith must remain slight for a considerable period to come. Pope Alexander VI, appealed to for guidance, fully recognized the fact, and counseled moderation. Immediately after the earliest baptisms, on May 30, 1497, the king had published a rescript promising that for a period of twenty years to come the New Christians should enjoy immunity from molestation for offences arising out of matters of Faith. After this period had elapsed, they were to be subjected to ordinary civil procedure only, no ecclesiastical tribunal being allowed to act against them. A general amnesty was meanwhile granted for all offences in religious matters of which they might have been guilty in the past. Above all, it was promised that at no time would there be any legislation against the New Christians as a separate race.

These regulations guaranteed the safety of the Portuguese Marranos for the moment. Meanwhile, it was inevitable that they should have continued to practice Judaism all but in public. Their physicians were even authorized to continue to possess Hebrew books for professional guidance, though the retention of other Jewish literature was forbidden. The more stalwart seized any opportunity of fleeing overseas to some place where they might practice their ancestral religion in peace. Large numbers made their way to Italy, Africa, and Turkey. To this period, probably, belongs the foundation of the "Portuguese" communities at Salonica, Smyrna, and elsewhere in the Levant. It soon became obvious that the royal policy would be circumvented, and that those who had been prevented from leaving the country as Jews would do so as Christians, reverting to the faith of their fathers as soon as they crossed the seas. There was only one logical course. On April 20, 1499, Manoel published a decree forbidding any New Christian to leave the country without special royal license. This was reinforced by a further provision forbidding the ordinary population to facilitate their flight by purchasing from them land or bills of exchange. This enactment continued to be enforced, with brief intermissions, through a large part of the sixteenth century. Thus, crypto-Judaism in the country was further strengthened. The New Christians were obliged to remain against their will in the midst of an alien

population which, already filled with hatred and contempt, regarded their successes with jealousy and was
constantly incited against them from the pulpit by a
fanatical clergy.

In 1503 the harvest was scanty. In the following
winter famine threatened the country; and the populace,
looking about for a scapegoat, found it in the unfortunate
Marranos, whose deceitful way of life had plainly aroused
the divine anger. On Whit-Sunday, a quarrel between
some New Christians and an insulting band of youths in
the Rua Nova, in Lisbon, led to a popular outbreak
which was suppressed only with difficulty. In the following April, there were similar disorders in Evora, where
the building which had previously served as a synagogue
was pulled down by the mob. All this led up to the
terrible scenes which took place at Lisbon early in 1506.

On the night of April 7, a number of New Christians
were surprised celebrating the Passover together. They
were arrested, but were released after only two days'
imprisonment. This display of mildness enraged the
populace. A few days later, on April 19, mass was
celebrated in the Jesus Chapel of the Church of
S. Domingo, to implore for cessation of the pestilence
which had recently begun to spread. A crucifix which
stood at the altar was observed to be unusually luminous.
Those present, wrought up to a high pitch of religious
enthusiasm, asserted that the phenomenon was caused
by a miracle. A New Christian among them tactlessly
laughed at the idea, saying that nothing more extraordinary was in question than the normal refraction
of light. His scepticism was taken as being equivalent to
blasphemy. He was dragged out of the church and

butchered, his body being dragged to the principal square (the *Rocio*) where it was burned. Attention was then turned to his brethren in disbelief. Two Dominican friars — one of them an Aragonese — paraded through the streets with an uplifted crucifix, crying *Heresia*, and summoning the people to avenge themselves on the enemies of the faith. The mob was joined by German, Dutch, and French sailors whose ships were lying in the harbor. A terrible massacre began. On the first day, over five hundred New Christians were murdered. Babes in the cradle were not spared. Women seeking refuge in the churches were dragged out and put to death, their bodies being committed to the flames. On the next day, the scenes were repeated. One of the last victims was the tax-farmer João Rodriguez Mascarenhas, the richest and most hated man in Lisbon, who was done to death in the Rua Nova amid the rejoicing of the mob, his house being subsequently demolished. Women showed themselves foremost amongst the rioters.

A German eye-witness — a Christian — gives a graphic description of the horrors which took place. "On Monday, I saw things that I would certainly not have believed had they been reported or written, or unless I had witnessed them myself. Women with child were flung from the windows and caught on spears by those standing underneath, their offspring being hurled away. The peasantry followed the example of the towns-people. Many women and girls were ravished in the fanatical pursuit. The number of New Christians slain is estimated at between 2,000 and 4,000 souls." Isaac ibn Farraj, a Hebrew writer, provides a gruesome side-light. He managed to remove from the ashes part of the burned skull of one of his dearest friends, which he was subsequently able to bury in the Jewish cemetery at Valona.

When the news reached the king, at Aviz, he was enraged. The disorders were sharply punished. The two friars who had instigated them were degraded, and then garroted and burned. Another twenty or thirty persons suffered capital punishment. The city temporarily lost its proud title, "Noble and Always Loyal," and its inhabitants were fined one-fifth of their property, as well as deprived of the right of electing their Town Councilors. Above all, the *Matança dos Christãos-Novos*, or "Massacre of the New Christians," as it was called, had displayed the utter inadequacy of the policy of forcible assimilation, which had been hitherto followed. Early in the following year (March 1, 1507), a royal edict restored to the New Christians the right of removing from the country like any other section of the population, at the same time confirming the immunities from penal procedure and special legislation granted ten years previously. In 1512, these were renewed for a further period of twenty years, during which no prosecution on the grounds of heresy might be allowed. The tide of emigration which consequently set in was however so great that in 1521 freedom of movement was again restricted.

This more moderate policy, which might in the end have resulted in assimilating the Marranos, continued to be followed up to the period of King Manoel's death in 1521. His son and successor, João III, was guided in the early years of his reign by his father's advisers. There was accordingly no drastic change in his attitude;

though in 1524 a secret inquiry amongst the parish priests confirmed the fact that the New Christians were still Jews in everything but name. In the following year, the young king married Catalina, a granddaughter of Ferdinand and Isabella and the sister of the Emperor Charles V, a strong-minded woman, with all the determination as well as the religious zeal characteristic of her family. She was the only Queen of Portugal ever to have a seat upon the Council of State, where she was thus able to bring decisive influence to bear. To one familiar with the state of affairs in Spain, only one satisfactory solution could be applied to the religious problems of Portugal: the introduction of an Inquisition on the Spanish model to cleanse the realm of heresy.

The idea was not a new one. Notwithstanding his repeated promise not to allow any ecclesiastical tribunal to take proceedings against them, Manoel had applied secretly to Rome in 1515 for the introduction of the Holy Office into his dominions; but nothing had come of it. His son, in spite of his confirmation on more than one occasion, in 1522 and 1524, of the immunities granted by his father, was thus provided with an example which he might piously follow.

The conduct of the minority was not altogether calculated to induce moderation. In 1524, a New Christian informer named Henrique Nuñes, who was acting as *agent provocateur* with the object of obtaining the introduction of the Inquisition, and had provided the king with lists of persons guilty of the practice of Judaism whose confidence he had obtained, was assassinated by a couple of Marranos disguised as friars. They were of course put to death, after having been tortured cruelly in order to discover the names of their accomplices. The memory of the crime was however kept alive, the remains of *Firme Fé* or "Firm-Faith" (as Nuñes was now generally called) being revered as those of a martyr. When in 1528 that incredible adventurer, David Reubeni, arrived in Portugal on a pretended mission from the independent Jewish tribes of the Far East to arrange joint action against the Turk, and armed with authentic letters of recommendation from the Pope, a great impression was naturally caused in crypto-Jewish circles. The report was even bruited abroad that he had been given permission to teach the "Law of Moses." Much to his personal annoyance, the Marranos flocked to him in large numbers wherever he went, showing him every sign of deference. A promising young government official, Diogo Pires, finding himself treated with some coldness, went so far as to circumcise himself; subsequently, he left the country, to become famous in the annals of Jewish history and martyrdom as Solomon Molcho, the pseudo-Messiah. A number of Spanish Marranos, who had fled to Campo-Mayor, were emboldened to make an armed raid on Badajoz, where they released by force a woman imprisoned in the dungeons of the Inquisition. Great unrest was spread through the country by a rumor that the New Christians had made common cause and were about to rise in arms. Attacks were made upon them by the populace in Alentejo, Santarem, and Gouvea, where an image of the Virgin had been found defaced. Serious riots, which were checked only by the efforts of the poet Gil Vicente, took place at Santarem. At Olivença, five Marranos found practicing "Mosaic" rites were arbitrarily burned by the Bishop of Ceuta, amid popular enthusiasm. There were disorders even in the Azores and at Madeira. At the beginning of the following year (1531) a large part of Lisbon was laid in ruins by a destructive earthquake. It seemed that the divine power was manifesting its indignation directly against the New Christian duplicity; and a further massacre was only narrowly averted.

This last event seems to have determined the king's mind. Early in the same year, Brás Neto, the Portuguese ambassador at Rome, was instructed to procure in strictest secrecy from Pope Clement VII the authorization for the establishment in Portugal of an Inquisition on the Spanish model. After prolonged negotiations, on December 17, 1531, Frei Diogo da Silva, the king's confessor, was formally appointed Inquisitor General. Meanwhile, the departure of the New Christians from the country, even to the Portuguese colonies, was again forbidden under heavy penalties.

Every endeavor had been made to keep the negotiations secret. The news inevitably leaked out and the New Christians, on their part, took energetic steps. They chose as their emissary a certain Duarte de Paz, an old soldier of Jewish extraction, a man of considerable ability and few scruples. Taking advantage of a foreign mission with which he had been entrusted by the king, he made his way to Rome, where he remained for ten years as the agent of his fellow New Christians. He was well supplied with money, the key to most things at the papal court. By dint of systematic propaganda backed up by bribes, the cause of the Marranos made great headway. The attitude which they adopted was simple, and from the religious point of view unimpeachable: that notwithstanding their origin, they were faithful adherents of Christianity, and that the proposed innovation was actuated entirely by jealousy and greed. In Portugal, they succeeded in buying over the Bishop of Sinigaglia (who had been sent to Lisbon as Papal Nuncio). Frei Diogo himself, who refused to take up the office to which he had been appointed, was also suspected of being in their pay.

At Rome, de Paz succeeded in procuring from the Pope a Brief suspending the action of that establishing the Holy Office, and forbidding any Inquisitorial action to be taken against the Marranos. This was reinforced by the famous Bull of Pardon (*Bulle de Perdão*) of April 7, 1533, which provided the New Christians with a complete amnesty for all past offences in matters of faith, coupled with the concession that those accused of heresy in future might justify themselves before the Papal Nuncio. The latter, naturally, reaped a handsome profit; within the next three years, he is said to have gained 30,000 crowns. Henceforth, the struggle centered about the *Bulle de Perdão*, which prevented serious Inquisitorial activity. It was confirmed in July and in October, suspended in December, but renewed by Clement on his death-bed in the following July. His successor, Paul III, referred the question to a commission of cardinals. They reported in favor of the Bull, recommending that the Inquisition should be authorized only under considerable limitations, coupled with the right of appeal to Rome. This last provision would have nullified the royal supremacy over the Tribunal, and was hence unacceptable to the Portuguese authorities. While negotiations were being carried on, the New Christians entered into a contract with the

Nuncio, promising to pay the Pope 30,000 ducats if he would prohibit the Inquisition and limit the power of prosecution to the bishops, who were to be confined to ordinary criminal procedure.

A deadlock had arisen, when the Emperor Charles V arrived in Rome, fresh from his triumph over the infidel at Tunis. He threw the weight of his authority, now almost omnipotent, into the scales on the side of his brother-in-law. This advocacy carried the day. After some slight further delay, a Brief was issued on May 23, 1536, repealing the previous temperate Bulls and definitely constituting in Portugal an Inquisition on the Spanish model. The only reservations made were that for the forthcoming three years the forms of secular law were to be observed, and that no confiscations of property (which struck at the family, as well as at the culprit himself) were to be allowed until a full decade had elapsed.

The struggle was, indeed, by no means over. The New Christians, a rare fit of parsimony on whose part had been partly responsible for the recent check, now redoubled their efforts. Thanks to lavish bribes, the new Nuncio, Girolamo Recanati Capodiferro, was authorized to hear appeals from the decisions of the Inquisition, and even to suspend its action altogether if he thought fit. He used his powers lavishly, to no small personal profit. Judaizers were occasionally prosecuted, and sentenced to light punishments. However, the establishment of an omnipotent tribunal like that of Spain seemed no nearer than it had been years before.

Once again, a piece of extravagance on the part of one of the persecuted minority nullified all their efforts.

One morning, in February 1539, placards were found
affixed to the doors of all the principal churches in Lisbon
bearing the following words:—"The Messiah has not
come. Jesus Christ was not the true Messiah." There
was, not unnaturally, a general wave of indignation.
Very considerable rewards were offered to any person
who discovered the culprit. Shortly after, a further
notice was found on the door of the Cathedral: "I am
neither Spaniard nor Portuguese, but an Englishman.
If instead of 10,000 *escudos* you offered 20,000, you would
not discover my name." It seemed obvious that this
was intended to divert suspicion from the Marranos,
who were generally regarded as being responsible for the
outrage. One of them, Manuel da Costa, was accused
of having perpetrated it. He was tortured until he confessed his guilt, after which he was burned with every
circumstance of cruelty.

Popular feeling against the *conversos* was now generally
aroused. The period of comparative mildness and humanity was at an end. The king appointed as Inquisitor
General his brother, Dom Henrique, thus plainly showing his own determination. The three years' delay
accorded in 1536 had now elapsed, the way being thus
open for the full and untrammeled exercise of Inquisitorial
power to begin. The New Christians indeed were still
busy at the papal Court, where the Bull *Pastoris Aeterni*,
allowing appeals to Rome and limiting the power of the
Inquisition in other ways, was issued on October 12, 1539.
However, owing to a quarrel between the New Christians and the rapacious Capodiferro, Nuncio at Lisbon,
this was never published.

Nothing now stood in the way of the initiation of

operations. Tribunals were speedily organized at Lisbon, Evora, and Coimbra, and temporarily also at Lamego, Thomar, and Oporto. (The three last-named were discontinued before long as being superfluous; though a contributory reason was the discovery of shameful irregularities and abuses in their administration.) On September 20, 1540, a formal Act of Faith took place at Lisbon: the earliest in Portugal, and the first of a long and gruesome series which extended over two and a half centuries. The Marranos had not indeed given up the fight, nor had the Pope altogether abandoned them. There was a further succession of quarrels and of bribery, culminating in the suspension of the Holy Office in 1544. The magnificent bribe of the revenues of the Archiepiscopal see of Visieu finally overcame the Pope's opposition. By the Bull *Meditatio Cordis* of July 16, 1547, the existence of a free and untrammeled Inquisition in Portugal was finally authorized. Negotiations still continued over the vexed question of the power of confiscation. This was one of the most deadly weapons in the hands of the Holy Office, and was considered by the New Christians to be a perpetual incitement to action against them. After prolonged negotiations and changes of policy, this too was finally conceded in 1579. From that date, Portugal was endowed with an independent Inquisition on the same model as that of Spain, capable of extremities of rigor not surpassed even by its more famous prototype. The work of the General Conversion could now be enforced.[3]

CHAPTER IV

THE HEYDAY OF THE INQUISITION

By the time that the Portuguese Inquisition was properly established, the original generation of forced converts had all but died out. A fresh generation had grown up, here as in Spain, of persons who had been born titular Christians, brought up in the full traditions of the dominant faith, and fully assimilated in externals to the mass of the population. In spite of this fact, and of the pledge made by King Manoel at the time of the General Conversion, they continued to be treated as a race apart. They were generally known as *"conversos,"* "Jews," or "Persons of the Nation." A close distinction was drawn between the "Old" and "New" Christians, the latter comprising the descendants — even after half a dozen generations or more — of those who had accepted baptism. The utmost prejudice prevailed against maintaining any connection with them, so that they were forced to marry in most cases only amongst themselves. Children of a mixed marriage would be designated (in the Inquisitional processes especially) as being "Half New Christian"; while a person with a grandparent of Jewish blood would be called "Quarter New Christian." Similarly, we find persons described as having "a part of the New Christian" if they possessed a single traceable Jewish ancestor, or as being "More than one half New Christian" if Jewish blood predominated. Occasionally, still more minute gradations were recorded. It is remarkable how the mere fact of consciousness of Jewish descent, however remote, determined large numbers of persons to brave all dangers and to throw in their lot with their persecuted kinsmen. Similarly, not a few individuals of undiluted Old Christian blood are known to have become martyrs for the cause of Judaism.

Conversely, Christians of old family prided themselves on their *limpieza*, or purity of blood — it will be recalled how Sancho Panza delighted in the fact. Among the functions of the Inquisition was that of giving certificates to this effect to persons who had no traceable Jewish or Moslem ancestor to contaminate their lineage. Certain offices — for example, commissions in the army, or employment under the Holy Office — were titularly confined to persons who could fulfill this condition; and, at one time, it was a condition of entrance into the faculty, or even the student-body, of certain universities. However, it was impossible in these inquiries to go back too far; and in fact not many houses can have been entirely pure. Thus it sometimes happened that the prosecution of a distant kinsman for Judaizing would reveal some unsuspected streak of infidel ancestry, which would throw obloquy upon a distinguished family and disqualify it for honorable office.

The prejudice against the *conversos* throughout the Peninsula was undiminished by the lapse of time. In Spain, they had been expelled from the districts of Guipúzcoa and Vizcaya early in the sixteenth century; and, as late as 1565, an attempt was made to repeat this. In Portugal, there were occasional outbreaks against them throughout the northern provinces (over one hundred towns of which contributed victims to the autos-da-fe between 1565 and 1595) — at Trancoso, Lamego, Miranda, Visieu, Guarda, Braga, and elsewhere. On one occasion, a plot was discovered for the extermination of all the New Christians on a single day. Anti-Semitic works, which refused to differentiate between *converso* and Jew, poured from the presses in a steady stream. In 1562, the Portuguese bishops presented a petition requesting that the New Christians should be compelled to wear special badges, and to be segregated in Ghettos, just as their unconverted ancestors had been.

In spite of all these restrictions and prejudices, there was no stratum of society to which the New Christians did not penetrate. This was the case even more in Portugal than in Spain. They were to be found in every walk of life — from beggars to statesmen, from playwrights to revenue-farmers, from cobblers to explorers. Their wealth was enormous. Early in the seventeenth century, they themselves admitted that they were worth between them no less than 80,000,000 ducats. They almost monopolized commerce. Within a few years of the General Conversion, one of the greatest banking houses in Europe was the establishment which the Mendes family had developed at Lisbon out of a comparatively small business in precious stones. The export trade of Portugal, especially, was very largely in Marrano hands. They provided politics and literature with important figures. Pedro Texeira, whose *Travels* are among the most important sources for our knowledge of the Orient at the beginning of the seventeenth century, was of Jewish extraction, and is believed to have reverted to his ancestral faith before his death. Duarte Gomez Solis, whose *Discourses on the Commerce of the*

Two Indies (Lisbon, 1622) gives him a place as one of the foremost economists of his age, was similarly a New Christian. The mathematician, Pedro Nuñes, Cosmographer Royal to King João III, was another, his grandchildren actually falling into the clutches of the Inquisition. The same was the fate of the poet, Serrão de Castro, who afterwards commemorated his experiences in his writings, and of Antonio Bocarro, the chronicler, who reverted to Christianity after a brief experience of Judaism.

A number of the most illustrious physicians of the day were of Jewish origin, and many of them devout Jews at heart; the profession was indeed adopted by some persons specifically by reason of the facilities which it afforded for the observance of the Sabbath. Thus, Tomas Rodrigues da Veiga (son of the *converso* Mestre Rodrigo da Veiga, body-physician to King Manoel, and grandson of Mestre Tomas de la Veiga, a Spanish exile of 1492) was medical attendant to King João III, and is described as the most famous professor of the University of Coimbra. Dr. Emmanuel Vaz was in the service of four Portuguese sovereigns in succession, from João III to Philip II. Garcia d'Orta, the founder of the study of tropical medicine and of Asiatic botany, has recently been discovered to have been a secret Jew, his body having been exhumed and burned by the Inquisition. When at the close of the sixteenth century the Grand Dukes of Tuscany set about the reorganization of the University of Pisa, it was especially to New Christian scholars from Portugal that they had recourse. Thus the eminent Estevão Rodrigues de Castro, professor of medicine successively there and at Padua, was in this category.

He was followed in both places by Antonio (Rodrigo) da Fonseca, author of an important work on fevers. Christoval Acosta, who was a native of one of the Portuguese settlements in Africa, composed a treatise on drugs which is still, after a lapse of three and a half centuries, regarded as authoritative. Further names in this sphere could be added almost indefinitely. Indeed, in an anti-Jewish work of the period, there was included a list of no less than fifty-one physicians and apothecaries who had been condemned by the Inquisition. In the Universities — particularly that of Coimbra — the proportion of New Christian professors was sometimes extraordinarily high.

In spite of all precautions, intermarriage with the nobility took place on a comparatively large scale. Thus the daughter of the *converso* Mestre Rodrigo da Veiga, body-physician of Manoel I, married a member of the Ximenes d'Arragon family, their descendants including nobles, statesmen, and ecclesiastics who were prominent in every part of Europe. There were however in Portugal a number of so-called "puritan" houses, who would contract family alliances with none who could not prove a lineage as unblemished as their own. Even in the army, notwithstanding the regulations to the contrary, the number of New Christians was considerable, and some of them rose to high rank. Many persons even adopted a clerical career, fancying perhaps that thus they would be safer from persecution. A lengthy list could be made of nuns and monks and friars, some of whom attained great distinction in the Church, who either suffered at the hands of the Inquisition, or else ended their lives as professing Jews.[1] At one single auto at Coimbra, which lasted over two days and at which over two hundred persons in all figured, the victims included professors, canons, priests, curates, vicars-general, friars, nuns, and even an unfrocked Franciscan who maintained his convictions to the last and was in consequence burned alive.[2] In the course of eight years, from 1619 to 1627, the 231 persons condemned to appear at public autos in Portugal included 15 doctors of the university, of whom two held professorial chairs; eleven other graduates; 20 advocates, and as many physicians and notaries; and above all forty-four nuns and fifteen beneficed clergy of whom seven were canons.

Launcelot Addison, the father of the great essayist, writing in 1675, gives the following graphic account:—

". . . I am assured that some *Jews* have gone herein so far as to enter into Holy Orders and the Profession of a *Religious Life*, who yet coming to places where the *Jews* have publick Toleration, have joyned themselves to the Synagogue.

"And of this we have a very late instance of two *Jews*, who in *Spain* having for several years professed the religion of Saint *Dominique*, coming to *Legorn* in their Fryar-Habits, they instantly changed their Cowl for a *Ganephe*[3] and of idle Fryers become progging[4] *Jews*. Another *Jew* (of my acquaintance, who for about five years had studied Physick at *Saragoza* in *Spain*) being asked how he could comply with the Religion, he merrily made this reply, *That his complyance was only the work of his Nerves and Muscles, and that his Anatomy told him nothing of the heart was therein concerned.*[5] Another *Jew* who in *Malaga* counterfeited Christianity so well as to be intrusted with the Sale of Indulgences, having made a good market thereof in *Spain*, came with what he had left to a Christian city in *Barbary*, where his Indulgences being all bought up by the *Irish* and others of the Papal perswasion, he declared his religion. The Papists who had bought his Indulgences impeach him to the Governur for a *Cheat*, and clamour to have him punished according to demerit. The *Jew* pleaded the Laws of the free Port, that he had neither imported nor sold any thing but his professed Merchandise, and therefore desired (and obtained) the Liberty and Priviledges of such as traffick'd to that Port. I report nothing but matter of personal knowledge.

"That there are many such Temporizing *Jews*, especially in *Spain* and *Portugal*, I have been assured from their own mouths: and what is more observable, some have ventured to affirm, that there want not *Jews* among the very Judges of the Inquisition, . . ."

(*The Present State of the Jews*, pp. 31–2)

It was upon this capable but extraordinarily motley element, by now inextricably intermingled with the general population, that the attentions of the Inquisition remained centered in the sixteenth and seventeenth centuries, both in Portugal and in Spain. In the latter country, its work had continued uninterrupted after the expulsion of the Jews. The immediate result of that cruel measure had been to increase the number of the insincere converts in the country. Large numbers of persons, despairing of finding any resting place abroad, had gained permission to remain behind at the price of conversion. The example was set by the sceptical Don Abraham Senior, the last *Rab de la Corte* in Castile and principal farmer of taxes, who was henceforth known as Fernando Perez Coronel. Many of those who chose exile turned back to Spain, after prolonged sufferings, and despairingly submitted to baptism. Sincerity could not be expected from persons who had embraced the Catholic religion under such circumstances. Thus, the field of labor of the Inquisition was further extended.

Thomás de Torquemada had been succeeded as Grand Inquisitor by the scholarly Diego Deza, the friend and patron of Columbus. Notwithstanding the fact that he himself (like his predecessor) was said to be of Jewish extraction on one side, the activity of the tribunal reached its zenith under his auspices. In 1500, an exalted Marrano woman, who pretended to be a prophetess, was arrested at Herrera.[6] This provided a unique opportunity for action. On February 22, 1501, a great auto was held at Toledo, at which 38 of her followers were burned; on the next day, 67 more — all of them women — suffered the same fate. Worse still were the excesses committed by Diego Rodrigues Lucero, Inquisitor of Cordova. Here, accusations were made wholesale. The severity shown was incredible. The grounds for prosecution were of the flimsiest nature, and the ruthless use of torture was generally sufficient to extract some sort of confession. No further cause was thus needed to condemn a man to the stake other than that he was of Jewish blood. Even the Archdeacon de Castro, whose mother was of an Old Christian family, while his father was a *converso* of high rank, was sentenced and made to perform public penance, his enormous fortune being confiscated. The climax came when no fewer than 107 persons were burned alive on the accusation of having listened to the sermons of one Membreque, a Bachelor of Divinity, who had sought to diffuse the doctrines of Judaism by this means. The Inquisitors, complained the Captain of Cordova, ". . . were able to defame the whole kingdom, to destroy, without God or justice, a great part of it, slaying and robbing and violating maids and wives, to the great dishonor of the Christian religion . . ."

Complaints against the atrocities which were being perpetrated became so rife that, on September 30, 1505, Philip and Juana, the Castilian sovereigns, suspended all action on the part of the Inquisition until they should return from Flanders. Meanwhile, the *conversos* spent money lavishly at Rome to induce the papal Curia to take a merciful view of their plight. It happened that, before anything definite could be done to ameliorate their position, Philip suddenly died, leaving his wife demented. Lucero now seized the opportunity to avenge himself for the check he had received, embarking upon fresh extravagances. He asserted categorically that most of the nobles and *caballeros* of Cordova and the other cities of Andalusia were Judaizers, and even maintained secret synagogues in their houses. A batch of reckless accusations followed, no rank or dignity being spared. The most illustrious of the victims was the saintly Hernando de Talavera, Archbishop of Granada (formerly confessor to Isabella the Catholic), who happened to have Jewish blood in his veins. The charge was ridiculous; but the old man died in consequence of the humiliation to which he was exposed. The popular outcry became so great that Ferdinand, who was now ruling over Castile in his daughter's name, was forced to dismiss Deza, and to appoint the Cardinal Ximenes as Inquisitor General for the country (1507). Proceedings were instituted against the inhuman Lucero, but they were ultimately allowed to drop.

Under Ximenes and his successors, the proceedings of the Inquisition in Spain were more regular, but no less zealous. Upon the accession to the throne of Charles V (1516–1556), the Spanish New Christians sent to him, promising an enormous subsidy if he would restrict the power of the Holy Office in his dominions. Above all, they desired the system of secret accusations to be abolished. Similar steps, backed up by lavish gifts, were taken at Rome. Here Pope Leo X, true to the tolerant tradition of the Medici, prepared a Bull embodying the desired concessions. Charles, on the other hand, after temporary vacillation, was ultimately decided by the narrow obscurantism which was to characterize him throughout life. Not only did he refuse to accede, but he even went so far as to prevent the publication of the Bull. Thereafter, there was never any serious threat to the authority of the Holy Office in Spain; and it could count, throughout, upon the implicit royal support. During Ximenes' tenure of office, 2,500 persons were given to the flames. Charles' son, Philip II (1556–1598), carried on and even enhanced his father's bigoted tradition, maintaining the tribunal, in spite of the protests of the Cortes, in all its terrible power. The Duke of Olivares, the reforming minister of Philip III (1598–1621), endeavored to restrict its might, which had by now become overpowering. It survived the attempt, however, with its status enhanced rather than otherwise. It was during this reign and that of the next monarch, Philip IV (1621–1665), that the Spanish Inquisition attained its greatest authority and pomp.

The number of Spanish tribunals ultimately totaled fifteen: Barcelona, Cordova, Cuenca, Granada, Logroño, Llerena, Madrid, Murcia, Santiago, Seville, Toledo, Valencia, Valladolid, and Saragossa, in addition to that situated at Palma, in the island of Majorca. All of these acted under the authority of the central Council, *Consejo de la Suprema y General Inquisición*—a title conveniently abbreviated to *La Suprema*. The activity was greatest, as far as the Jews were concerned, in Old Castile and Andalusia; it was least in Catalonia, where the New Christians never attained any great number. As time advanced, the exclusive preoccupation of the Inquisition with Judaizers, on whose account it had been founded, was very much diminished. From 1525, when the practice of Mohammedanism was forbidden in Spain, Moors who remained secretly faithful to the religion of their fathers also came within its scope. As the century advanced, there was an increasing number of Protestants and of the licentious mystics known as the Alumbrados. It dealt besides with what were considered to be less serious offenses, such as bigamy. Sorcery also fell within its province; but, under its moderating influence, Spain remained the one country in Europe where the persecution of so-called witches in the seventeenth and eighteenth centuries never generally obtained. In this respect, Spain compared very favorably with England or North America; and the debt which she owes on this account to the Holy Office is not to be underestimated.

The Jews, however, continued to be the main object of attention, particularly in the south of the country. Thus, at Cordova, between 1655 and 1700, out of 399 persons who figured in the public autos, 324 had been charged with Judaizing. In Toledo, out of 855 cases tried in the second half of the seventeenth century, 556 were for the same offence. At Valladolid, 78 out of the 85 cases pending in 1699 were of Judaizers. In Aragon and Old Castile, the proportions were definitely less, but they were by no means insignificant.

Of all those who fell within its scope, moreover, it was the Marranos whom the Spanish Inquisition hounded down with the greatest ferocity. Such indeed was its initial zeal against them in the first few decades of its existence that, to a large extent, it succeeded in its object. By the middle of the sixteenth century, the native Spanish Judaizers — the descendants of the renegades of 1391 and the succeeding years — had disappeared. The most steadfast had perished at the stake, or else had fled overseas. The remainder, cut off from direct association with their Jewish kinsfolk, had become completely absorbed. The apostates of 1492 survived a little longer, but their ultimate fate was identical. It is not, as a matter of fact, a very remarkable phenomenon. As we have seen, the Spanish New Christians, unlike the Portuguese counterparts, comprised mainly those Jews of the weaker sort who had embraced Christianity in order to save their lives, and sometimes on even less pardonable grounds. Their descendants did not therefore possess the full measure of devotion and self-sacrifice which generally characterized their race. Inevitably, therefore, the great majority in the end gave way to force of circumstances. But the labors of the Inquisition were not lightened thereby. Their place was taken by immigrants from Portugal, attracted by the economic possibilities of the wealthier country, or else seeking refuge where they were less known. From the second half of the sixteenth century, native Spanish Judaizers figure less and less frequently; those Marranos who so largely engaged the attention of the Holy Office in Madrid, in Toledo, or in Seville being in the over-whelming majority immigrants from Portugal or else their immediate descendants. History had achieved its usual irony. The Forced Conversion in Portugal, brought about by Ferdinand and Isabella in order to purge their dominions of even the propinquity of unbelief, ultimately resulted in perpetuating the Judaizing tradition there long after the Inquisitional Tribunal which they had founded had completed its immediate work. King Manoel had consented in the hopes of bringing the whole of the Peninsula under the rule of his house. His grandson, Sebastian, however, fell in battle in Africa in 1578, his nobles thinking themselves fortunate if they became the slaves of the humane Jews whose fathers had been chased out of the Peninsula; and ultimately, instead of the larger country falling into the hands of the rulers of the smaller, the match resulted in the temporary absorption of the smaller by the larger.

After the unification of the two countries, in 1580, the tide of emigration naturally increased. In Seville and Madrid, there were whole streets where nothing but Portuguese was spoken; and the fact of origin from the smaller country was in itself regarded as ground for suspicion. Insofar as the Inquisition busied itself with

Judaizers, it was these immigrants who were mainly in question. Every now and again, a fresh covey of suspects would be discovered. Thus, in 1630, a secret community was unearthed at Madrid, presided over by Miguel Rodriguez and his wife, Isabel Nuñez Alvarez. Services were regularly held in their house in the *Calle de las Infantas*, at which, according to the ridiculous report, a crucifix was formally scourged.[7] The members of the group figured amongst the fifty-three persons who appeared at the great auto held at Madrid on July 4, 1632, in the presence of the King, Queen, and foreign ambassadors, seven of them being burned in person and four more in effigy. In the same month, the Infant Carlos died; and Jewish observers were not slow to note the coincidence, which they considered to be a judgment from God. The house in which the outrage was alleged to have taken place was ceremoniously destroyed, a Capuchin convent aptly known as *La Paciencia* being subsequently erected on its site.

In 1635 another Jewish conventicle was discovered in the Capital, where the Day of Atonement services were held in the home of a certain Diego Ximenes. That same year a further group of Portuguese was unearthed in the city of Badajoz. One hundred and fifty of the persons implicated managed to avoid trial by flight or otherwise; and the tribunal of Llerena was engaged for three or four years afterwards in trying the rest. In 1647, a gaol-bird in prison at Valladolid, in the hopes of securing his own release, gave information concerning an alleged secret congregation at Ciudad Real. Its principal member was Pablo de Herrera, the paymaster of the army on the Portuguese frontier. In his house, it was alleged,

his fellow New Christians met each Friday for the purpose of scourging images of Christ and the Virgin, which
were ceremonially burned during Holy Week! Large
numbers of arrests were carried out in consequence of
this ridiculous story. A lavish employment of torture
secured ample confirmatory evidence, parents testifying
against their own children and brothers against sisters.
The trials dragged on for four years. Finally, it was
established that the story of the image-scourging was a
spiteful invention. Nevertheless, there were several convictions; and the tribunal was enriched by enormous fines.

In the township of Beas, meanwhile, a small colony of
Portuguese had established themselves. For about ten
years, they lived without disturbance. Ultimately, the
attention of the neighboring tribunal of Cuenca was
drawn to them. Thirteen were arrested and put on trial;
nine more fled just in time to escape the same fate,
leaving all their property behind. Their effigies were
burned in the great Seville auto of 1660, when eighty-one
Judaizers (nearly all Portuguese) figured, seven of them
perishing at the stake. Two or three of the Beas fugitives,
who had settled at Malaga, were tried by the Inquisition
of Toledo in 1667; a couple more, who had taken the
precaution to change their names, were arrested after
long adventures at Daimiel in 1677 — seventeen years
after they had been burned in effigy at Seville; and,
after a two and a half years' trial, they were condemned
to perpetual imprisonment. Similar little groups were
continually being unearthed. At a Seville auto of 1660,
eight of the Portuguese Judaizers who figured were from
Utrera, and as many as thirty-seven — nearly one-half
of the total — from Osuna. In 1679, in the course of

his trial at Toledo, one Simon Múnoz gave the names of twenty-two accomplices residing at Pastrana, nearly all of whom figured at an auto on December 21, 1680. In 1676, a similar group of over twenty persons was unearthed at Berin (Orense), where they had been long settled. Two of them — Baltasar López Cardoso and his cousin, Felipa López — who proudly confessed their attachment to Judaism, were burned alive at the auto at Madrid in 1680.

In Portugal, the persecution of the Marranos had entered upon a new phase with the Spanish conquest. A nominee of the new rulers — the Cardinal-Archduke Albrecht of Austria, who was also governor of the country — succeeded to the office of Inquisitor General. Under his direction, the activity of the Inquisition increased. In twenty years, the three tribunals held in all fifty autos-da-fè. Of these, the records of five are lost; but, in the other forty-five, there were 162 "relaxations" in person, fifty-nine in effigy, and 2979 less ferocious punishments, or "reconciliations."[8] The Tribunal of Evora particularly distinguished itself for its ferocity, being responsible for nearly two-thirds of the burnings alive, though for considerably less than one-half of the total number of trials.

This activity, coupled with the impoverishment of the realm under Spanish rule, was responsible for the wholesale flight of the Portuguese Marranos across the frontier, which gave the tribunals of the larger country a growing field of activity in the coming years. At the same time, it tended to make the Portuguese Marranos fiercely opposed to the new regime, and favor every attempt to secure independence. The nominee of the national party was Antonio, Prior of Crato. He was himself as a matter of fact partly of Jewish origin, being the son of a member of the old royal house through an irregular union with a beautiful New Christian, Violante Gomez. Down to his death in 1595 he remained a prominent figure in current politics, intriguing in every court of Europe for assistance to gain the Portuguese throne. Everywhere, both at home and abroad, the Marranos strove their utmost to assist him. So notorious were their sympathies, indeed, that Drake's forays were generally said to have been plotted by the Marranos. Dom Antonio's failure was therefore regarded by them as a general disaster. After his death, a more constitutional method of obtaining relief was attempted. A dazzling bribe to the Crown of nearly two million ducats secured application to the Pope for a Brief authorizing the reconciliation of all Portuguese New Christians, wherever they might be found, after undergoing only spiritual penances (1605). This was, in effect, a General Pardon for all past offences. Under its terms, on January 16, 1605, the Portuguese tribunals simultaneously liberated 410 prisoners after imposing formal penance. At Seville, on the eve of an auto, for which the inhabitants of all the surrounding countryside had streamed into the city, the Inquisitor was aroused from his bed by a courier, who had broken all records on the journey, and was informed that the celebration had to be suspended. On the same day, the silver-fleet under Don Luis de Córdova was destroyed with enormous loss. It was considered by the pious that this disaster was an expression of the divine disapproval of the ill-advised display of clemency.

The intermission was only temporary. After the stipulated period of twelve months had elapsed, the tribunals were again occupied in prosecuting those who had not taken advantage of the General Pardon by coming forward spontaneously to confess their wrongdoing, or had reverted to their former practices since it had been issued. The prejudices against the New Christians tended to increase rather than otherwise. In 1621, a Portuguese named Vincente da Costa Mattos published a work, *Breve Discurso contra a Heretica Perfidia do Judaismo* (A Brief Discourse against the Heretical Perfidy of Judaism), in which he roundly accused the Portuguese New Christians of perpetuating all of the most dastardly crimes, as well as the disbeliefs, of their Jewish ancestors, and seriously suggested that they should be expelled from the country. Notwithstanding its extravagant tone, the work was a great success, being translated into Spanish, and frequently republished. The Inquisitional watchfulness was unrelaxing. In 1618 the whole of Oporto was thrown into confusion by the arrest of nearly all the New Christian merchants of the city, who controlled the trade with the colonies. A few years later three hundred children were left destitute at Trancoso through the arrest of their parents, whose houses were sacked. In the little town of Montemor o Novo, where the Jewish tradition seems to have been peculiarly tenacious, no less than one hundred persons were seized almost simultaneously in 1623. The Portuguese autos outdid in scale those of contemporary Spain, and busied themselves with little else than Jews. Thus one was held by the tribunal of Coimbra, on August 16, 1626, in which two hundred and forty-seven persons in all appeared, and another on May 6, 1629, with 218. In 1627 and 1630, by dint of heavy payments, two further General Pardons were obtained; but their benefits were only temporary.

One winter's morning, in 1630, it was discovered that the Church of Santa Engracia, at Lisbon, had been broken into overnight, and that a silver pyx holding the consecrated elements had been stolen. It was assumed that no ordinary thief would have the hardihood to perform so sacrilegious an action. In consequence, suspicion automatically fell upon the Marranos, who were alleged to have obtained possession of the Host for the purpose of perpetrating a ritual outrage upon it. It happened that a New Christian youth of good family named Simão Pires Solis had been observed passing that way on the previous night, on his way to visit a lady. He was arrested, and submitted to terrible tortures. Finally, the hands suspected to have committed the outrage were chopped off, and the mutilated body was dragged through the streets and burned. Some time afterwards, a common thief confessed at the foot of the gallows that he had himself been guilty of the crime. In the meantime, the consequences upon the New Christians had been terrible. The popular passions against them were aroused to an unprecedented degree. The streets of Lisbon were placarded with inflammatory proclamations. At Santarem and Torres Novas, there were riots in which some persons lost their lives. At several places, the students prevented New Christian youths from entering the lecture halls, the University of Coimbra being temporarily closed in consequence. From all the pulpits, the preachers incited the people against those whom they now openly designated as Jews. The flight from the country increased; from a single parish of Lisbon, no less than 2,000 persons were said to have fled. The agitation for the expulsion of the New Christians, which had been gathering weight during the last decade, and which had been seriously recommended to Philip IV by the Portuguese bishops in 1628, attained such proportions as to have given the impression that it was actually carried into effect in 1631.⁹ Meanwhile, the activities of the Inquisition received a further stimulus. At the auto of Coimbra on August 17, 1631, no less than 247 persons appeared. In ten only of the series held between 1620 and 1640, no less than 230 New Christians lost their lives, while over 5,000 persons figured all told. A bitterly anti-Jewish memorial, drawn up in the middle of the century, makes the assertion — no doubt exaggerated, but none the less highly suggestive — that the Inquisitional zeal in this period had partly depopulated many of the greatest cities of the country, including Coimbra, Oporto, Evora, Santarem, and some districts of Lisbon. It was only after the accession of the House of Braganza in 1640, and the recovery of Portuguese independence (in which the labors of the New Christians played a prominent part), that the activities of the Holy Office were to any extent restrained.

In the Balearic Islands, subject to the crown of Aragon, the activity of the Inquisition reached its climax at the close of the seventeenth century. The original Jewish community of Majorca had come to an end after the terrible massacre which took place on August 24, 1391, in consequence of which a very large proportion had submitted to baptism. The commercial advantages of the place had speedily attracted fresh settlers. In 1435, however, there had been a ritual murder charge, the Jews being accused of having crucified a Saracen on Good Friday in mockery of the Passion. The principal members of the community were cruelly put to death, after a grotesquely partial trial, all the rest were compelled to submit to baptism. After that date, no declared Jews lived on the island. Nevertheless, the descendants of the converts remained true to their ancestral faith, providing the Inquisition (which was introduced in 1488) with an ample field for activity. At the initial solemnity, on August 18, 1488, no less than 338 persons were forced to do public penance. In the following year, serious work began, seven autos taking place and a considerable number of New Christians being burned, either in person or in effigy. Between 1489 and 1535, a total of nearly seven hundred and fifty persons were penanced, 460 burned in effigy, and 99 (all but five of whom were Judaizers) in person. After this date, the persecution languished, so that there was some question of allowing the vacant posts on the Tribunal to remain empty.[10]

This inactivity emboldened the native New Christians, who still remained numerous on the island, to become less cautious. In 1678, the Inquisitor's attention was attracted to a meeting held in a garden, outside the city, where there was rumored to be a synagogue. Investigations resulted in a very large number of arrests of New Christians suspected of Judaizing. There was obviously no spirit of martyrdom abroad. All those accused confessed their sin and professed contrition. In a series of four public autos in 1678, 219 of them figured as penitents, none however being condemned to death. They comprised all the wealthiest business men in the island. Their property, to the value of at least a million and a half *pesos*, was confiscated; and, out of the proceeds, the Tribunal built itself a new Palace, which was considered to be one of the finest in Spain.

The subsequent degradation and ill-treatment of those convicted and their families led many of them to form a plot to leave the island on an English ship; but storms delayed the boat, and they were arrested. As they had not obtained the requisite license to leave Spain, their action was taken as a confession of guilt, and all were put on trial. This time, they were treated as heretics who had "relapsed" into guilt, and there could be no question of mercy for them. A series of four autos was held in March, May and July, 1691. A huge *quemadero*, eighty feet square and eight feet high, provided with twenty-five stakes for the victims, was erected to serve as the stage for the last act of the tragedy. With a truly sardonic consideration for the comfort of the ordinary population, this was situated on the sea-shore, two miles from the city, so that the stench should not cause any inconvenience. In all, thirty-seven persons were burned, while fifty suffered lesser punishment. The majority of those convicted professed repentance, as on a previous occasion, and thus secured the grace of being garroted before their bodies were committed to the flames. Only three held out defiantly to the last, and were burned alive. These were Raphael Valls, the spiritual leader of the secret community, with his pupil, Raphael Benito Terongi, and the latter's sister, Catalina. All of these suffered, with nine of their less heroic brethren in faith, at the principal auto of the series, on May 6, 1691. Catalina Terongi, who had confessed proudly that she was a Jewess and wished to remain one, cried out pathetically for mercy from the middle of the flames; but it was noticed that in her worst extremity she never allowed the name of Jesus to cross her lips. Her brother, a stalwart youth of twenty-one, struggled hard to escape, and ultimately succeeded in snapping his bonds; but as he broke loose, he fell back on the pyre. Old Raphael Valls, a simple soap-maker, who had succeeded in holding his own against all the most erudite theologians of the island, maintained a stoic attitude until the flames reached him, when (as the old chronicler jubilantly records) his body flared up like a torch. The local poets celebrated these victims in popular ballads, which continued until quite recently to be chanted by the women of the island, as they went about their work.

By this awful lesson, crypto-Judaism in Majorca was finally blotted out; and, though the tribunal celebrated one or two further autos, only three native Judaizers figured in them. Nevertheless, though their orthodoxy was henceforth unimpeachable, the descendants of the New Christians to the number of three hundred families continued to be treated with the acme of degradation and contempt. They were scornfully designated as *Chuetas*, or "swine."[11] They were not allowed to live outside the old Jewish quarter, or *Calle* (hence the other title applied to them: *Individuos de la Calle*, or Ghetto Folk). They were excluded from all public office and from all honorable professions. The ordinary population refused to approach them unnecessarily, or to do any but the most pressing business with them. Inevitably, they were forced to marry only amongst themselves. At public worship they sat apart. Even in the cemetery, their bodies were isolated. The Church did everything to keep alive the prejudice against them, preserving in the Dominican convent the effigies of those of their fathers who had suffered at the hands of the Inquisition, and repeatedly publishing a list of all those who had been condemned by it. They were treated in every respect as though they were still Jews, though their fidelity to Catholicism was never seriously questioned.

No attempt was made to ameliorate their condition until late in the eighteenth century. In 1773, following on a pathetic appeal to the Crown, an edict was issued taking them under the royal protection. In 1782, they were formally permitted to reside outside the *Calle*, in any part of the city of Palma or of the island; and it was forbidden to call them Jews, Hebrews, or *Chuetas* under severe penalties. Three years later, they were declared eligible for all public office, as well as to enter the Army and Navy. A further *Real Cedula* (royal decree) to a similar effect was issued in 1788. But this carried little weight. Local prejudices still remained so strong as to nullify the good intentions of the Madrid government. The *Chuetas* continued to live largely in the old *Calle*, no houses being rented to them in any other part of the island. They remained excluded from all offices and honorable professions. They were still forced to inter-marry amongst themselves. The pillar which marked the site of the secret synagogue discovered in 1679 was re-erected in 1814. The passage of generations and the progress of civilization made little difference to the island prejudices. As late as 1857, a book *La Sinagoga Balear*

(The Balearic Synagogue), was directed against them, recapitulating the lists of those condemned two centuries before and maintaining that their descendants still adhered to their old Jewish practices and were unworthy to be reckoned as Christians. The main purpose of the work was blackmail; and the *Chuetas* bought up almost the whole edition.

Even in the present generation, the prejudice continues, no self-respecting family consenting to ally itself with them by marriage.[12] Until very recently, the three hundred families remained cooped up in their *Calle* known by the same contemptuous name as their condemned ancestors of many generations before, and following mainly the solitary craft of goldsmith to which only they were admitted. In spite of all this, they were sincere Catholics at heart, ultra-observant in public, and blankly ignorant of the Judaism of their fathers, for which they themselves still suffered. In very recent years, their condition has considerably improved; but still the *Individuos de la Calle* remain, a pathetic relic of the community which once flourished in the Balearic Islands, and a living record of the heavy hand of the Holy Office of the Inquisition.[13]

CHAPTER V

THE INQUISITIONAL PROCEDURE AND THE AUTO-DA-FÈ

WITHIN comparatively few years of its establishment, the Inquisition had evolved an elaborate procedure of its own. This was laid down in a number of handbooks, of which that of 1561 became authoritative in Spain. In Portugal, the organization of the tribunals of the neighboring country served as model, the differences being negligible.[1]

When a new tribunal was established at any place, an "Edict of Grace" would generally be published, inviting those persons conscious of having committed heretical actions in the past to come forward and confess their crimes, on the understanding that they would receive merciful treatment. A time limit, generally of thirty or forty days, known as the "Term of Grace," was assigned for this purpose. After the lapse of this period, guilty persons were liable to be proceeded against with all the rigor of the Inquisition. Those who presented themselves under the Edict of Grace would be required to denounce all others with whom they had associated or whom they knew to be guilty of similar offences; hence the Holy Office was generally provided with a vast mass of information which kept it busy for some time to come.

At later stages, an "Edict of Faith" would periodically be issued. This summoned all the faithful, under pain of excommunication, to denounce to the Inquisitional authorities any person of whom they had cognizance who was guilty of certain specified heretical offences. The latter invariably comprised, even down to the final period, all those practices popularly associated with Judaism, such as lighting special lamps on Friday evening, changing linen on the Sabbath, abstaining from forbidden food, observing the Day of Atonement or other fasts, laying out the dead according to the Jewish method, etc. By this means, the whole population became enlisted as accomplices of the Holy Office in its task of eradicating heresy; and the denunciation of some trivial action, performed absent-mindedly or by mere force of habit, was frequently sufficient to bring a man to the stake. The relevant portion of a typical "Edict of Faith," throwing a vivid light upon Marrano customs, is here appended:—

". . . If they observe the Sabbath, putting on clean or festive clothes, clean and washed shirts and headdress; arranging and cleaning their houses on Friday afternoon, and in the evening lighting new candles, with new tapers and torches, earlier than on other evenings of the week; cooking on the said Fridays such food as is required for the Saturday, and on the latter eating the meat thus cooked on the Friday, as is the manner of the Jews; keeping the Jewish fasts, not touching food the whole day until nightfall, and especially the Fast of Queen Esther, and the chief fast of *Cinquepur*[2] and other Jewish fasts, laid down by their Law; and keeping other fasts in the week, especially Mondays and Thursdays, kept by them as devotional fasts; eating on (the conclu-

sion of?) such fast days such meats and other viands as
are customary with the Jews; and on the said fast days
asking pardon of one another in the Jewish manner, the
younger ones to the elders, the latter placing their hands
on the heads of the former, but without signing them
with the sign of the Cross; . . . keeping the feasts and
festivals of the Jews, in particular the feast of unleavened
bread, which falls in Holy Week, upon which festival
they eat unleavened bread, beginning their meal with
lettuce and celery; keeping the feast of Tabernacles
which falls in the month of September; saying Jewish
prayers . . . reciting these with the face turned to the
wall, moving the head backwards and forwards as the
Jews do; cutting the nails and keeping, burning or
burying the parings; cleansing, or causing meat to be
cleaned, cutting away from it all fat and grease, and
cutting away the nerve or sinew from the leg; cutting
the throats of fowls as is the manner of the Jews, reciting
certain words during the process and passing the knife
across the nail; killing oxen as the Jews do, covering the
blood with cinders or with earth; giving the Jewish
blessing before eating, called the *baraha*; reciting certain
words over the cup or vase of wine, after which each
person sips a little, according to the custom of the Jews;
not eating pork, hare, rabbit, strangled birds, conger-eel,
cuttlefish, nor eels or other scaleless fish, as laid down in
Jewish law; and upon the death of parents and others
eating, on the floor or on very low tables, such things
as boiled eggs, olives, and other viands, as do the Jews;
. . . pouring water from jars and pitchers when someone
has died, believing that the soul of such persons will
come and bathe in the water; and who when kneading

bread will throw particles of dough in the fire, which the Jews call *Hallah*; making divinations for children born to them, on the seventh day; not baptizing them, and when they have been baptized scraping off the chrism put on them in the sacrament of baptism; ... If they give Old Testament names to the children, or bless them by the laying on of hands; if the women do not attend Church within forty days after a confinement; if the dying turn towards the wall; if they wash a corpse with warm water; if they recite the Psalms without adding the *Gloria Patri* at the close; who say that the dead Law of Moses is good, and can bring about their salvation, and perform other rites and ceremonies of the same . . ."[3]

The Tribunal of the Inquisition was, theoretically, an impartial one. Hence the formal function of prosecution was assumed by a special official, known as the *Promotor Fiscal*. In this manner, the fiction of a fair trial was preserved, though it was not always necessary to await his formal denunciation before initiating proceedings. Before the case came up for consideration, the charges were examined by *calificadores* to determine whether they presented *calidad de oficio*, or justification for further action. If it were found that they did (as was almost invariably the case, though occasionally a little revision might be needed), the way was clear for the *Promotor Fiscal* to present his *clamosa*, or formal demand for the opening of proceedings. Judaizers and other pernicious heretics were however deprived even of this slender safeguard. The next step was the arrest of the persons accused.

The HALL of the INQUISITION in which the Prisoners are examined.

The trial, and everything connected with it, took place under conditions of the greatest secrecy. This, indeed, became one of the greatest terrors of the Inquisition according to the Spanish model. All the parties concerned — witnesses, accusers, and accused — were sworn to observe the most profound confidence. Any breach which came to the ears of the authorities was liable to be punished with the utmost severity, just as heresy itself. It can easily be realized how this system lent itself to groundless denunciations, prompted only by private enmity. As a natural consequence, from the moment of arrest the utmost segregation was enforced, it being regarded as a very serious offence for prisoners to communicate with one another. The accused were confined in the dungeons of the Palace of the Inquisition, such as may still be seen in Evora and elsewhere. As was inevitable, there were sometimes terrible abuses, female prisoners suffering especially; and it not infrequently happened that a woman was dragged pregnant to the stake. All the expense connected with the imprisonment, which sometimes lasted over a period of years, was supposed to be borne by the prisoner. Thus, even if a man were acquitted, he might find himself utterly ruined. At the same time, in cases which might ultimately involve confiscation, all the possessions of the accused were sequestered at the moment of arrest; sometimes with very serious effects upon the economic life of a whole town or province. When a condemnation resulted, all this property devolved on the Holy Office, which thus had every inducement to bring in a verdict of guilty.

The rules of evidence were so devised as to exclude all witnesses likely to be serviceable to the accused, on the ground that their testimony would be untrustworthy. No such scruples prevailed with regard to witnesses for the prosecution, who were frequently inspired by mere venom. Moreover, the names of the accusers were suppressed. This provision was originally introduced only in the case of "powerful persons," who might intimidate the witnesses. Ultimately, all Judaizers and similar dangerous heretics had been included in this category, precisely those persons who most needed protection being hence deprived of it. The accusers and accused were never confronted — a practice inconceivable in modern jurisprudence. Thus, any attempt upon the part of the prisoner to invalidate the evidence, while his life was at stake, had to be based upon utter conjecture. It was necessary for him to search his memory for the name of some personal enemy who might have denounced him without cause, and to demonstrate that any evidence which might have been received from this quarter or from that ought not to obtain credence so far as he was concerned.[4]

The details admitted were flimsy in the extreme. Thus mere regard for personal cleanliness might be enough to convict a person of secretly practicing Judaism or Islam, and so cost him his life. The system naturally lent itself to false accusations, sometimes on an enormous scale. In the early years of the eighteenth century, a certain physician from Faro, named Francisco de Sá e Mesquita, denounced a number of persons at Beja who, he alleged, had come together to practice Jewish rites — on one occasion, sixty-six, and on another ninety-two. They were arrested; several of them died in prison as a result of their sufferings. Ultimately it was found that the accusation was utterly baseless. It is only fair to add that the Inquisition punished the crime rigorously, the informer being executed at Lisbon in the auto of October 10,1723.[5] Such exhibitions of severity in cases of this description were not, however, common.

Once the formal accusation was made, the whole of the subsequent procedure was based upon a desire to make the accused person confess his crime and so be admitted to penitence. Thus, though his body might suffer, his immortal soul would be saved. If confession were not forthcoming voluntarily, torture might be applied. This was in fullest accordance with the spirit of the age.[6] As a matter of fact, in this particular instance the Spanish Inquisition, notorious though its cruelties were, compared favorably with that of Rome, where torture might be continued even after confession in order to obtain the names of presumed accomplices or associates. Nevertheless, in those cases where the confession did not cover other persons who were implicated in the same charge, the torture would frequently be continued *in caput alienum* (as it was termed), so as to extort fresh evidence against them.

In the earlier period, the most common methods of torture were the *strappado* (in which the victim was let fall from a beam to which he was attached by a short rope, being brought up with a jerk before he reached the ground), and the water-torment. Afterwards, fresh and (as they were considered) more humane fashions came into vogue — notably the *cordeles* and the *garrotes*. An eighteenth-century English account gives some idea of the procedure, and will spare the unpleasant necessity of embarking upon an original description: —

The place of TORMENTS and manner of giving the TORTURE

An Account of the Process of the Inquisition and its Management By Torture

"When the prisoner has been examined three times and still persists in the negative, it often happens that he is detained a whole year or longer before he is admitted to another audience, that being wearied with his imprisonment, he may more readily confess what is desired; but if he still persists in the negative his accusation is at length delivered to him intermixt with a number of pretended crimes of a heinous nature, which composition of truth and falsehood is a snare for the unhappy wretch; for as he seldom fails to exclaim against the feigned crimes, his judges thence conclude the others of which he makes less complaint are true. When his trial comes on in good earnest, the witnesses are examined afresh, a copy of the depositions is delivered to him with those circumstances suprest as might discover the evidence; he replies to each particular, and gives interrogatories to which he would have the witnesses examined and the names of others that he would have examined in his behalf; an advocate is appointed for him, which tho' it has the appearance of Justice is really of no use to the prisoner — for the advocate is under oath to the office, is not admitted to speak to his client but in presence of the inquisitor, nor to alledge anything in his favour but what he thinks proper. After the process has been carried on in this manner for a considerable time, the judges with their assessors examine the proofs and determine the fate of the Prisoner; if his answers and exceptions are not satisfactory, nor the proofs against him sufficient for conviction, he is condemned to the TORTURE. The scene of this diabolical cruelty is a dark underground vault, the prisoner upon his arrival there is immediately seized by a torturer, who forthwith strips him. Whilst he is stripping, and while under the torture, the inquisitor strongly exhorts him to confess his guilt, yet neither to bear false witness against himself or others. The first TORTURE is that of ye ROPE which is performed in this manner. The prisoner's hands are bound behind him, and by means of a rope fastened to them and running through a pulley, he is raised up to the ceiling, where having hung for some time with weights tyed to his feet, he is let down almost to the ground with such sudden jerks as disjoints his arms and legs, whereby he is put to the most exquisite pain, and is forced to cry out in a terrible manner. If the prisoner's strength holds out, they usually torture him in this manner about an hour, and if it does not force a confession from him to their liking, they have recourse to the next torture, viz.: WATER. The prisoner is now laid upon his back in a wooden trough which has a barr running through ye midst of it upon which his back lies, and upon occasion his back bone is hereby broke and puts him to incredible pain. The torture of Water is sometimes performed by forcing the prisoner to swallow a quantity of water and then pressing his body by screwing ye sides of ye trough closer; at other times a wet cloth is laid over the prisoners mouth and nostrils, and a small stream of water constantly descending upon it he sucks ye cloth into his throat, which being suddenly removed draws away

with it water and blood and puts ye unhappy wretch
into the AGONIES OF DEATH. The next torture, viz,:
that of FIRE, is thus performed, the prisoner being
placed on the ground his feet are held towards a fire
and rubbed with unctious and cumbustible matter,
by which means, ye heat penetrating into those parts,
HE SUFFERS PAINS WORSE THAN DEATH ITSELF."

As may be imagined, death under torture was by no
means uncommon, though in most instances the physician
in attendance enforced sufficient moderation to avoid a
fatal conclusion. But in any case the sufferings were
terrible. Even pregnancy was not regarded as a sufficient
reason to save a woman from the ordeal. It is worth
while to quote at some length the official record of the
torture of Elvira del Campo, wife of the scrivener Alonso
de Moya, who was tried by the Inquisition of Toledo
in 1567–9 on a charge of not eating pork and of putting
on clean linen on Saturdays. She admitted having been
guilty of these heinous practices, but pleaded that she
had no heretical intention. Naturally, she was not
believed. When the sentence of torture was read out to
her, she fell to her knees and begged to know what they
wanted her to say. This was obviously unsatisfactory,
and orders were given for the proceedings to begin.
It may be added that the administration of one *jarra*
(jug) of water in this particular variety of torture was
unusually lenient, the number sometimes reaching six or
eight. The present case is one which omits the screams
and cries of horror, which are usually set forth in excru-
ciating detail. The cold, unmoved tone in which the
official account proceeds is worth noting:—

She was carried to the torture chamber, and told to tell the truth, when she said that she had nothing to say. She was ordered to be stripped and again admonished, but was silent. When stripped, she said "Señores, I have done all that is said of me and I bear false-witness against myself, for I do not want to see myself in such trouble; please God, I have done nothing." She was told not to bring false testimony against herself but to tell the truth. The tying of the arms commenced; she said "I have told the truth; what have I to tell?" She was told to tell the truth and replied "I have told the truth and have nothing to tell." One cord was applied to the arms and twisted and she was admonished to tell the truth but said she had nothing to tell. Then she screamed and said "I have done all they say." Told to tell in detail what she had done she replied "I have already told the truth." Then she screamed and said "Tell me what you want for I don't know what to say." She was told to tell what she had done, for she was tortured because she had not done so, and another turn of the cord was ordered. She cried: "Loosen me, Señores, and tell me what I have to say: I do not know what I have done, O Lord have mercy on me, a sinner!" Another turn was given and she said "Loosen me a little that I may remember what I have to tell; I don't know what I have done; I did not eat pork, for it made me sick; I have done everything; loosen me and I will tell the truth." Another turn of the cord was ordered, when she said "Loosen me and I will tell the truth; I don't know what I have to tell — loosen me for the sake of God — tell me what

I have to say — I did it, I did it, — they hurt me
Señor — loosen me, loosen me and I will tell it." She
was told to tell it and said "I don't know what I have
to tell — Señor I did it — I have nothing to tell —
O my arms! release me and I will tell it." She was
asked to tell what she did and said "I don't know, I
did not eat because I did not wish to." She was asked
why she did not wish to and replied "Ay! loosen me,
loosen me — take me from here and I will tell it when
I am taken away — I say that I did not eat it." She
was told to speak and said "I did not eat it, I don't
know why." Another turn was ordered and she said
"Señor I did not eat it because I did not wish to —
release me and I will tell it." She was told to tell what
she had done contrary to our holy Catholic faith. She
said "Take me from here and tell me what I have to
say — they hurt me — Oh my arms, my arms!" which
repeated many times and went on "I don't remember
— tell me what I have to say — O wretched me! — I
will tell all that is wanted, Señores — they are breaking my arms — loosen me a little — I did everything
that is said of me." She was told to tell in detail
truly what she did. She said "What am I wanted to
tell? I did everything — loosen me for I don't remember what I have to tell — don't you see what a weak
woman I am? Oh! Oh! my arms are breaking."
More turns were ordered and as they were given she
cried, "Oh, Oh, loosen me for I don't know what I
have to say — Oh, my arms! I don't know what I
have to say — if I did I would tell it." The cords were
ordered to be tightened when she said "Señores have
you no pity on a sinful woman?" She was told, yes,

if she would tell the truth. She said, "Señor tell me, tell me it." The cords were tightened again, and she said "I have already said that I did it." She was ordered to tell in detail, to which she said "I don't know how to tell it señor, I don't know." Then the cords were separated and counted, and there were sixteen turns, and in giving the last turn the cord broke.

She was then ordered to be placed on the *potro* (frame). She said: "Señores, why will you not tell me what I have to say? Señor, put me on the ground — have I not said that I did it all?" She was told to tell it. She said: "I don't remember — take me away I did what the witnesses say." She was told to tell in detail what the witnesses said. She said "Señor, as I have told you, I do not know for certain." I have said that I did all that the witnesses say. Señores release me, for I do not remember it." She was told to tell it. She said "I do not know it. Oh, Oh, they are tearing me to pieces — I have said that I did it — let me go." She was told to tell it. She said "Señores, it does not help me to say that I did it, and I have admitted that what I have done has brought me to this suffering — Señor, you know the truth — Señores, for God's sake have mercy on me. Oh Señor, take these things from my arms — Señor release me, they are killing me." She was tied on the *potro* with the cords, she was admonished to tell the truth and the garrotes were ordered to be tightened. She said "Señor do you not see how these people are killing me? Señor, I did it — for God's sake let me go." She was told to tell it. She said "Señor, remind me

of what I did not know — Señores have mercy upon
me — let me go for God's sake — they have no pity
on me — I did it — take me from here and I will
remember what I cannot here." She was told to tell
the truth or the cords would be tightened. She said
"Remind me of what I have to say for I don't know
it — I said that I did not want to eat it — I know
only that I did not want to eat it," and this she
repeated many times. She was told to tell why she
did not want to eat it. She said "For the reason that
the witnesses say — I don't know how to tell it —
miserable that I am that I don't know how to tell it.
I say I did it and my God how can I tell it?" Then
she said that, as she did not do it, how could she tell
it —"They will not listen to me — these people want
to kill me — release me and I will tell the truth."
She was again admonished to tell the truth. She said,
"I did it, I don't know how I did it — I did it for
what the witnesses say — let me go — I have lost
my senses and I don't know how to tell it — loosen
me and I will tell the truth." Then she said "Señor,
I did it, I don't know how I have to tell it, but I tell
it as the witnesses say — I wish to tell it — take me
from here. Señor as the witnesses say, so I say and
confess it." She was told to declare it. She said "I
don't know how to say it — I have no memory —
Lord, you are witness that if I knew how to say
anything else I would say it. I know nothing more
to say than that I did it and God knows it." She
said many times, "Señores, Señores, nothing helps
me. You, Lord, hear that I tell the truth and can
say no more,— they are tearing out my soul — order

them to loosen me." Then she said, "I do not say that I did it — I said no more." Then she said, "Señor, I did it to observe that Law." She was asked what Law. She said, "The Law that the witnesses say — I ·declare it all Señor, and don't remember what Law it was — O, wretched was the mother that bore me." She was asked what was the Law she meant and what was the Law she said the witnesses say. This was asked repeatedly, but she was silent and at last said that she did not know. She was told to tell the truth or the garrotes would be tightened but she did not answer. Another turn was ordered on the garrotes and she was admonished to say what Law it was. She said "If I knew what to say I would say it. Oh Señor, I don't know what I have to say — Oh, Oh, they are killing me — if they would tell me what — Oh, Señores! Oh, my heart!" Then she asked why they wished her to tell what she could not tell and cried repeatedly "O, miserable me!" Then she said "Lord bear witness that they are killing me without my being able to confess." She was told that if she wished to tell the truth before the water was poured she should do so and discharge her conscience. She said that she could not speak and that she was a sinner. Then the linen *toca* (funnel) was placed (in her throat) and she said "Take it away, I am strangling and am sick in the stomach." A jar of water* was then poured down, after which she was told to tell the truth. She clamoured for confession, saying that she was dying. She was told that the torture would be continued till she told the truth and was admonished to tell it, but though she was

questioned repeatedly she remained silent. Then the
inquisitor, seeing her exhausted by the torture, ordered
it to be suspended.

The unhappy woman's sufferings were by no means
at an end. Four days were allowed to elapse before her
next appearance; for long experience had shown that in
the interval the limbs would be stiffened, and repetition
of the torture thereby rendered more painful. The
miserable victim was again brought to the torture-
chamber; but she broke down when she was stripped,
and piteously begged to have her nakedness covered.
The interrogation was resumed. Under torture, her
replies were even more rambling and incoherent than
before. Ultimately, her powers of resistance broke down,
so that the Inquisitors were able to elicit the confession
of Judaism at which they had been aiming, coupled
with a prayer for mercy and penance.[7] It may be imagined with what feelings of attachment to the Christian
Faith she emerged from the auto-de-fé at which she was
formally reconciled to the Holy Catholic Church. Indeed,
in one or two well-authenticated instances, the sufferings
endured during the course of an unjust imprisonment
finally caused the victims to turn to Judaism, for which
they had previously had no inclination. There was
generally ample opportunity for meditation, as the
Inquisition proceeded with southern leisureliness. Persons sometimes languished in prison for as long as fourteen years, at the close of which period they might be
acquitted!

It may readily be understood that the torture was
generally abundantly sufficient to elicit a confession, if

RELACION
DE CAUSAS DE LOS REOS, QUE
salieron en el Auto Particular de Fè, que celebrò
el Santo Oficio de la Inquisicion de Sevilla,
el Domingo cinco de Julio de
este año de 1722.
EN EL REAL CONVENTO DE SAN PABLO
de esta Ciudad.

Vendese en Sevilla, en casa de Manuel de los Rios,
Mercader de Libros, en calle de Genova.

Title Page of an Account of the Auto held in
Seville on July 5, 1722.
(See p. 120)

one had been withheld up to that point. It is however
only right to add that the Inquisition, however cruel
and relentless, was just according to its own severe
standards. It generally proceeded only after having
collected ample evidence of crime; and the student of
any Inquisitional process is impressed by the care and
deliberation with which the case progresses. Torture was
imposed, in most instances, only to procure confirmation
of what the Inquisitors already knew; for, without
confession, penitence was out of the question, and there
was no alternative but death. The cases in which a
condemnation did not result were thus extremely few.
Thus, in the Toledo Tribunal, the acquittals between
the years 1484 and 1531 averaged less than two yearly.
In the Portuguese Inquisition, the number of condemnations comes to well over three-quarters of the total
number of cases tried. But even when the Inquisitors
were convinced that the silence of the accused under
torture was based on innocence, in most instances a
certain measure of culpability was nevertheless assumed,
and formal penance was required.

In the case of any convicted person who professed
repentance, whether spontaneously or as the result of
torture, "reconciliation" to the bosom of the Church
followed as a matter of course. The culprit had to swear
before a crucifix that he accepted the Catholic religion
in its every detail; that he anathematized every sort of
heresy, particularly that of which he had been convicted; and that he accepted fully the punishment which
had been imposed upon him in token of penitence. This
"abjuration," as it was termed, might be "light" or
"vehement." In the former case (*de levi*) the person con-

victed added that in case of failure in his undertaking
to comply with the sentence he should be held impenitent; in the latter (*de vehementi*), that in such case he
should be considered and treated as a relapsed heretic.
Logically, a reconciliation of this sort could be performed
only once. Any subsequent conviction was taken as a
clear proof that the original penitence had been insincere;
and the culprit was *ipso facto* condemned to the stake.[8]

The reconciliation was invariably accompanied by a
punishment, of varying intensity. The spiritual penances,
such as fasting each Friday for six months or reciting a
certain number of Ave Marias or Paternosters, were the
most infrequent: a curious paradox, considering the fact
that the offences were not of a material nature. In any
case, they would not figure to any appreciable extent in
the sentences of those convicted for so heinous a sin as
Judaizing. For these, harsher penalties existed. Among
these was that of scourging — very common in the
earlier period, but remitted more and more frequently as
time went on. This was executed publicly, with every
circumstance of humiliation. Similar, with the omission
of the lashes, was the *verguenza* ("shaming"), imposed
both on men and women. This consisted in parading
the town stripped to the waist and bearing the insignia
of the offence; the town-crier meanwhile proclaiming the
sentence. The *mordaza*, or gag, was sometimes applied,
this being regarded as enhancing the humiliation of the
punishment. More severe was the penalty of the galleys,
an economical device of Ferdinand the Catholic, whereby
the punishment of heresy was turned to the benefit of
the State. In 1573, and again in 1591, the *Suprema*
ordered that all convicted New Christians, even when

RELAXADOS EN ESTATVA.

1 FRancisco de la Peña, natural de Malaga, vezino de Cadiz, de oficio Mercader , judayzante fugitivo, salió al Auto vna Estatua, que representaba su persona, y nombre, con insignias de relaxado, y fue entregado à la Justicia, y brazo Seglar.

2. Juan de la Peña, hijo del antecedente, natural de Arazena, y vezino de Cadiz, de oficio Mercader, de edad de veinte y seis años, fugitivo de las Carceles de este Santo Oficio, judayzante : se sacó à al Auto vna Estatua, que representaba su persona, y nombre, con insignias de relaxado, se le leyó su sentencia con meritos, y fue entregado à la Justicia, y brazo Seglar.

3 Leonor de la Peña, hermana del antecedente , natural de Malaga, y vezina de Cadiz, de edad de treinta y seis años, judayzante, difunta en las Carceles de este Santo Oficio, salió al Auto vna Estatua , que representaba su persona, y nombre, con insignias de relaxada, se le leyó su sentencia con meritos, y sus huessos fueron exhumados, y entregados con su Estatua à la Justicia Seglar.

RELAXADOS EN PERSONA.

4 MAnuel de Andrade, natural de Lisboa, vezino de esta Ciudad , Agente de Rentas Reales, de edad de quarenta años, de estado casado , reconciliado que fue por la Inquisicion de Corte, judayzante relapso ; salió al Auto con insignias de tal , y relaxado

à

Beginning of List of those "Relaxed" to be Burned.
Seville, July 5, 1722.
(See p. 117; for the Penha family, p. 217.)

they confessed their crime freely, should be sent to the galleys; and it remained a punishment very commonly inflicted upon secret Jews. The sentences ranged from three years to life; but these terms frequently approximated, as the sufferings involved often resulted fatally. In the course of the eighteenth century, other types of penal servitude were substituted. For women the most frequent alternative was forced service in hospitals or houses of correction. Perpetual incarceration was another usual form of punishment; though the prison was known by the euphemistic title of *casa de la penitência* or *de la misericordia*.[9] At a later period, the duration of the imprisonment was generally decreased, those convicted being released at the close of eight years, or even less.[10] The title of the punishment, however, "perpetual imprisonment," officially remained as before. Among the other penalties may be mentioned that of exile (frequently to the colonies), exclusion from certain cities, and the practice of rasing to the ground the house of any peculiarly heinous offender, or one in which heretical services — particularly Jewish — had been held.

It was not only in his own person that anyone convicted by the Inquisition of a serious offence was punished. A number of disabilities were entailed which fell not only on those penanced, but also on their children and their descendants for some generations to come. They were not allowed to enter Holy Orders. They were excluded from any public dignity. They were not permitted to become physicians, apothecaries, tutors of the young, advocates, scriveners, or farmers of revenue. They were submitted to certain sumptuary regulations, not being allowed to be dressed in cloth of gold or silver,

or to wear jewelry, or to ride on horse-back. Neglect
of these provisions, sometimes after the lapse of several
generations, brought the offender once more into the
clutches of the Holy Office. Generally, infractions were
punished in such cases by fine only; and the granting of
rehabilitations, in return for a monetary consideration,
ultimately became very common.

But the most terrible weapon of the Inquisition,
other than the power of inflicting the death sentence,
was the right it enjoyed of confiscating the property of
those whom it convicted. At the beginning, the proceeds
were devoted to the use of the sovereign. Gradually,
they devolved upon the Holy Office itself, only a very
small proportion reaching the public treasury. In the
earlier period, general compositions on the part of the
New Christians, to save themselves from the possibility
of arbitrary confiscation, were not uncommon. Later,
conditions changed, and concerted action became impossible. We have seen how the *conversos* and their descendants, particularly in Portugal, struggled against this
right of confiscation, which they considered to be a perpetual incitement to proceed against them, however
unimpeachable their orthodoxy might be. It was through
this means that the Inquisition was raised into a corporation of such vast influence and wealth. Above all, it
thus became overwhelmingly to its interest to procure
the conviction of all who were brought before it, especially
when they were persons of great means. It was a weapon
which struck at the whole of a man's family, reducing
them at one stroke from affluence to beggary; while
through such action the economic life of the whole
country was liable to be thrown into sudden disorganiza-

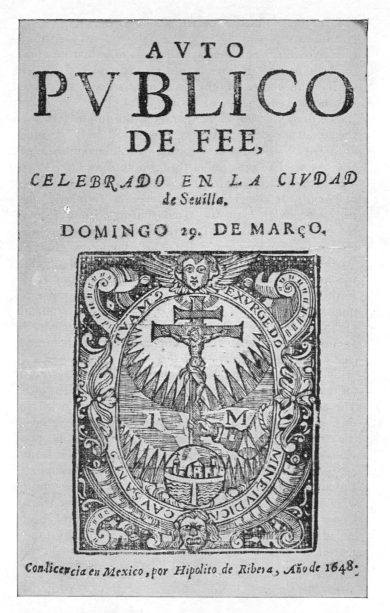

AVTO
PVBLICO
DE FEE,
CELEBRADO EN LA CIVDAD
de Seuilla.

DOMINGO 29. DE MARÇO.

Con licencia en Mexico, por Hipolito de Ribera, Año de 1648.

Title Page of List of Victims of Auto held at Seville on March 29, 1648;
Printed in Mexico in 1648.

[123]

tion. No other single factor, perhaps, was so instrumental in draining the ·Peninsula of its accumulated wealth during the course of the sixteenth, seventeenth, and eighteenth centuries.

The final sanction in the hands of the Inquisition was the penalty of death. As an ecclesiastical body, it could not itself be a direct party to this (it will be remembered how the warlike prelates of the Middle Ages used to go into battle armed with a mace, so as to avoid the shedding of blood!). It therefore handed over, or "relaxed," the persons convicted to the secular arm, with a formal recommendation that, if it were found necessary· to proceed to the extreme penalty, this should be effected "without effusion of blood"— that is, by burning. This was an ancient legal fiction of the Church, dating back to the eleventh or twelfth century. The actual mode of punishment was justified by a text of the New Testament (John, 15.6): "If a man abide not in me, he is cast forth as a branch and is withered: and men gather them and cast them into the fire, *and they are burned*."

Generally speaking, the extreme penalty was reserved for such as refused the opportunity for repentance. These comprised the "contumacious," who gloried in their crime, and died true martyrs to their convictions; the "relapsed," who had been reconciled on some previous occasion, and whose backsliding proved their insincerity; the "*diminutos*," whose confession was incomplete, and who shielded their accomplices;[11] or the *negativos*, who refused to confess the charges made against them. Under this heading there must necessarily have been included on occasion persons who were absolutely innocent of the crimes imputed to them, and who would not

The place and manner of EXECUTIONS

[125]

confess falsely to the sin of heresy even to escape death. The fact that those who came under this last category were condemned to the flames shows more clearly than anything else on what sure ground the Inquisition generally found itself. "Dogmatizers," or those who propagated heretical views, whether baptized or no, were also marked out as victims; and, in the earliest Inquisitional period, many fervent professing Jews suffered under this head.[12] On the other hand, by no means all of those persons upon whom a capital sentence was pronounced were burned alive. A profession of repentance, even after condemnation, was, except in the case of relapsed heretics, almost sufficient to secure the preliminary mercy of garroting, only the corpse being burned at the stake. The effigies of fugitives, with the bones of those who had escaped justice by death (sometimes in prison, or else under torture), would similarly be committed to the flames. Those burned in effigy often numbered nearly as many as those burned in person, sometimes even more. This was not, indeed, a barren formality, as the condemnation even of the dead secured the confiscation of their property, no matter how much time had elapsed since the alleged offence had been committed; while reconciliation in such cases was obviously outside the bounds of possibility.

Under the circumstances, it is obviously incorrect to consider all the victims of the Inquisition as martyrs to their faith. The "contumacious," who went to the stake proudly confessing their Judaism, were a comparatively insignificant minority. As we have seen, on the occasion of the great persecution in Majorca, in 1691, only three persons out of a total of some forty were burned alive. All the rest saved themselves the worst agonies by a very timely repentance, so that only their garroted bodies were committed to the flames. The proportion was not peculiarly high. It was not to be expected that persons who had lived a life of subterfuge would suddenly acquire the spirit of martyrdom in their last moments, though that sometimes happened. The general impression that the Inquisition burned Jews must be classed as a popular misconception. Normally, as we have seen, the Jews did not come within the scope of its activity, provided that they did not interfere in matters of faith; and sometimes the defence of persons put on trial was that they had been born Jews, that they had never been baptized, and that they were accordingly guilty of no crime except that of being in the country illegally. Of those who died at the stake, an overwhelming majority had denied Judaism while they lived; while a very large proportion repudiated it even in the hour of death. The proportion of real martyrs amongst the Inquisitional victims was not large. Even of the minority who were burned alive, some were *diminutos* or *relapsados*, whose profession of repentance was now insufficient to procure mercy; while others were *negativos* who stoutly disclaimed the charges brought against them, and sometimes were indubitably innocent. In either case, such victims died professing the Catholic faith with their last breath. It was as a matter of fact sometimes agreed upon among the Marranos, as being the safest course, to deny all charges brought against them. Thus they would have at least some possibility of escaping sentence, and would not implicate their accomplices. It is this which explains the strange silence of some persons, indubitably guilty, who forewent by their persistently negative attitude even the full satisfaction of martyrdom.[13]

The sentences of the Inquisition were announced at the so-called Act of Faith: *Auto de Fé* as it was termed in Spain, and *Auto-da-fè* in Portugal. It is the latter title which has obtained universal currency — a fact which throws a vivid light upon the unenviable prominence in Inquisitional activity which the smaller country ultimately attained. For lighter offences, involving abjuration *de levi*, the ceremonial might be private (*auto particular*, or *autillo*). In these cases it would be held in a church, with a minimum of publicity. This was however rarely resorted to for so heinous a crime as Judaizing; particularly as it was considered wrong to pronounce in the sacred precincts a sentence ultimately involving capital punishment. In most cases, therefore, the ceremony was public (*auto publico general*). This ultimately became the subject of elaborate organization. The ceremony would be arranged to take place on some feast-day, in the principal square of the city. Ample notice was given so as to attract as large a concourse of spectators as was possible, spiritual benefits being promised to all those present. Two stagings were erected, at considerable expense, for the accommodation of the principal actors — one for those convicted and their spiritual attendants, and the other for the Inquisitors and the rest of the authorities, civil and ecclesiastical. Pulpits and a temporary altar, draped in black, were set up between them.

The proceedings would be opened at dawn by a procession, in which all the clergy of the city would take

The Habit of a PENITENT called SAMBENITO.

The Habit of a RELAPSE or IMPENITENT going to be burnt.

part, headed by the great standard of the Inquisition. Behind followed those condemned to appear at the ceremony. Those abjuring *de vehementi* had to carry lighted tapers in their hands and to wear the *sambenito*, or *saco bendito*[14] (the *abito*, as it was called in the official sentence). This, an innovation of the Spanish Inquisition, consisted of a long yellow robe, transversed by a black cross (in the case of those convicted of only formal heresy, only one of the diagonal arms was necessary). Where the heretic had escaped the stake by confession, flames pointing downwards (*fuego revuelto*) were painted on the garment, which in these instances were sometimes of black. Those condemned to be burned bore a representation of devils thrusting heretics into the fires of hell. All wore in addition tall mitres (*coraza*), similarly adorned. In certain cases, as an additional punishment, the *sambenito* had to be worn in public, particularly on Sundays and festivals, even after the release of the prisoner, exposing him to universal scorn and derision. After its immediate utility had passed, it was generally hung up in the parish church of the delinquent, accompanied by a fitting inscription; the wearer and his family being thus marked out for lasting humiliation. These memorials of shame were destroyed only with the abolition of the Inquisition in the early years of the nineteenth century.[15]

When, amid the universal obsecration, the procession had arrived in the square where the auto was to be celebrated, the penitents and dignitaries would take their place on the respective scaffoldings reserved for them. Thereupon, a notary would administer a solemn oath to all present to defend the Catholic faith and to support the Holy Office. A sermon would then be delivered by some distinguished ecclesiastic. Its object was not so much the edification of the audience as the humiliation of the penitents, upon whose heads a torrent of the most unsparing insults, revoltingly cruel under the circumstances, would be poured. They would then appear one by one before the pulpit to hear their sentences, which had hitherto been kept a profound secret. The reading of the sentences took some time, the proceedings being often protracted into the night, and sometimes spread over two or even three days. The formal acts of abjuration would generally take place in batches, half a dozen prisoners appearing before the altar at a time.

Only those who were to be "relaxed" to the secular arm had known their fate before, being brought from their dungeons in the Palace of the Inquisition to hear it, on the previous evening. From that time, a couple of eloquent Confessors were permanently attached to the person of each one, in the hope of persuading him to a last-minute repentance. For the more steadfast, this cannot have been the least part of the sufferings involved. At the auto, the sentences of relaxation were left to the last. Those so fated were then formally condemned to death by the civil magistrate and escorted to the *quemadero*, or place of burning,[16] by a detachment of soldiers whose presence was sometimes necessary to save them from a violent (but indeed more humane) death at the hands of the infuriated mob. With them were borne the effigies of any who had anticipated their fate by flight or death, as well as the exhumed bones of the latter, all of which were formally committed to the flames. To light the brand with which the pyre was set afire was

The Celebration of an ACT of FAITH in the Great Square of MADRID as it was solemnized in honour of ye Nuptials of Charles 2d of Spain

[133]

The seventeenth-century Portuguese Synagogue in Amsterdam; from an etching.

considered an honor, or rather a religious duty, of the highest magnitude and usually fell to the lot of some distinguished visitor. It should be noted that the execution of sentence did not, as is generally imagined, form an integral part of the solemnity, being carried out at a different place (generally outside the city-walls), and some time later. The windows of the nearest houses were let out at high prices to those who desired to enjoy the spectacle, or else reserved for honored guests. At some places, such as Toledo, the *Plaza do Quemadero* still retains its old name. At Lisbon, the place of burning was the great square on the sea-front, formerly called the *Terreiro do Paço* (now the *Praça do Municipio*), adjacent to the royal palace. The ashes of the victims were supposed to be scattered to the winds. However, masses of bones have more than once been found during the course of recent excavations near the place of execution — notably at Saragossa — showing that the fire did not always complete its task. It was the fiendish custom of the populace to set fire to the beards of the condemned persons before the pyre was lighted, so as to increase their sufferings. This they called "shaving the New Christians."

During the course of the sixteenth and seventeenth centuries, the auto came to be reckoned a great public spectacle in the Peninsula and its dependencies, vying in popular appeal with bull-fights. Tens of thousands of people, of every sort and degree; would stream in from the surrounding countryside to take advantage of the spiritual benefits which were involved. The splendor was extreme. At one great auto at Cordova, on June 29, 1665, nearly 400,000 *maravedis* were expended on the entertainment of the Inquisitors, their servants, and the numerous guests. The proceedings lasted from seven in the morning to nine o'clock at night; and fifty-five Judaizers were "relaxed" either in person or in effigy, three of them being burned alive. Another especially noteworthy auto took place at Seville in 1660. It continued over three days, from April 11 to April 13, and was with only few exceptions the greatest yet known. A throng estimated at no less than 100,000 persons is said to have witnessed it. Forty-seven Judaizers (mostly Portuguese) figured in it, of whom seven were burned — three of them alive. Besides these, thirty fugitives were burned in effigy, including one of the best known dramatists and one of the greatest physicians of the day.[17] Special celebrations would sometimes be arranged in honor of royalty. Thus, on February 24, 1570, and the following day, one was held at Toledo to celebrate the visit of Philip II and his bride, Isabella of Valois. In Madrid on July 4, 1632, an auto was held in celebration (could fanatical unimaginativeness go further?) of the safe delivery of the Queen; it was on this occasion that the members of the secret synagogue in the capital were punished. But the climax was reached on June 30, 1680, on the Plaza Mayor of the same city, in the presence of the young Carlos II and his young bride, Louise Marie d'Orléans, newly arrived from France. At this auto, which began at six o'clock in the morning and lasted for fourteen hours, no less than fifty-one persons (most of them Judaizers) were "relaxed" either in person or in effigy; while sixty-seven penitents were reconciled. It is said that one strikingly beautiful girl of about seventeen called out, as she passed the royal stand: "Noble Queen,

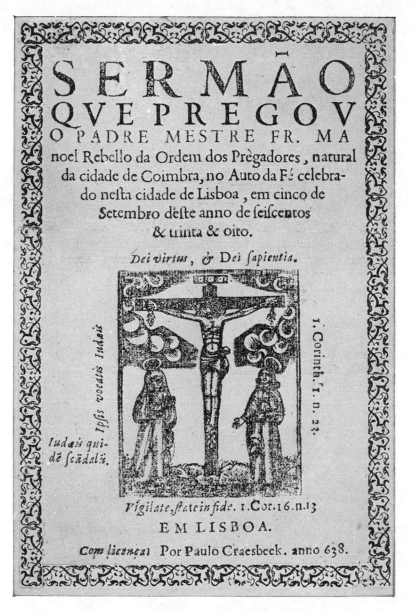

SERMÃO
QVE PREGOV
O PADRE MESTRE FR. MA
noel Rebello da Ordem dos Prègadores, natural
da cidade de Coimbra, no Auto da Fé celebrado nesta cidade de Lisboa, em cinco de
Setembro deste anno de seiscentos
& trinta & oito.

Dei virtus, & Dei sapientia.

Iudæis quidē scādalū.

Ipsis vocatis Iudæis

1. Corinth. 1. n. 23.

Vigilate, state in fide. 1. Cor. 16. n. 13

EM LISBOA.

Com licença. Por Paulo Craesbeck. anno 638.

Title Page of Sermon preached by the Dominican Manuel Rebello
at Auto held at Lisbon, September 5, 1638.

cannot your royal presence save me from this? I sucked in my religion with my mother's milk; must I now die for it?" In spite of this, the king himself set light to the brand which kindled the *quemadero* on which she perished. This, as a great Court spectacle, formed the subject of a painting by Rici, and of a triumphant description by Olmo. It was, however, as matters turned out, the last great solemnity of its kind.

The sermons preached at the autos were often published subsequently; in Portuguese alone, about seventy-five are extant in print. They usually speak of the penitents as Jews, and in terms of the utmost vituperation. Similarly, "Relations" of the autos, containing full details of the proceedings, or more succinct "*Listas*" of the persons who appeared, were usually printed and hawked about the streets in order to satisfy the ghoulish tastes of the populace. They are among our main sources of knowledge for the history of the period, giving full information as to the names of the victims and the nature of their crimes, with gruesome details as to who was burned alive, who after garroting, and who in effigy.

These publications had their counterparts in the Jewish communities of the free world abroad. When the news of the autos-da-fè reached them, special services would often be held; an elegy especially composed for such an occasion by Ezekiel Rosa would be recited; a sermon would be preached by some eminent rabbi; and the local poetasters would celebrate the martyrs in touching elegies. When on May 3, 1655, Manuel (Abraham) Nuñez Bernal was burned at Cordova, all the litterateurs of the community of Amsterdam collaborated in a

Title Page of Columbus' Letter to Sanchez, Basle, 1493.

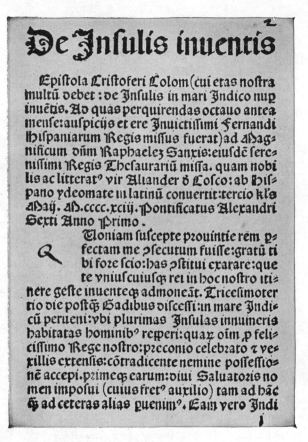

De Insulis inuentis

Epistola Cristoferi Colom (cui etas nostra multū debet : de Insulis in mari Indico nup inuētis. Ad quas perquirendas octauo antea mense: auspicijs et ere Inuictissimi Fernandi Hispaniarum Regis missus fuerat)ad Magnificum dūm Raphaelez Sanxis: eiusdē serenissimi Regis Thesaurariū missa. quam nobilis ac litterat⁹ vir Aliander d Cosco : ab Hispano ydeomate in latinū conuertit: tercio kl's Maij. M.cccc.xciij. Pontificatus Alexandri Sexti Anno Primo.

Qloniam suscepte prouintie rēm pfectam me ᴐsecutum fuisse: gratū tibi fore scio: has ᴐstitui exarare: que te vniuscuiusᶜᷘ rei in hoc nostro itinere gēste inuenteᶜᷘ admoneāt. Tricesimotertio die postᶜᷘ Gadibus discessi: in mare Indicū perueni: vbi plurimas Insulas innumeris habitatas hominib⁹ resperi: quaꝝ oīm p felicissimo Rege nostro: preconio celebrato ꞇ vexillis extensis: cōtradicente nemine possessionē accepi. primeᶜᷘ earum: diui Saluatoris nomen imposui (cuius fret⁹ auxilio) tam ad hāc ᶜᷘ ad ceteras alias puenim⁹. Eam vero Indi

First Page of Columbus' Letter to Sanchez.

[140]

memorial volume which was published in his honor and
that of his nephew, Isaac de Almeyda, who perished
about the same time.[18] In the prayer-books of the time,
a special form of *Hascaba*, or Memorial Prayer, was in-
serted, to be recited in commemoration of those "Burned
for the sanctification of the Divine Name:" "God of
Vengeance! O Lord, God of Vengeance! Shine forth!"
it begins, after a formal opening. A number of other
similar verses follow, and then the final prayer:—

> "May the great, mighty, and terrible God avenge
> the vengeance of His holy servant . . . . who was
> burned alive for the sanctified unity of His name.
> May He seek his blood from his enemies by His
> mighty arm and repay his foes according to their
> deserts. May the King, in His mercy, remember
> unto us His merit, as it is written: 'Rejoice, O ye
> nations, His people, for He will avenge the blood of
> His servants, and will render vengeance to His
> adversaries, and will absolve the land and His
> People.' "[19]

The organization, and the thoroughness, of the Inquisition cannot but excite a certain admiration. No lapse
of years nor alteration of circumstances nor completeness
of disguise could apparently baffle it. It knew no distinction of age or sex or degree. Its memory could be incredibly long; its relentlessness and its conscientiousness
were worthy of a better cause. We read of a fugitive Portuguese family implicated in a case in 1656, burned in
effigy in 1660, finally arrested in a different part of the
country under a disguised name in 1677, and being
sentenced to lifelong imprisonment in expiation of their

crime in 1679 — twenty-four years after the opening of
the case! A certain woman — Isabella, wife of Francisco
Palos of Ciudad Real — was tried by the Valladolid
tribunal in 1608, when 22 years of age. Subsequently,
she was again tried five times — twice at Llerena, twice
at Cuenca, and finally at Toledo. Altogether, about
eighteen years of her life were thus passed. The last trial
began in 1665, when she was in her eightieth year, and
lasted until 1670. During its course, notwithstanding
her advanced age, she was tortured three times, ultimately succumbing (as was not remarkable) to her
sufferings. Nevertheless, the tribunal would not be
baulked of its revenge; and she was burned in effigy,
with her bones, as one who had died in sin.

The tentacles of the Tribunal were stretched out
to every part of the known world. Denunciations
were regularly received, from informers or from spies,
from France, England, Holland, Italy, Turkey, Africa,
and even India and the New World. The disclosures
made in one trial might involve whole families, or even
communities, which would methodically and mercilessly
be tracked down in their turn. Cases are on record of
persons who denounced under torture as many as five
or six hundred of their relatives or acquaintances, though
this did not always save their own lives. During the
case at Toledo in 1669–70, against Fernando Gil de
Espinosa, alias Benjamin Gil, of Madrid, information
was elicited which led to the issue of warrants for the
arrest of no less than 213 persons, without counting
numerous others who had left the country. If the Inquisition was no respecter of persons, it was even less so of
years. In this respect, the record is perhaps held by the

venerable Anna Rodriguez, of Chaves, who figured as a penitent at the auto-da-fè held at Lisbon on May 10, 1682, at the hoary age of ninety-seven years; but she has a close second in Maria Barbara Carillo, who was actually burned alive at Madrid on May 18, 1721, in her ninety-sixth year. In 1726 Blasca Gomez Fernandez, who had died in prison at the age of one hundred, was relaxed in effigy at Cordova. Maria Alejandra Rodriguez, a woman of ninety, was similarly "relaxed" at Granada in 1721.[20] At the Lisbon auto of thirty-nine years previously, a woman of seventy was sentenced to deportation to Brazil! At the other end of the scale, we frequently find children of twelve or thirteen of both sexes similarly condemned, and forced to implicate their whole families in their confessions. In 1659, two girls only ten years old were reconciled by the Tribunal of Toledo.

The extent of the devastation achieved by the Inquisition can best be conveyed only by brutal figures. As far as Spain is concerned, the estimates given vary immensely. Llorente, the earliest scientific historian of the institution, states that all told, from its foundation down to 1808, the number of heretics burned in person in that country totaled 31,912; those burned in effigy, 17,659; and those reconciled *de vehementi* 291,450 — a total of 341,021 in all. These huge figures are open to suspicion. However, they are exceeded by the indications given by the intensely Catholic Amador de los Rios, usually most moderate in his views. He estimates that up to 1525, when the Moriscos first began to suffer, the number of those burned in person came to 28,540; those burned in effigy to 16,520; and those penanced to 303,847; making a total of 348,907 condemnations exclusively for Judaism in less than half a century of existence. Rodrigo, the apologist of the Inquisition, on the other hand, puts forward the impossible assertion that less than 400 persons were burned in the whole course of the existence of the Inquisition in Spain. Even if this refers to those true martyrs who remained steadfast to the last and so were burned alive, it is a manifest understatement; but the total number of victims enormously outnumbered those in this category. It was in the earlier and most ferocious period of the Inquisitional activity that the secret Jews especially suffered, being at that time the almost exclusive object of its persecutions. They furnish therefore a disproportionate number of the victims. In the later period, their contribution progressively declined. In the very last years, as will be seen, only a very small proportion of the cases were for Judaizing; but the majority of the charges at this period were trivial ones, and the sentences imposed were in most cases negligible.

As far as Portugal and its dependencies are concerned, the figures can be given with a much greater approach to precision. There are extant the records of approximately 40,000 cases tried before the Inquisition in that country in the sixteenth, seventeenth, and eighteenth centuries, the archives embodying them being virtually complete so far as the tribunals of Coimbra and Lisbon are concerned. Of these, upwards of 30,000 resulted in condemnations. The sentences were carried at recorded autos-da-fè totaling approximately 750 in all. In these, 1,808 culprits were burned at the stake (633 in effigy and 1,175 in person) and 29,590 were reconciled.[21] Of those who suffered at the hands of the Portuguese Inquisition, down to its last days, an overwhelming proportion were Judaizers. Lists have been compiled of little less than 2,000 autos which took place in the Peninsula and its dependencies from 1480 to 1825. This figure can be increased even further. All told, the Judaizers who were put to death by the Inquisition in Spain and Portugal during its three centuries of activity probably totaled more than 30,000. Of these, a goodly number were burned alive, true martyrs to their faith. Since history began, perhaps, in no spot on the earth's surface has so systematic and so protracted a persecution ever been perpetrated for so innocent a cause.

CHAPTER VI

SAINTS, HEROES AND MARTYRS

THE victims of the Inquisition were recruited from every walk of life and every section of society, from the highest to the lowest. They included priests and nobles, poets and statesmen, nuns and friars, farmers of the revenue, beggars, merchants, craftsmen, pastry-cooks, peddlers, scriveners, attorneys, booksellers, professors, university students, uneducated women, children scarcely out of school, old men with one foot in the grave, knights of the various military orders, aristocrats allied to the noblest families in the land. Each story embodies its own tragedy, set down with incredible callousness by the functionary who reported the trial or the chronicler who recorded it. Some of the cases are of more universal interest than the rest; and a few of them, illustrating in a larger measure the pathetic romance of Marrano history, will be described here at greater length.[1]

The earliest of the Portuguese autos-da-fè witnessed the martyrdom of a succession of extraordinary popular religious leaders. During the period which preceded the establishment of the Inquisition in that country, a considerable amount of disturbance had been caused on account of a certain Luis Dias, a poor and uneducated New Christian tailor of the sea-port of Setubal, to the south of Lisbon. His mind was filled with confused Jewish ideas which he had heard from his parents. These worked on him to such an extent that he began to consider himself a prophet. Ultimately, he persuaded himself that he was the promised Messiah, who was to deliver his people from oppression. As such, he was looked up to with reverence by his fellow New Christians, both in his native place and in the capital, which he frequently visited. Many Old Christians of all ranks also believed in his claims. Wherever he went, he was treated with extravagant signs of respect, his followers kissing his hand devoutly when they encountered him in the street. He received mystical letters from persons in all parts of the country who believed in his pretensions. He was reported to work miracles. An even more serious accusation made against him was that he circumcised the children of his adherents. These reports reached the ears of the authorities, and he was arrested. However, at this period the Inquisition had not yet attained its plenary power. In consequence, after confessing his wrong and undergoing formal penance, he was released.

Very soon he was found reverting to his previous practices, and was again arrested. By this time, the Holy Office had acquired plenary authority, and was fully embarked upon its career of blood. On this occasion there was no mercy for him. He was accordingly sentenced to death, and was burned at the second auto-da-fè held at Lisbon, in 1542. Eighty-three of his associates and adherents, Old Christians and New, suffered with him. Among the latter was the pseudo-prophet "Master Gabriel," a physician, who had gone about from house to house preaching the Law of Moses, and making many proselytes. Gonçalo Eannes Bandarra of Trancoso, a popular mystical poet, who was in close relations with him, though apparently not of Jewish descent, was similarly burned. His fate did not destroy his influence among the people; and his rhymes were largely responsible for the curious semi-Messianic belief which became current in Portugal that Dom Sebastian, who had fallen in battle against the Moors in 1578, was not really dead, but would one day return to deliver his people from oppression. The most illustrious member of the group was a government official, the *Desembargador* Gil Vaz Bugalho, an Old Christian of good family, who occupied a high position in the government service. Through the influence of "the Messiah of Setubal" (as Luis Dias was termed), he became converted into a conforming Jew, translating parts of the Bible into the vernacular, composing a handbook of religious practice for the use of the New Christians, and observing the "Law of Moses" as far as lay in his power. Meanwhile, he kept up an intimate mystical correspondence with Dias himself. He too ultimately died at the stake, in 1551; while Francisco Mendes, physician to the Infant Alfonso, escaped the same fate only by flight.

Another Messianic adventurer who met his end at the hands of the Inquisition was David Reubeni, the self-styled emissary from the independent Jewish tribes of the East. He had been arrested while endeavoring to approach the Emperor Charles V at Ratisbon, and was finally carried off in chains to Spain, and lodged in the dungeons of the Inquisition at Llerena. From this point, he disappears from view. However, among the victims of the first auto held at Evora, in 1542, was "the Jew of the Sabbath (*O Judeu do Sapato*[2]), who came from India to Portugal to manifest himself to his people, saying that he was the promised Messiah, and that he

came from the Euphrates; whence all the Jews believed
in him." There can be little doubt that the reference is to
David Reubeni, who suffered presumably on the charge
of having caused the New Christians to weaken in their
devotion to their new faith. As far as his former associate,
Solomon Molcho, alias Diogo Pires, is concerned, we are
on surer ground. He perished in Italy, at Mantua, in
December, 1532, as a Judaizing apostate from the Holy
Catholic Church.

A further martyr of the sixteenth century who created
a great deal of attention in his day was Diego Lopes,
of Pinancos, near La Guardia, who suffered at Coimbra
about the year 1580. From the moment of his arrest, he
proclaimed proudly that he was a Jew, and desired to
live and die in the Law of Moses. The efforts of all
the theologians whose assistance was summoned against
him could not convince him of his error, and he was
"relaxed" to the secular arm for punishment. As the
flames began to get a hold on the pyre, a curious thing
happened. The chains with which he was bound fell into
the flames, but the body was nowhere to be seen. The
Catholic population had a ready explanation: that the
devils, unable to restrain their eagerness to have so pernicious a heretic in their clutches, had carried him off
to Hell, before the soul had been dissociated from the
flesh. His fellow New Christians, to be sure, had a more
comforting interpretation of what had occurred; and,
for a century after, the memory of this event continued
to inspire them at the hour of trial.

One of the most illustrious and distinguished martyrs
of the Inquisition in Portugal was Frei Diogo da Assumpção, a young Franciscan friar, born at Viana in

1579. He had in his veins only a small amount of Jewish blood. Nevertheless, his attention had become attracted to Judaism by reason of the ferocity with which its adherents were persecuted. His own studies convinced him of the untenability of the principal doctrines of Christianity, and the immeasurable superiority of the older faith. It was impossible for him to keep his views to himself. Finding his position increasingly dangerous, he endeavored to make his escape to England or to France, but was apprehended on the way. Brought before the Inquisition, he freely confessed all that was alleged against him, and at first professed repentance. Ultimately his attitude changed, and he proudly confessed himself an adherent of the Law of Moses, "in which he lived and wished to die, and to which he looked for salvation." His impressions of Judaism were based only upon a literal interpretation of the Bible; but all attempts to shake his belief proved powerless. Even when in prison, he refused to take any oath on the Gospels, fasted every Friday, found means to light the Sabbath lamp at nightfall, made some differentiation on Saturday to mark the sanctity of the day, worked ostentatiously on Sunday, and removed the fat meticulously from all the meat brought to him, in accordance with his impression of the Mosaic code. A succession of theologians was called in to argue with him and to persuade him to abandon his heretical views, but he was able to hold his own against them all. The ultimate conclusion was inevitable. He was condemned, and handed over to the secular arm for punishment "without effusion of blood." On August 3, 1603, in his twenty-fifth year, he was burned alive at Lisbon "for the

Sanctification of the Name," remaining constant to the end.

This episode created a profound impression. Too late, the Inquisitors realized the error which they had committed in publishing his arguments against Christianity, as well as the confutation; for they were by now widely circulated. Abroad, the martyr was generally mourned, numerous elegies being composed and published to celebrate his heroism and his devotion. A number of Marranos in Portugal formed a religious association in his memory (called, in order to divert suspicion, the Brotherhood of S. Diogo), which kept a lamp perpetually burning before the Ark of the Law of the synagogue in some place of greater freedom. Thus, by the blood of the victim, the faith of the secret Jews was fertilized and strengthened.

The cult of the martyr was strongest in the city of Coimbra. Here there was a considerable group of New Christians attached to the famous University—all, or nearly all, devoted adherents to their ancestral faith. The principal among them was Antonio Homem, one of the most gifted figures in the learned society of the age. He had been born at Coimbra in 1564, being the son of Jorge Vaz Brandão and great-grandson of Moses Boino (Bueno), a Jewish merchant and physician of Oporto, a victim of the general conversion of 1497. He was brought up by his mother, Isabel Nuñez de Almeida, who belonged to an Old Christian family. Antonio Homem was educated by the Jesuits and studied in the famous University of his native place, where he graduated in Canon Law in 1584. In 1592 he obtained an appointment on the faculty. On the occasion of the great Plague of 1599, he was able to render considerable services. In reward for these, the University granted him an ecclesiastical benefice, to enjoy which he entered into Holy Orders, becoming a deacon. In 1614, he was appointed Professor of Canon Law at the University. In this capacity, he enjoyed an unrivaled reputation. His opinion was widely consulted on all matters concerned with ecclesiastical law. Several of his treatises are extant in manuscript. He was even called upon, in 1612, to make a deposition in connection with the proposed canonization of Queen Isabella of Portugal. At the same time, he attained a considerable reputation as preacher and confessor. In 1616, accusations of improper conduct were brought against him, and he was punished by a fine; but his intellectual reputation was unimpaired.

During the period when he was at the height of his fame as a theologian, Antonio Homem became the leading spirit of the Marrano group which flourished at Coimbra. This comprised several of the most distinguished figures in the University. There was André d'Avelar, Reader in Mathematics in the University, author of a couple of scientific works, and, like Homem, a clerk in Holy Orders—at this time, an old man of seventy-six. Antonio Gomez, born at Alcobaça in the middle of the sixteenth century, had been Professor of Medicine in the University since 1584. Tomé Vaz was a distinguished author and jurist, in practice at Oporto. He was a cousin of Homem's, who had brought him over to his own beliefs. Francisco Dias was Reader in Canon Law. A younger, but very illustrious member of the circle was Francisco Vaz (Velasco) de Gouvea, son of the eminent New Christian jurist Alvaro Vaz.

Francisco de Gouvea had been born at Lisbon in 1580.
After a distinguished career as a student, he became
Reader in Canon Law at the University of Coimbra, as
well as Archdeacon of Vila Nova de Cerveira, holding
besides other minor appointments. He had already
written one important work, and was subsequently to
publish many others. The then Inquisitor General
thought highly of him, and specially recommended him
to the Pope. Several others connected with the University were also members of the little group, including,
all told, half a dozen canons, as many eminent physicians, and several priests.

They held regular services at a house in the Largo das
Olarias in Coimbra. These were attended by as many
as a couple of dozen persons, including some students
at the University. They were conducted by one Diogo
Lopes da Rosa. Antonio Homem seems to have acted as
the rabbi, or priest. A graphic description has come down
of the service held here on the Day of Atonement.
The ritual seems to have been very far from Jewish
tradition, being based largely on a literal interpretation
of the Pentateuch. A prominent part appears to have
been played by the cult of the martyred Frei Diogo da
Assumpção. In the confraternity formed in his memory
Antonio Homem played an important part.

Ultimately the secret was betrayed. On November 24,
1619, Homem was arrested by the Inquisition and sent
to Lisbon for trial. After four and a half years of imprisonment, he was sentenced to death as a "contumacious and negative" heretic. He was put to death, by
garroting, at the auto-da-fè held at Lisbon on May 5,
1624, without having admitted his sin in any way;

and his body was subsequently burned. At the same time, eight other members of the circle (one of whom had died in prison) were relaxed to the secular arm. These included two priests, both of them Half New Christians, like Homem himself. None of these, as it appears, followed the example set by the martyred Frei Diogo by holding out to the last. Seventy-five other persons—42 men and 33 women—were condemned at the auto to less severe sentences.

The other members of the Coimbra group were more fortunate than their spiritual leader had been. Tomé Vaz had professed penitence, and had been reconciled at Coimbra on March 29, 1620, when Antonio d'Avelar similarly appeared. The latter however was promptly rearrested, in consequence of fresh facts discovered during the trial of his own children. At the age of eighty, he was despatched to Lisbon, there to undergo perpetual imprisonment. His two sons and his four daughters, three of whom were nuns, were meanwhile put on trial on the same charge, and were reconciled at successive autos. Francisco de Gouvea was not implicated for the moment. He was nevertheless arrested in 1626 on a charge of Judaizing and, after five years of imprisonment accompanied by torture, was penanced and deprived of his Chair at the University. Subsequently, he became one of the most important polemists on behalf of the royal House of Braganza. Antonio Gomez, whose wife Maria had perished with Homem, managed to escape to Spain. Here the long arm of the Holy Office overtook him, and he was penanced *de vehementi* at an auto held at Toledo in 1629, being in consequence deprived of his Chair. The house at Coimbra in which the secret synagogue had been situated was pulled down, a pillar suitably inscribed being erected on the site; and Antonio Homem went down to posterity as the *Praeceptor Infelix* — the Unhappy Doctor. His Marrano brethren subsequently founded a Fraternity in his honor, as they had done in that of Frei Diogo, under the name of the *Confraria de S. Antonio.*

The scandal had far-reaching repercussions. On April 30, 1620, the Portuguese tribunals had sent to Philip III, intimating that at the recent autos held by them, there had appeared several lawyers, three friars, and as many Canons of Coimbra: while six more—all nominees. of the Pope — were under arrest. The king was therefore requested not to allow any New Christian to be admitted henceforth to benefices or to Holy Orders. The petition, indeed, was not acceded to; but the palmy days of the Marranos at the University of Coimbra were henceforth at an end.

A parallel case to that of Frei Diogo da Assumpção, but if anything more remarkable, took place in Spain half a century later. Don Lope de Vera was the son of Don Fernando de Vera y Alarcon, a gentleman of San Clemente, not far from Cuenca. He was of gentle birth and of unsullied *limpieza*, having no Jewish blood in his veins. Of a studious nature, he had been sent at the age of fourteen to the University of Salamanca. Here he studied Hebrew (among other tongues) with such zeal that at the age of nineteen he actually competed for a chair in the University. His reading of the Scriptures inclined him, without any outside persuasion, towards Judaism. It was natural for him to attempt to win over his brother to his new way of thinking. The latter, a bigoted Catholic, denounced him to the Inquisition. He was arrested at Valladolid, on June 24, 1639. After a short interval of hesitation, he suddenly announced to the Inquisitors that he wished to be a Jew and to hold all that the Jews believed, for all other religions were false. He was kept in prison for five years, while earnest endeavors were made to win his soul back for the Catholic faith. All was fruitless. In his cell, he managed to circumcise himself with a bone and to abstain from meat. From this time, he changed his name to Judah the Believer, refusing to answer to any other. In spite of flogging, he maintained complete silence when called upon to meet the eminent Catholic theologians who came to convince him of his error, refusing to set forth his arguments except in writing. Even for this, he would not make use of a quill pen, on the ground that it was an animal product, and so forbidden. Over a long period, the only words which crossed his lips when the Inquisitors made their weekly visit was: *Viva la ley de Moisen!*[3] Ultimately, after five years' imprisonment, the attempt to convince him was abandoned. In the auto held at Valladolid on July 25, 1644, he was burned alive, in his twenty-sixth year, maintaining his constancy to the end. As he was led to his death through the streets, he recited Hebrew prayers to the amazement of the spectators; and from the middle of the flames he was heard to chant, literally with his last breath, the Psalm, "Unto Thee, O Lord, do I lift up my soul." In the middle of this, he expired.

His heroic end created a profound impression. As in the case of Frei Diogo, the Marrano poets and historians celebrated it in their writings, so that his martyrdom became one of the best-known episodes of contemporary history. "He was the greatest Jewish heretic that I think has been in the Church," wrote the Inquisitor Mirezo to the Countess of Monterrey; but he was not able to conceal his admiration for the firmness displayed in the final scene. Long after, a youth on trial before the Inquisition in the same city referred repeatedly to Don Lope de Vera and declared that he had seen him in a vision after death, riding on a mule and glistening with the sweat that was on him when he was taken to the *quemadero*.

Different from this case in all but its heroism was that of Isaac de Castro Tartas. His father, a native of Braganza named Christovão Luis, or Abraham de Castro, had emigrated to France with his wife, Isabel de Paz, settling down at Tartas, in Guienne. There, in 1626, was born their son, Thomas Luiz, alias Isaac de Castro, who adopted the name of Tartas from his birth-place. He had studied the elements of philosophy and medicine at the Universities of Paris and Bordeaux, and had afterwards removed, with his parents, to Amsterdam. Thence he sailed to seek his fortune in the Dutch possessions in Brazil. Having got into a scrape at Paraiba, where he had settled, he took it into his head to pay a visit to Bahia, which was in Portuguese hands. Here he was arrested, and after a little time was sent to Lisbon for trial. He attempted to defend himself at first by stating that he was a Jew by birth, and hence could not be proceeded against as a heretic. Ultimately he was forced to admit that, like all the children of the Portuguese *émigrés* in France, he had been baptized at birth. From this point, he took up a more heroic attitude. He proudly proclaimed his Judaism, and his determination to remain true to his faith. All attempts to reconvert him to Christianity failed, and he was condemned to death. On December 15, 1647, the heroic youth (he was only twenty-one years old) was relaxed to the secular arm, with five others, at the great auto-da-fè held at Lisbon. He retained his constancy to the last. As the fire leapt up round him, there was heard from the midst of the flames a strange cry, which was repeated about the town by the populace until the Inquisition ordered them to desist. It was the Jewish confession of faith, the *Shema'*: "Hear, O Israel! The Lord, our God, the Lord is One!" It is said that the heroic end of this youth so affected the Inquisitors that for some time to come they refrained from burning any further persons alive. Of all martyrdoms at the hands of the Inquisition, none was more generally mourned abroad. In Amsterdam, poets, preachers, and chroniclers vied with one another in celebrating the tragic end. It was told that, in order to relieve his parents' mind of anxiety, he had written to them after his arrest, before he left Brazil, saying that he was going to Rio de Janeiro to see whether he could induce some of his relatives who were living there to embrace Judaism, and that they would not hear from him for some years. By a curious error, on the day when the memorial sermon was to be delivered for him in the synagogue of Amsterdam, his name was drawn by lot for the coveted honor of opening the doors of the Ark.

Another true martyr who deserves to be remembered (though, unlike those who have preceded, his memory was entirely forgotten in after years) was Antonio Cabicho, a Spaniard, who was relaxed in person at

Lisbon on December 26, 1684. He marched to the pyre loudly proclaiming his constancy to the Law of Moses. A high wind was blowing, which kept the flames from consuming his body. Over a period of three hours he remained in agony, fearfully scorched and half suffocated by the smoke. Meanwhile the populace expressed its detestation by pelting him with stones and pieces of wood, from which he vainly endeavored to shield his face. Nevertheless, he continued steadfast to the very end. His clerk, Manoel de Sandoval, was condemned to go to the stake with him. On the morning of the auto-da-fè, he requested an audience. He was asked whether he believed in God the Father, and said that he did; but nothing would persuade him to admit belief in God the son. They inquired in what religion he desired to die. "In the same as my Master," he replied. The faithful souls thus went together, after the same agonizing martyrdom, to greet eternity.

None of the victims of the Inquisition in Portugal was more distinguished than Manuel Fernandes Villareal. A native of Lisbon, he studied at the University of Madrid, and served for a number of years in the army, rising to the rank of Captain. He became one of the foremost champions of the restoration of the House of Braganza in Portugal, and was rewarded by being sent to Paris as Consul-General. Here he became a friend and admirer of the great Cardinal Richelieu, upon whose family and career he wrote a panegyric which enjoyed no little vogue. He was the author of a number of other works, historical and political, in addition to some able plays. Thus he became known not only as a rising diplomat but also as one of the foremost Portuguese men of letters of his day. In 1650, he returned to Lisbon on a visit. Just as he was on the point of being sent abroad on an important mission, he was denounced to the Inquisition by a certain literary friar, a rabid personal enemy of his. Searching inquiries revealed the fact that this eminent public servant was not only of New Christian blood, but also a devoted adherent of the faith of his fathers. He had worked to obtain some amelioration in the condition of the New Christians in Portugal, publicly condemned the rigor of the Inquisition, boasted that he was of the tribe of Levi, and had been in the habit of going to Rouen to celebrate the Passover with his wife. The case against him was damning enough; it was made worse by his imprudence in allowing it to become known that he had discovered the spy-hole through which he was watched in his cell. He was not cast in the heroic mould. He confessed his crimes, professed repentance, and endeavored to shield himself by giving information against several other New Christians, including his own wife. All, however, were living in France, this coincidence giving rise to the very natural suspicion that he was concealing any fact which might be of material assistance to the Holy Office. Moreover, his discovery of the system of espionage, it was frankly confessed, made it dangerous to set him at liberty. Accordingly he was condemned. As a member of the nobility, he was spared the additional indignity of being burned; but, on December 1, 1652, he was garroted. The king, for whom he had worked so devotedly, had done nothing to protect him.[4]

Balthasar Lopez introduces an element of humor into the grim story. He was a native of Valladolid, who had amassed a considerable fortune as court sad-

dler. Betaking himself to Bayonne, he joined the Jewish community of that place, and was received into the
Covenant of Abraham. However, in 1645 he ventured
back into Spain, with the object of persuading some of
his kinsmen to embrace Judaism. He was discovered,
arrested, and relaxed to the secular arm in the great
auto held at Cuenca on June 29, 1654, at which there
figured in all 57 persons (almost all of them Portuguese
Judaizers), ten being burned. The confessor, who remained
in attendance on him from the moment that the sentence
was communicated, persuaded him to avoid the worst
agonies by a profession of repentance. As they approached
the *quemadero*, the priest exhorted him to rejoice, since
through this action the gates of Paradise were opening
for him freely. "Freely say you, Father?" retorted
Lopez, indignantly. "The confiscation of my property
has cost me two hundred thousand ducats; am I to
believe that I struck a bad bargain?" At the *brasero*,
he looked on critically, while the executioner, Pedro de
Alcalá, bungled in garroting two of his fellow-victims,
Violante Rodriguez and Ana de Guevara. "Pedro," he
said, in mild reproach, "if you strangle me no better
than those two poor souls, I had rather be burned alive."

When his turn came, the executioner began to fasten
his feet. Lopez struggled against this indignity. "*Per
Dios!*" he cried. "If you bind me, I won't believe in
your Jesus. Take this crucifix away!" Suiting the action
to the word, he threw it from him. His attendant priest,
horrified, succeeded after some little trouble in persuading
him to take it back again, and to ask its forgiveness.
The last moment approached. As the executioner began
to do his work, the priest asked whether he was truly

repentant. The dying man looked at him, in reproof. "Father," he said, sadly, "do you think this a time to joke?"

The New World, too, had its martyrs. At the splendid auto held in the city of Mexico on April 11, 1649, the only one of the thirteen persons relaxed who had the fortitude to hold out to the end was the wealthy Tomás Treviño, of Sobremonte. He belonged to a family of martyrs. His mother had been burned at Valladolid, and nearly all of his kindred, as well as that of his wife, had suffered at the hands of the Inquisition. Already in 1625 he had been reconciled for the crime of Judaizing, but had been subsequently implicated in the confessions of a tortured child and was arrested again. During the five years that he lay in prison on trial, he persisted in denying his guilt. On the night before the auto was to take place, his sentence was communicated to him. Though a relapsed apostate, he could have secured by professing repentance the preliminary grace of strangulation before he was burned. At the last moment, however, his attitude changed. He proudly proclaimed himself a Jew, and declared his intention to die as such. All the assembled confessors combined to persuade him to reconsider his decision, but without effect. To silence his blasphemies, as they were called, he was gagged as he was taken to the auto. In spite of this, he managed to express audibly his attachment to Judaism and his contempt for Christianity. Even the patient beasts of burden, it was afterwards related, joined the populace in expressing their abhorrence of so great a sinner; for, one after the other, the mules assigned to bear him to the *quemadero* refused to submit to the load, so that he was obliged to walk until a broken-down horse could be found.[5] There was mounted behind him an Indian, who made a final attempt to convert him as they went. Enraged at his failure, he beat the condemned man about the mouth, so as to check his blasphemies. On the pyre, Treviño continued to mock the Pope and his hirelings. As the flames leaped up, he drew the blazing brands towards him with his feet. "Pile on the wood! How much my money costs me!" he was heard to say, sarcastic to the end. They were his last audible words.

An even more remarkable character was Francisco Maldonado da Silva. He was a surgeon of considerable reputation in Concepción de Chile. His father, who was of Portuguese birth, had been reconciled for the crime of Judaizing, and, warned by the experience, had brought up his children as good Christians. At the age of eighteen, Francisco happened to read the conversionist work of the renegade Pablo de Santa Maria, Bishop of Burgos, the *Scrutinium Scripturarum* (Examination of the Scriptures). Paradoxically, this drew his attention to the very views which it was intended to confute. He naturally consulted his father, who advised him to read the Bible and instructed him, as far as lay in his power, in the Law of Moses. In consequence, he became an ardent Judaizer, going so far as to circumcise himself with a pair of scissors, and to give himself the biblical name of Eli. He kept the secret even from his own wife, but, nevertheless, ultimately thought it his duty to bring over his sister to his way of thinking. The latter, a bigoted Catholic, overcame her natural affection and denounced him to the Holy Office. Early in 1627, he was arrested, and sent to Lima for trial. Here, he made no secret of his convictions, averring that he was an adherent of the faith of his fathers, and refusing to be sworn on a crucifix. The ablest theologians of the country, in repeated audiences, were unable to shake him in his beliefs; and, on January 26, 1633, he was unanimously condemned to be relaxed to the secular arm for punishment.

The most amazing portion of the whole episode now followed. So great was the pressure of business, that year after year elapsed before the sentence was carried out. Meanwhile, the condemned man continued to practice Judaism to the utmost limit of his ability. He observed the Day of Atonement with excessive rigor, fasting for four days instead of one in penitence for his sins. He took the biblical vows of a Nazirite, allowing his hair to grow long and not touching any meat. In his depositions, he refused to sign his name excepting as: "The unworthy servant of God, Eli Nazareno, alias Silva." A special fast of eighty days which he imposed upon himself undermined his constitution and reduced him to little more than a skeleton, covered with sores. Asking for maize husks instead of his usual ration of bread, he fashioned with them a rope. By means of this, he managed to get out through a window. Instead of making good his escape, he visited two neighboring cells and urged the inmates (both Old Christians accused on minor charges) to become converted to Judaism. With marvelous ingenuity, he pieced together out of scraps of paper two books (each of more than one hundred leaves) "so neat, that they seemed to have come out of a stationer's shop." In these he wrote, with ink made from charcoal, and pens cut out of a chicken-bone[6] with a knife fashioned from a nail, long treatises vindicating his attitude. At last, after an imprisonment of nearly twelve years, he was relaxed, with ten others, in the auto of January 23, 1639 — the greatest as yet known in the New World.

Seven of those who suffered on this occasion joined with him in proclaiming their convictions to the end, and were therefore burned alive. As the sentences were being read, a sudden whirlwind tore away the awning from overhead. "This is the doing of the Lord God of Israel," Maldonado da Silva exclaimed, "so that I may now look upon Him, face to face." On the *quemadero*, his two paper books were hung around his neck so that they might assist the flames, and that the record of his heretical views might perish with him.[7]

One of the most illustrious of all the victims of the Inquisition, and one of the last of the long series, combines European and American interest. Antonio José da Silva had been born in Brazil, at Rio de Janeiro, in 1705. His father, João Mendes da Silva, was an eminent lawyer and poet. His mother, Lourença Coutinho, was a persistent Judaizer. She had already been condemned once by the Tribunal of Valladolid. In 1713, she was again arrested and carried off to Lisbon for trial, together with her family. On July 9, at a public auto, she was reconciled for a second time (the Inquisitional methods had now lost something of their rigor). Antonio José da Silva studied Canon Law at the University of Coimbra, where he graduated in 1726, at the age of twenty-one. It was natural that the actions of a member of such a family should be closely scrutinized. The result was seen later in the same year, when he was arraigned before the Inquisition in consequence of an unwelcome satire which he had written, as well as on a suspicion of Judaizing. Under torture, which left him so crippled that he was unable to sign his name, he denounced several members of his family. On October 13, he appeared as a penitent at a public auto.

Upon his release, besides practicing as an advocate, Da Silva turned his attention to literature. He wrote numbers of comedies and operas, making a reputation as one of the foremost playwrights of his day. From 1733, his productions were amongst those most favored by the theater-goers of Lisbon; and he has been styled the Portuguese Plautus. But from the moment of his first release, he was a marked man. On October 5, 1737, he was again arrested, together with his young wife, then pregnant. The latter was released, but rearrested and condemned to public reconciliation, her mother-in-law simultaneously abjuring for the third time. For the poet, whose mordant pen had gained him many enemies, there could be no such lenience. The principal witness against him was a negro slave-girl who alleged that he had been accustomed to change his linen and even to abstain from work on the Sabbath, besides observing fasts which did not coincide with those of the Church. Watch kept upon him in prison showed that even there he abstained from food on certain days and practiced certain other unfamiliar rites. He was again submitted to torture; but, during recent years, his character had become firmer, and nothing was elicited from him. Accordingly, he was condemned as a convicted, negative, and relapsed Judaizer. The general sympathy, the efforts of distinguished statesmen and litterateurs, and even the intervention of the king himself, were now insufficient to save him. On October 1, 1739, he was relaxed to the secular arm at an auto held at Lisbon, being garroted and subsequently burned. On the same night, by a tragic but hardly unintentional coincidence, one of his comedies was produced at the principal theater of the town. Antonio José da Silva is still remembered in the annals of Portuguese literature as *O Judeu* — "The Jew."

CHAPTER VII

THE RELIGION OF THE MARRANOS

A PICTURE of the Marranos cannot be complete without an attempt to describe, not only the vicissitudes through which they passed, but in addition the actual practices and beliefs which they cherished; not merely what happened to them, but also what they were. The popular conception of a subterranean Judaism, entirely cut off from the outer world, but in secret clinging with the utmost fidelity to every jot and tittle of the ancestral rites and ceremonies, is obviously untrue. Uninstructed and isolated, cut off from the outside world, and deprived even of the guidance of literature, it was impossible for them to preserve the traditions of Judaism in anything like entirety. This did not indeed apply to the earliest generations. Down to the middle of the sixteenth century, both in Spain and in Portugal, the influence of Judaism remained strong, and, though observances were restricted by fear, they were not warped by ignorance. The Marranos of this period retained some knowledge of the Hebrew language. They continued to possess Hebrew books. They observed the dietary laws in full, when it was possible. Private synagogues were maintained, the services being conducted perhaps by former rabbis. Sabbath and festivals were kept with all possible rigor. They would do their utmost to be buried near their unconverted fathers, and would follow Jewish funeral rites.

As the sixteenth century progressed, such an approach to conformity became exceptional. A new generation grew up, with no first-hand acquaintance of official Judaism, no knowledge of the traditional language of prayer, and no literature for their guidance. All that they had to go upon was oral tradition and the authority of the Jewish Scriptures, which remained accessible to them in the Latin version. To this we may perhaps add the edicts and fulminations of the Inquisition itself, which in certain cases demonstrably served to indicate to those wavering in their faith what they should do, instead of the practices which they should avoid. It is from this point that the "religion" of the Marranos (for it was little less) had of necessity to begin; and from that time onwards we can trace an uninterrupted tradition.

Complete uniformity, of course, is not to be expected. Cut off as they were from one another, and lacking the unifying influence of books, it was inevitable that the degree and nature of observance should have differed from generation to generation, from place to place, and even from family to family. Nor is the information upon the subject which is to be found in contemporary sources to be relied upon implicitly. The nature of the Inquisitorial suspicions, largely based upon biblical reminiscence, naturally colored the accusations on the one hand and the enforced confessions on the other, so that the latter, in many cases, must inevitably be suspect. There are discernible, however, certain main tendencies, which may be utilized in drawing a consistent picture, to be applied with more or less fidelity to the whole period.[1]

The new religion did not lack what may perhaps be termed its "theology." In the last chapter of the apocry-

phal Book of Baruch, the Epistle of Jeremy, there occurs
a passage in which the prophet exhorts his brethren of
the Babylonian exile: "When ye see a multitude before
you and behind bowing down ye shall say in your hearts:
Thou alone art to be praised, O Lord." We are informed
by an erudite contemporary that the Marranos of his
generation applied the words "bowing down" to the Jews
instead of to their Babylonian enemies, interpreting the
passage as a divine license to worship strange gods in
case of necessity, so long as the heart remains inclined
to the God of Heaven. Equally informative is the sermon
preached by Antonio Homem, the *Praeceptor Infelix*, at
the secret service at which he officiated at Coimbra on
the Day of Atonement in 1615, as reported by an informer
who was present. He taught, it appears, that the essential difference between Judaism and Christianity lay in
the two questions of the observance of the Sabbath and
the worship of images; and that, while living in persecution, it was sufficient to have in mind the intention
of performing those precepts of the Law which could not
safely be observed.

The doctrine of the ordinary Marrano was, however,
simpler than this by far. It lay in one sentence — that
salvation was possible through the Law of Moses, and
not through the Law of Christ. This phrase is of constant
recurrence throughout the Inquisitional records, occur-
ring with an insistence which it is impossible to ignore.
It is pathetic in the extreme. Intended as a confession
of the Jewish faith, it employed nevertheless the language
and the conceptions of Catholic theology. To observe
one's religion merely in order to secure salvation unat-
tainable to followers of another faith, is an intolerant

conception entirely alien to the traditional Jewish spirit.

In some other points of considerable importance, the Marranos were profoundly influenced by their environment. Victims of the Inquisition were revered as martyrs. In honor of certain outstanding figures, religious confraternities were actually formed, very much as though some Christian saint were in question. "St. Raphael," "St. Esther," and "St. Tobit" (the last-named being considered the patron of travel) actually found their way into the Marrano liturgy. Catholic in inspiration, too, was the usage of fasting "for the living and for the dead;" and even more so, the custom of paying a third person, or even leaving a legacy, for vicarious affliction, as was sometimes done. We even read of a Mexican woman who acted as a professional faster, charging one piece-of-eight on each occasion.

Nevertheless, Jewish doctrine was not by any means submerged. Though persecution may have embittered some to the point of sacrilege and blasphemy, others managed to retain the traditional Jewish tolerance for the views of others, no matter how difficult the conditions. "A man will be saved by his works, whatever his creed," asserted a simple Marrano woman; and a zealous priest denounced Antonio Fernando Carvajal, the founder of English Jewry, for the heretical statement: "Don Mathias, although I am a Jew, we shall meet in heaven." Similar instances could be multiplied.

The Messianic idea did not exhaust itself with the mere denial of the claims of Jesus. Restoration of the "Land of Promise" continued to occupy an important part in Marrano hopes and prayers. In its early generations, as we have seen, the Marranos had their pseudo-Messiah, Luis Dias of Setubal, and their prophetess, the Maid of Herrera, to mention only two. As late as the middle of the seventeenth century, the reports which reached the Peninsula of Sabbatai Zevi, the Turkish pretender who set all the Levant in a blaze, were sufficient to attract a concourse of adherents. A special watch was set at all the sea-ports to detain those who set out to join him; and a muleteer of Toledo was punished severely for conducting suspected Judaizers clandestinely out of the country for that purpose. A few years later, the Mogadouro family, seven members of which suffered at successive autos at Lisbon, were fortified in their Judaism by the report that the astrologers of Holland had asserted the existence of undiscovered lands, where the Jews were in instant expectation of the coming of the Messiah. In Mexico, the Messiah had been confidently expected for 1642 ·or 1643; and extravagant hopes were centered in the person of Gaspar Vaez Sevilla, a known descendant of the tribe of Levi, who had been born there of devout parentage in 1624.

Judaism, even at its least traditional, is necessarily to a large extent a rule of life, rather than a mere creed; and Marranism never ceased to partake of this nature. A preliminary inquiry which suggests itself is the nature of the initiation into its practices. Children were frequently brought up as devout Catholics, being allowed by their parents to be introduced fortuitously into the secrets of their faith by outside influences. Thus in some families the various members tacitly assumed that all the others were Judaizers, or "Portuguese," but never ventured to communicate together on the subject. Sometimes, the rational tendency inherent in the Jew seems to have sufficed to bring out doubts which ultimately led automatically to reversion to the ancestral faith (an instance of this we have already seen above, in the case of Maldonado da Silva). One person who appeared before the Inquisition, half a New Christian, frankly confessed that "his blood on his mother's side had inclined him to entertain doubts in matters of faith, and, if anybody had informed him that there was a Law of Moses, doubtless he would have followed it." Some persons braved all perils to proselytize amongst those whom they knew to be of Jewish stock. Finally, the fulminations of the Inquisition itself, and natural feeling for the persecuted, led in some cases to sympathetic attention to the very beliefs and practices which it was desired to suppress; this was indeed the case sometimes with Old Christians as well as New.

Parents must obviously have been unwilling to risk the eternal damnation of their children (as they considered it) by leaving the matter to chance. Yet, whichever way they turned, they were faced with danger. If the younger generation were initiated into their secret from earliest youth, their childish prattle was likely to jeopardize the lives of the whole family. If they waited until maturity, Catholicism might be so deeply instilled in them that disclosure would be dangerous as well as useless; for religious zeal was no respecter of so trivial a consideration as family ties, and cases where children accused their parents, or even husbands their wives, are by no means uncommon. The obvious compromise between the two alternatives was to wait until adolescence, when parental authority on the one hand was still strong, and on the other discretion might be expected. For this purpose, the ancient Jewish rite of *Bar Mizvah*, at the end of the thirteenth year, when a boy entered upon his full religious responsibilities, was naturally indicated. It appears highly probable that the traditional introduction at this age to full performance of the precepts of the Law became transformed into initiation to the secret rites and mysteries of Marranism. Thus Gabriel de Granada, tried in Mexico for Judaizing in 1642-3, stated specifically that "when he was at the age of thirteen years, Dona Maria de Rivera, his mother, called him and, when alone with him in the house in which they lived in the Alcayceria, she told him how the law of Our Lord Jesus Christ which he followed was not good, nor true, but that of Moses . . . because it is the true, good, and necessary law for his salvation . . ." One of the charges brought against Antonio Roiz de Castello, who was martyred at Lisbon in 1647, was that he had been in the habit of instructing children in Jewish practices at the age of thirteen. It may be assumed that this was the common, if not the invariable, practice.

The religion into which a child was thus initiated was necessarily far removed from integral Judaism. The fundamental rite of circumcision was obviously an impossibility; for its discovery was tantamount to a sentence of death. Although therefore some neophyte of especial zeal might perform the operation on himself, or some venturesome youth might be initiated overseas, or isolated groups at distant spots might show a greater hardihood, the generality dispensed with the rite. They found, indeed, some justification in the Bible. God did not account it a sin that the children of Israel born in

the wilderness were not circumcised until they reached
the Promised Land, by reason of the inconvenience of
their circumstances. Assuredly, their own unwilling non-
compliance would be judged with equal lenience.

The weaker sex were fully as steadfast in their observance as men, or even more so. At the earliest Inquisitional period in Spain, we are informed how women
comprised the vast majority of the few who maintained
their Judaism to the end and thus died the deaths of
true martyrs. It is significant that women took a
prominent part in initiation to Judaism in several known
cases, showed an especial familiarity with the prayers,
and were in some instances peculiarly meticulous in
their observance. It was by the mothers and the wives
that the Marrano circle in Mexico, in the first half of
the seventeenth century, was presided over and inspired.
Ultimately it became customary for a woman to act as
the spiritual leader of the Marrano groups. It is a
striking manifestation of the vital position occupied by
the woman in Jewish life.

Any knowledge of Hebrew, the traditional language of
prayer, was almost out of the question. True, in the
earlier period, we frequently read of the seizure of
Hebrew books, and even the use of Hebrew speech;
while on one occasion we are informed of a person
against whom no other complaint could be made, except
that he could sign his name only in Hebrew! However,
in the subsequent generation, any acquaintance with that
tongue must have been a rare phenomenon, except
that not inconsiderable class which endeavored to
dissimulate its disbelief by entering Holy Orders. Even
the possession of Jewish works in translation would

have exposed the owner to persecution; indeed, in the
whole vast Inquisitional literature, there is barely a
mention of the seizure of Judaistic writings after the
sixteenth century. The place of the voluminous ancient
sacred literature was now taken by the Latin version of
the Bible. The New Testament was of course neglected;
but so far was Jewish tradition forgotten that the Apocrypha seems to have been treated with the same
reverence as the Old Testament. It was from the Bible
alone, fortified by fragmentary tradition, that the
Marranos derived encouragement and guidance. Observance was almost exclusively based upon its literal
interpretation, even in points when it was at variance
with catholic Jewish teaching. Of the Hebrew language,
only the very fewest fragments were preserved in oral
tradition. *Adonai* continued to be used for the Divine
Name; and one solitary complete phrase in which it
figures was remembered, though in a mutilated form.
With these trivial exceptions, which had long since lost
their full meaning, the prayers of the Marranos were
in the vernacular. Of necessity, they had to be handed
down by word of mouth. No books were used in their
services: and the couple of manuscripts of the liturgy
which have been preserved are late in date, and most
exceptional. Sometimes the prayers were original, especially those composed in verse which, it may be imagined,
are the latest in date. Many, however, and especially
those in prose, seem to have been based upon memories
of the ancient Hebrew texts.

The number of prayers was most exiguous. A full
compilation of the Marrano liturgy so far as it is known
does not fill more than forty printed pages. Sometimes,

a neophyte seems to have been taught only one prayer
as the whole of his spiritual panoply. A new specimen
was regarded as treasure-trove, and a person who
learned one hastened to communicate it to his confidants.
On special occasions, it appears, the whole repertory had
to be repeated, time after time, with pathetic monotony.
Nevertheless, there was a perpetual store of spiritual
comfort in the Psalms of David, accessible to all in the
Vulgate version; though the Inquisition was always lying
in wait for such as should be heard repeating them
without the *gloria patri* at the close.[2] In the secret
conventicle at Coimbra, psalms comprised a very large
part of the service on the Day of Atonement. Vernacular
versions, in prose and verse, form a considerable proportion of the Marrano liturgy of the later period, and
inspire the majority of the remainder. Instead of the
Christological concluding formula repeated by their
neighbors, the Marranos were accustomed to recite some
similar, but less objectionable, phrase, such as: "In the
name of the Lord, *Adonai*: amen!" Another manner of
making up the liturgical dearth was by reciting familiar
prayers of the Church, with any necessary omissions:
thus we are told of a certain New Christian youth who
confessed that he used to commend himself to God with
the "orations" of the Christians. The Lord's Prayer,
in its primitive simplicity, obtained a definite place in
liturgical usage. Meetings for prayer were generally
informal. However, we read occasionally of the existence
of secret synagogues or conventicles, at which services
were held at more or less regular intervals.

In worship, Jewish and Christian practices were intermingled. At the earliest period, it was customary to

cover the head; but this soon fell into desuetude. The preliminary washing of the hands, whereby Judaism made cleanliness precede Godliness, remained usual; indeed, it was at one time taken as a sign of Judaizing. Facing towards the East was another practice which was perpetuated. Covering the head during prayer with a white cloth, in imitation of the traditional *tallit*, managed to survive, at least locally, up to a very late period. On the other hand, kneeling during service, contrary to Jewish usage, became so prevalent as to receive specific mention in the liturgy. Prayers were recited rather than chanted in the traditional fashion; obviously, in part from oblivion of the old tunes, and in part from fear of attracting attention. Highly characteristic was the loyal preservation of the custom of blessing the children, the father passing his hands over their faces at the close.

Of the ceremonial Jewish rites, the most characteristic are those connected with food. In this, too, some of the Marranos of the first generation were meticulous, a *shohet* or ritual slaughterer being occasionally found continuing his activities although baptized. Detailed observance in so public a matter would have been equivalent to suicide at a later period. The flesh of the unclean beasts mentioned in the Mosaic code could indeed be omitted from the diet without too much difficulty. Hence the Inquisition was always especially on watch for such as abstained from pork, rabbit, and scaleless fish. Yielding to circumstances, however, the Marrano had to abandon the idea of procuring food killed in the Jewish manner. One or two things remained possible. In the Bible, he could read (Gen. 32.33)

how the children of Israel do not eat the sinew of the
thigh; and it was customary accordingly, whenever it
could be done without suspicion, to "porge" the leg
before preparing it for food. Moreover, when chickens
were killed at home, their heads were chopped off instead
of their necks being wrung — an approximation to the
ritual regulations. A prayer even existed to be recited
before killing animals for food. In over-meticulous conformity with the Levitical ordinance, the Marranos
refused to touch any animal fat. Hence they were
forced to utilize oil only in cooking, this coming to be
recognized as one of the regular practices of Judaism.
All meat was regularly washed, in order to remove
every trace of blood.

From pork, the Marranos of the earlier generations
would try to abstain, going so far as to destroy any dish
in which it had been inadvertently prepared, and telling
their children that those who ate pork would be turned
into pigs. The intense suspicion attaching to this,
coupled with the fact that in a large part of the Peninsula
the flesh of the pig in some form or other is the staple
food of the majority of the population, ultimately made
rigid observance in this respect impossible. Yet for all
this, the regulations concerning it did not entirely
disappear. Though forced to contaminate themselves
with "impure" food for the major part of the year, the
Marranos refused to do so on any occasion of especial
sanctity. Thus it became customary with them to
abstain from pork at least on Sabbaths, and during the
periods leading up to the Passover and to the Day of
Atonement; while they avoided eating any meat during
the seven days of mourning upon the death of a parent

and immediately before or after any fast. The origin of this custom was ultimately so completely forgotten that it came to be considered an integral observance of Judaism. On those days when any individual kept a minor fast, he was restricted to supping off fish and vegetables; while the rest of his family, who had not fasted, had no scruples against partaking of meat.

The difference between Judaism and Christianity consisted principally, according to the doctrine of Antonio Homem, in the two questions of the worship of images and the observance of the Sabbath. The latter continued to be one of the main cares of the Inquisition. To abstain from ordinary occupations on Saturday was an obvious indication of guilt. Nevertheless, food was prepared as far as possible on the previous day; and Marrano ladies would sit idle before their spinning-wheels, taking up their work only when a stranger appeared. It was usual to make a point of changing linen on Friday night, though the imprudence might bring a man to the stake. This, indeed, figured foremost among the charges which cost the illustrious Antonio José da Silva his life. In the circumstances, observance became more and more difficult. It was clung to, nevertheless, with pathetic eagerness. Angela Nuñez Marques, a devout Marrano woman of Pastrana, tried at Toledo in 1680, admitted that in spite of all her efforts she had been unable to keep more than fifteen Sabbaths in twenty years. Regular meetings for prayer on Saturdays were obviously dangerous. They were however held, as far as possible, in the months before the Passover and the Day of Atonement.

But the most persistent of all traditions relating to

the observance of the day was the kindling of the Sabbath light on Friday evening. This, in the eyes of the Inquisition, was the most damning proof of Judaism. The observant Jew would not extinguish a light after the Sabbath was inaugurated. This was a rigor the continued observance of which was not possible in time of oppression. Nevertheless, the Marranos would not couple what they conceived to be a transgression with the performance of a religious action. Hence the Sabbatical light, at all events, was allowed to burn itself out; and, long after the origin of the practice was lost, this continued to be considered an essential. Such was the veneration with which the Sabbath light was regarded (as indicated by its name, "the candle of the Lord") that it became customary to prepare the wicks with special prayers, as a religious rite. Naturally, only pure olive oil, not animal fat, was to be used in kindling it. To conceal it from prying eyes, it was customary locally to kindle the light in a cellar, or to place it inside a pitcher; this similarly coming to be regarded as an essential observance.

Preoccupied with the salvation of their souls, and living under the conditions in which they did, the Marranos could not be expected to appreciate Judaism in its comprehensive whole. Prohibitions took a greater share in their outlook than practices. They attached more importance to fasting than to feasting. With one exception, therefore, the festivals seem to have fallen into considerable desuetude. Even the New Year, despite its traditional solemnity, appears to have been absolutely neglected — largely, no doubt, on account of its comparative inconspicuousness in the Bible. The only annual celebrations which retained their importance were the Passover and the Day of Atonement.

At this point, an obvious problem arises. How were the dates calculated? The Jewish calendar, with its careful adjustment of the solar and lunar systems by means of sporadic intercalary months, was far too complicated to be preserved orally. Had twelve lunar months been reckoned to every year, the preservation of the reckoning would have been difficult, and in any case the cycle of seasons would have become ridiculously inaccurate within a very short period. We have one clue to the solution of this mystery. In the Inquisitional records, the Day of Atonement is consistently referred to as being celebrated on the tenth day after the New Moon of September, and the Passover as coinciding with the Full Moon of March. What seems to have happened was, that the Marranos made use of the current solar calendar as a basis for their lunar reckoning. Thus they celebrated the Day of Atonement on the tenth day after the New Moon which fell in the month of September, and the Passover on the fourteenth day after the New Moon of March. In most cases, this reckoning would have been accurate, within a day or two; but sometimes it must have been nearly a month out. Thus in 1606, when the Day of Atonement actually fell on October 12, it was celebrated at Coimbra some time between the tenth and the fifteenth of the previous month; and in 1618, when Passover occurred on April 10, it was observed some time in the month of March. In Mexico, on one occasion, there was a great dispute in the Marrano community relative to the date of an approaching celebration, one faction wishing to observe it ten days before the other.

Ultimately, a further complication was introduced. At the time of the more solemn celebrations of the Jewish year, the Inquisition and its myrmidons became more vigilant. In order to evade their watchfulness, it became customary to wait for a day or two, until their attention was relaxed. Then the customary rites could be observed with comparative impunity. Thus the Day of Atonement was kept on the eleventh day after the New Moon of September, instead of the tenth; while the major solemnities of the Passover were observed after the first two days had expired, on the night of the sixteenth of the lunar month instead of the fourteenth. This curious perversion was ultimately regarded as mandatory, its origin being forgotten. For fixing the dates, the authority of some person of especial piety or learning was followed. Thus we hear that the New Christians of Guadalajara in New Galicia, when they were desirous of knowing whether they should fast on one day or another, watched the house of Violante Juarez (subsequently reconciled at the auto in Mexico City in 1648). If the door was closed and she was idle, they knew that some religious celebration fell on that day.

The Day of Atonement, in particular, retained all of its solemnity amongst the Marranos, who braved all perils in order to celebrate it together. On the previous day, they bathed, in accordance with the traditional practice. In the evening, candles were lighted in abundance "for the living and for the dead," being placed upon clean white cloths. The entire day was spent in one another's company, in complete abstention from food. Meanwhile, all the prayers they knew were repeated, time after time, or the Messianic prophecies of the Bible were discussed. Among the ancient traditions of the day preserved was that of having four services between sunrise and sundown, instead of the normal three. Though the practice of wearing no shoes was retained, they did not recognize it as one of the traditional deprivations, but considered it a tribute to the sanctity of the place of prayer; finding biblical precedent in the conduct of Moses before the Burning Bush (Ex. 3.5). The title given to the day was *Dia Pura* or "Day of Purity"— an obvious corruption of the Hebrew *Kippur*, but giving nevertheless an impression of the special character with which it was invested in their eyes. The traditional Jewish characterization as the Day of Pardon (from Heaven) seems to have been slightly misinterpreted; for an outstanding feature of the celebration was the formal forgiving of one another for offences received.[3] Thus, at the prayer-meeting at Coimbra in 1616, all the congregation were urged to pardon one another: "for that was the Day of Pardon." It was natural for the dates of the various celebrations of the coming year to be publicly announced at the general assemblage on this occasion. Before and after the fast, as has been pointed out, it was customary to make a meal of fish and vegetables; not meat, since none was available which had been prepared according to the ritually prescribed fashion.

The other great biblical celebration was the Passover. The observance of this, locally at least, was obviously dictated by biblical reminiscence, a meal being prepared in which the principal dish was a lamb cooked whole. Those partaking of it stood, booted, with staffs in their hands, in literal fulfillment of the biblical precept: practices long since abandoned in Jewish usage. In Mexico, persons went so far as to smear their doorposts with the blood of the sacrifice. The traditional three cakes of unleavened bread was consumed at the same time as the lamb. A special ritual grew up in time about the preparation of this "Holy Bread," as it was called. A fragment separated from it, symbolizing the ancient offering (Num. 15.17–21), was thrown into the fire: a survival of a regular Jewish religious practice which had originally caused the Inquisition grave preoccupation, and which had survived sporadically in its old form up to the close of the seventeenth century. In order to elude the Inquisitional vigilance, it became customary to perform the ceremony of baking the unleavened bread two days late, on the sixteenth of the month; so that on the first two days of the feast no bread, leavened or unleavened, was eaten. This ceremony ultimately assumed the prominence of the traditional *Seder*-service on the first evening of the festival. Such elaborate observance was possible however only under unusual conditions of security.

Of the observance of the other biblical feasts, we hear virtually nothing. Tabernacles is occasionally mentioned, but without details. Pentecost disappeared entirely, or nearly so. The minor celebration of Hanukkah seems to have remained (though no details are given) as the Feast of Candles. Except for these scant remains, the festive cycle which plays so prominent a part in traditional Jewish life was utterly submerged.

Notwithstanding this general diminution, there was one occasion of the Jewish year which attained an enhanced importance in Marrano eyes. Although the joyous minor feast of Purim was entirely forgotten, the so-called Fast of Esther (observed, as a sort of antidote, upon its eve) attracted their attention to a remarkable degree; and the importance which it ultimately acquired rivaled that of the Day of Atonement itself. The reason is not far to seek. Was not the case of Esther "telling not her race nor her birth," yet still faithful to the religion of her fathers in an alien environment, almost identical with their own? Moreover, the touching prayer ascribed to her in the Apocrypha (to them equal in sanctity with the Bible itself) seemed exactly adapted to their needs. So much significance was attached to it that, we read, one of the daughters of Francisco Rodríguez Mattos, "dogmatist and Rabbi of the Jewish sect," burned in effigy in Mexico in 1592, could actually repeat it backwards. The phraseology of the passage* explains the popularity which it enjoyed: —

"And she prayed unto the Lord God of Israel, saying, O my Lord, Thou only art our King: help me, desolate woman, which have no helper but Thee: For my danger is in mine hand. From my youth up I have heard in the tribe of my family, that Thou, O Lord, tookest Israel from among all people, and our fathers from all their predecessors, for a perpetual inheritance, and Thou hast performed whatsoever Thou didst promise them. And now we have sinned before Thee: therefore hast Thou given us into the

*The Rest of Esther, 14.3–19.

hands of our enemies, because we worshipped their
gods: O Lord Thou art righteous. Nevertheless it
satisfieth them not, that we are in bitter captivity:
but they have stricken hands with their idols, that
they will abolish the thing that Thou with Thy
mouth hast ordained, and destroy Thine inheritance,
and stop the mouth of them that praise Thee, and
quench the glory of Thy house, and of Thine altar,
and open the mouths of the heathen to set forth the
praises of the idols, and to magnify a fleshly king for
ever. O Lord, give not Thy sceptre unto them that
be nothing, and let them not laugh at our fall; but
turn their device upon themselves, and make him an
example, that hath begun this against us. Remember,
O Lord, make Thyself known in time of our affliction,
and give me boldness, O King of the nations, and
Lord of all power. Give me eloquent speech in my
mouth before the lion: turn his heart to hate him
that fighteth against us, that there may be an end of
him, and of all that are likeminded to him: But deliver
us with Thine hand, and help me that am desolate,
and which have no other help but Thee. Thou
knowest all things, O Lord: Thou knowest that I hate
the glory of the unrighteous, and abhor the bed of
the uncircumcised, and of all the heathen. Thou
knowest my necessity: for I abhor the sign of my
high estate, which is upon mine head in the days
wherein I shew myself, and that I abhor it as a
menstruous rag, and that I wear it not when I am
private by myself, and that Thine handmaid hath
not eaten at Aman's table, and that I have not greatly
esteemed the king's feast, nor drunk the wine of the

drink offerings. Neither had Thine handmaid any
joy since the day that I was brought hither to this
present, but in Thee, O Lord God of Abraham.
O Thou mighty God above all, hear the voice of the
forlorn, and deliver us out of the hands of the
mischievous, and deliver me out of my fear."

The fast associated with the name of Esther thus
attracted the Marranos in an especial degree; and in the
Inquisitional records it has an importance second to
no other day in the Marrano calendar. It was generally
observed on the Full Moon of February, precisely a
month before the Passover. According to the biblical
account, Esther herself fasted on three consecutive
days — not, as a matter of fact, in the month of Adar,
when the commemoration is observed, but three months
later. So greatly did the parallel with their case affect
the Marranos that some at least of them followed the
example, keeping a three-days' fast, with an austerity
unknown to traditional Judaism. Thus we hear of a
woman of good family, who died young by reason of
observing the three days of this fast.

Without any biblical authority, it had been customary
in former ages for certain ultra-pietists to fast twice
every week, on Mondays and Thursdays, in atonement
for their presumed sins. No sin, obviously, could be
greater than that of apostasy. Some of the original
forced converts seem accordingly to have taken up the
observance of these biweekly fasts, which, though recognized as voluntary, became an institution amongst the
Marranos. They are repeatedly mentioned in the Inquisitional records; and even lukewarm Judaizers in distant
Mexico observed several of them in the course of com-

paratively brief periods of conformity. Such fasts were observed "for the living and for the dead"— in atonement for a departed kinsman, or for the welfare of some person in the clutches of the Inquisition. Other minor fasts which were observed, locally at least, were that of the First-born on the eve of Passover (transformed, with an excess of rigor, into a general celebration) and that of Gedaliah, on the day following the New Year. Special pietists inflicted additional austerities upon themselves, eating only every third day, besides spending two nights each week absorbed in prayer. All these fasts were kept, with characteristic severity, from sundown to sundown.

The expedients resorted to, in order to conceal the fact that a fast was being observed, were numerous. The simplest was to go out into the country, or else to feign a headache. In other cases, the servants would be sent out of the house on a trifling errand, the plates and cutlery being carefully greased during their absence in order to make it appear that the household had eaten. The most convincing and elaborate scheme was to stage a family quarrel just before mealtime, one person rushing out of the house in an assumed fit of rage, and the rest following at his heels to appease him.

Though the Marranos had to be buried with Catholic rites, they would do their best to be interred in virgin ground, or amongst their own people. On the death-bed, Jewish practices retained their hold. The Inquisition was especially concerned with those who turned their faces to the wall in their last moments; though biblical, rather than Jewish, reminiscence would appear to be reflected in this. When all was over, a piece of gold, or a jewel, was placed in the mouth of the dead person, as the toll to be paid on being ferried over the Jordan — an extraordinary garbled survival of classical, not Hebrew, mythology. All standing water about the house was meanwhile emptied out. The traditional *taharah*, or ritual laving of the body, remained customary. No doubt all strangers, including of course the priest, were hurried out of the death-chamber before the last moments arrived, so that the dying man might end his days, at least, in an atmosphere of sincerity. It is possible that the ridiculous legend prevalent among the Portuguese, that the end was hastened by suffocation, may be traceable to this fact.

After the funeral, certain of the rites of the traditional Jewish week of mourning were observed. The first meal of hard-boiled eggs — the customary mourning fare — was served to the family by a stranger after their return home, just as orthodox practice prescribes. During the whole week, they would remain at home, no meat being eaten, so as to avoid a direct breach of the dietary laws at this period. Ample charity would be given. On the last of the seven days, a fast would be observed. Other fasts "for the dead" were repeated at intervals, either by the mourners themselves or else by some other person, paid for his services. Money was sometimes left with this object.

The matrimonial customs of the country had perforce to be accepted. In the earliest period, however, there were instances of New Christians who were guilty of polygamy, as was still permitted (though not by any means usual) amongst the Jews of Spain; this coming to be considered one of the symptoms of Judaizing.

Even later, Catholic matrimonial regulations were treated lightly, persons sometimes marrying their near kindred "according to the Law of Moses." Fasting on the part of the bridal couple remained usual. The ceremony was inevitably performed in Church, though it was supplemented by a very simple home function. Nevertheless, the idea was always cherished that it should be confirmed in some proper community according to full Jewish rites when the occasion should arise. Down to the close of the eighteenth century, cases were common in the great Marrano centers overseas of the remarriage of couples "come from Portugal." As a matter of course, alliances were contracted as far as possible amongst themselves. Somewhat amusing accounts may be read of the efforts made to find out whether a prospective bridegroom was a secret Jew, or the expedients resorted to in order to get rid of him when it was discovered that he was not, or the difficulties experienced in finding a suitable husband for a Marrano girl who was ignorant of the traditional practices, or the anger of the parents if a mixed marriage were contracted. We read how on one occasion an apathetic youth, who had fallen in love with a Marrano maiden of observant family, was taken to the principal church and shown his grandfather's *sambenito*, as an inducement to Judaize. Manuel Alvarez de Arellano, who was almoner for the secret community in Mexico, also acted as *medianero* or marriage-broker to contract matches between the various New Christian families.

A Jewish life without charity is an unknown phenomenon. It was something with which not even Marrano observance could dispense. Accordingly, they used to pay particular attention to their own "New Christian" poor, giving them preference over others, and making additional distributions to them on all special occasions. So great was the importance attached to this that an apposite prayer was prescribed, to be recited on the occasion of giving alms.

For a prolonged period, the Marranos handed on from father to son the secret of their old family name (generally of Hebrew or Arabic origin), though they were known to the outside world by the Gothic appellations which they had assumed from some noble sponsor at baptism. On escaping to freedom, they hastened to reassume them (witness the Abendana, Abrabanel, Musaphia, and Usque families, to cite only a very few examples). At a later period, when the hidalgo tradition had become more deeply rooted, some families combined the two elements, like the Aboab da Fonseca. Ultimately, the Hebraic tradition died out in the Peninsula. Some enthusiasts now invented fresh, characteristically Jewish appellations for themselves, or else had to rely upon the information of graybeards who had known their families. Thus a well-born youth named d'Oliveira, a nephew of Mestre Pedro, the Queen's physician, was assured when he reached Safed at the close of the sixteenth century that his proper family name should be Gedaliah. The less fortunate had to content themselves with the recently acquired Spanish or Portuguese surnames which are considered characteristic of them in Northern Europe. It was long, however, before the tradition of descent from the houses of Levi or of Aaron died out. We have seen how Villareal prided himself upon his semi-priestly ancestry; and, outside the Peninsula, incongruous juxtapositions of the Hebrew and the Gothic, such as Levi Ximenes or Cohen Herrera, became common.

As far as the first names were concerned, biblical ones (generally patriarchal) were apparently adopted in secret at the time of baptism. The story was current of a Marrano youth who, asked his name, ingenuously inquired if he should say that by which he was known out of doors, or that by which he was called at home. Thus, more than one Inquisitional martyr was mourned abroad by a name different from that under which he had suffered at the stake.

Occasional attendance at Church was of course necessary. To be sure, it was reduced to a minimum. At service time, for the benefit of the neighbors, the parents would summon their children in a loud voice to go to mass. They would then sally into the street together, but would employ their time in going for a walk or paying a call. Thus it was possible for a child in one authenticated case to reach the age of fourteen without having attended a Christian service more than once. This, however, must have been exceptional. For those occasions when they were forced to enter a Church, it is not surprising that they had an uncomplimentary formula to recite, specifying that they bowed down, not to the images, but to the God of Heaven. Curious expedients were resorted to so as to avoid any active participation in the service. Thus when the Host was elevated, they would happen to be wiping their eyes, and thus would be unable to see it in time to perform the customary genuflexion.

From what has been said above, it should not be imagined that the religion of the Marranos was simply a negative one, consisting in the denial of a few Catholic doctrines coupled with the observance of a number of dry, meaningless survivals. It is true that theirs was inevitably a narrowed, atrophied existence. In some cases, perhaps, the conception of Judaism that was current was not far removed from that of a mystical secret society, adherence to which would entail, notwithstanding its perils, considerable advantages both in this world and in the next. On the other hand, even at its furthest from traditional Judaism, the religion of the Marranos had its positive side. Notwithstanding the progressive diminution in doctrine and in practice, the fundamental Jewish conceptions retained their importance. At the constant peril of their lives, the Marranos sternly upheld the unity of God in a country where the worship of images had obscured the essentials of monotheism. They conceived divine service as something to be carried out and realized, not in prayer alone, but in the actions of daily life. They retained a vivid realization of the brotherhood of Israel and of their own identity with the great mass of their people, wheresoever they might be found. They hoped eagerly for the final Deliverance, which they bound up with the recollection of the former national center in the Land of Promise. Thus, notwithstanding oppression, all the characteristic features of traditional Judaism were preserved; and the appellation "Jews," applied by the Inquisitors to the Marranos in scorn, may be vindicated for them as their rightful due.

CHAPTER VIII

THE MARRANO DIASPORA

THE most natural method by which the Peninsula could have been purged of the taint of disbelief, at the period of the introduction of the Holy Office and after, was obviously by encouraging those persons who refused to conform to the dominant faith to emigrate. This simple expedient would have been at variance with the ideals of the period. Had the recent converts been allowed to revert to their ancestral beliefs and practices, their souls would have been endangered, and all the work of recent years would have been wasted. Heresy was, moreover, in contemporary eyes a positive crime — indeed the greatest of all crimes; and to permit persons guilty of it to go unscathed was no more to be thought of than to allow deliberately a thief or a murderer to escape from justice. A secondary consideration, though by no means without its weight, was that flight would have robbed the Holy Office of the confiscations and profits which must have followed upon condemnation. Hence, a logical consequence of the general policy which was adopted towards the New Christians was to keep them in the country at all costs. Accordingly, in the period following upon the establishment of the Inquisition in Spain, orders were continually issued prohibiting emigration on the part of the *conversos*, and imposing heavy fines, of as much as five hundred florins, on persons conveying them. In 1499, the Archbishop of

Messina issued an order that no ship-captain or merchant should transport any New Christian overseas without royal license, under pain of excommunication, confiscation, and prosecution as a *fautor* or favorer of heresy. This was confirmed and sporadically enforced in succeeding years, would-be emigrants being sometimes arrested at the sea-ports as they were about to embark.

In Portugal, a more consistent policy was followed. There, from the moment of the General Conversion, the prohibition of emigration had been a logical necessity if the efforts of King Manoel to secure the Christianization of his Jewish subjects were not to be nullified within a few years. Accordingly, as we have seen, a decree was published in 1499 forbidding any New Christian to leave the country without special license, and prohibiting the general population to facilitate their flight, however indirectly. After the massacre of 1507 in Lisbon, freedom of movement was restored; but emigration immediately attained such proportions that in 1521 it was again forbidden. The prohibition was again renewed, generally for three- or ten-year periods in 1532, 1535, 1547, 1567, and 1573, and perhaps at other intermediate dates. It was suspended in 1577, but reënacted again in 1580 and 1587. In 1601, on the payment of the enormous bribe of 200,000 ducats to Philip III, the prohibition was removed, the king promising that it would never again be enforced; and the right of the New Christians to emigrate to the colonies of both Spain and Portugal was expressly guaranteed. This "irrevocable" permission was canceled in 1610. Freedom of movement was, however, restored in 1629 — on this occasion, never to be withdrawn again. This did not of course apply to suspected persons, who continued to have great difficulty in leaving the country. Over a large part of the period, evasion was prevented by a provision forbidding the purchase of land or bills of exchange from New Christians, who by clandestine emigration would thus sacrifice a large part of their substance.

It was not impossible, of course, to evade this prohibition. There were many methods. The ports and frontiers could not be guarded so closely as to prevent flight on the part of those who were willing to leave their property behind. The necessary royal license could generally be purchased without too much difficulty. Authorization to travel might be obtained for several plausible causes, such as trade or personal business abroad. Most characteristic, perhaps, was the plea of pilgrimage. Several cases are known of persons, who, leaving the country on a pious voyage to Rome, became pillars of the Synagogue in some place outside the realm. In 1500, a whole party of Portuguese New Christians was arrested at Malaga, where they had assembled with the ostensible intention of going to the capital of Christendom to celebrate the jubilee!

Accordingly, almost from the moment of the forced conversions in Spain, at the close of the fourteenth century, the Mediterranean ports, especially along the neighboring coasts of northern Africa, became filled with Marrano refugees who had fled in order to return to Judaism.¹ Their number was naturally greatest in the Moroccan ports, across the Straits of Gibraltar. After the establishment of the Inquisition, the flight was accentuated. Thus Obadiah di Bertinoro, a celebrated Italian rabbi who visited Egypt, on his way to Palestine, in 1484, writes: "There are in Cairo today about fifty householders belonging to the *Anusim* that were in Spain. All were truly penitent. The majority of them are paupers, having left their houses and their substance and their sires and their grandsires, who observed the laws of the Gentiles, to come to take refuge beneath the wings of the Divine Presence." Large numbers fled to the Aragonese possessions overseas — Sicily, Sardinia, and ultimately Naples. Their presence was the pretext for the introduction of the Holy Office into these two islands, in 1487 and 1492 respectively. In Sicily, real activity began on June 6, 1511, when an auto was held at which eight persons lost their lives. In 1513, there were three autos, thirty-nine persons all told (mostly relapsed penitents) being burned. After a period of disturbance and inactivity, the persecution began again. The climax was reached at the great auto of May 30, 1541, at which twenty-one persons appeared — nineteen of them New Christians, almost all refugees from Spain. Thereafter, cases of Judaizing gradually diminished, ultimately ceasing entirely. Notwithstanding its close connection with the Spanish throne, or perhaps because of it, Sicily had become too dangerous to commend itself as a place of refuge. Very similar was the case in Sardinia, where the branch of the Holy Office founded in 1492 lapsed into inaction for want of material at the beginning of the sixteenth century. In Naples, no independent tribunal was introduced, owing to the popular opposition. However, the papal Inquisition was active there, Waldensian heretics sharing attention with the native Judaizing *neofiti*[2] and immigrant Marranos from Spain. In 1572, seven of them were sent to Rome and burned at the stake. By the middle of the seventeenth century, all heresy had been virtually rooted out of the country.

The importance, and the diffusion, of the refugees from Portugal was very much greater. The latter were not likely to escape to a Christian country, where they could practice their religion only under the same limitations from which they already suffered. They made their way therefore in the first instance to the Moslem countries of the Mediterranean littoral. We read of many of them fleeing to the neighboring coast of northern Africa. In Turkey, they were numerous enough to form their own separate communities in many towns — Constantinople, Valona, Arta, Smyrna. In Salonica and Adrianople, the refugees from Evora and Lisbon were sufficiently influential to form additional congregations of their own. Owing to the circumstances of the mis-named "expulsion" from Portugal, it is obvious that the majority of those who sought refuge in these places must have lived as professing Christians at one period of their lives. This fact itself is enough to indicate the magnitude of the migration. At a later period, these communities were reinforced by new arrivals, who had been born and brought up as Catholics. When owing to the suspicions of the government direct migration became impossible, or dangerous, an indirect flow began. The Marranos would obtain permission to leave the country in a direction diametrically opposite to the goal for which they were bound — generally for Flanders. Hence they would go overland, across the Alps, to Turkey, their ultimate objective; sometimes, by way of Italy. In due course, a regular organization was set up to facilitate the migration. When the vessels put in at some English port on their way to Flanders, the fugitives would be informed whether it was safe to continue their journey or no. Agents were stationed here and there on the route. Letters were drawn up and circulated, giving minute instructions as to the journey, specifying what roads should be taken, what inns chosen, and where the refugees could obtain help and advice in case of need.[3]

It did not take long for the secret of this roundabout migration to be penetrated. Soon, it began to become dangerous. Convoys were periodically arrested and mal-treated en route. In 1532, the Emperor Charles V forbade admittance to the Low Countries to New Christians on their way to Turkey. Naturally, after the introduction of the Inquisition to Portugal, matters became worse. The New Christians were accused of taking with them, to aid the enemy of Christendom, not only their persons and their fortunes, but also munitions of war and the art of manufacturing them. In 1540, a commission was appointed at Milan to investigate the migration, and wholesale arrests were made in Italy of persons on their way to the Levant. Jean de la Foix, who was in charge in Lombardy, made himself especially notorious for his barbarous treatment of those who fell into his hands. Four years later, orders were given for the arrest through-out the Empire of New Christians who sold arms to the Grand Turk. In pursuance of this, a convoy of forty-three persons traveling in four wagons was arrested at Colmar, in 1547, and released only upon giving an undertaking that they would settle in some Christian country.

Those Marranos who directed their steps to the East generally became swallowed up in the great Jewish communities which were already to be found in all of the more important cities of the Turkish Empire and the Balkans, thus leaving no separate trace. They were however to be found all over the Levant. In 1544, a whole shipload arrived at Ragusa. A little settlement was to be found in Cyprus. They were numerous in Palestine. There was a considerable colony among the mystics of Safed. In 1620, a Portuguese bishop, on his way home from the Indies, met one at Aleppo, whose ingenuous conversation enabled him to give information, on his return to Portugal, which led to the arrest of several Judaizers all over the country. Many naturally found their way to Constantinople. But the greatest place of refuge was Salonica, at this period the leading Jewish center of Europe. Here, at the close of the sixteenth century, there was a large Portuguese-speaking colony, which has left its mark to the present day upon the Ladino dialect of the region. So frequent was the phenomenon of the arrival of repentant New Christians that special regulations were required to deal with the problems which arose in consequence from time to time. For example, the local scholars decided that marriages contracted among the Marranos in the Iberian Peninsula, even in those cases where a fully traditional home ceremony supplemented that carried out in Church, were of no validity. This decision is by no means as harsh and unsympathetic as appears at first glance. If a couple escaped to freedom together, it was easy for them to be married again. If only the wife had the hardihood or the conviction to flee, then she could find another partner, and not remain tied down to a person with whom all sympathy and all connection had ceased.

The responsa of the Levantine rabbis of the period are filled with discussions relating to the position of the Marranos in Jewish law. Very characteristic was one as to whether a person who had escaped to freedom and reverted to his Jewish name might continue to make use of his previous appellation for purposes of trade. In certain matters, a differentiation was made between the *conversos* of Spain, who had adopted Christianity more or less voluntarily, and those of Portugal, who had it thrust upon them. The emigration to Turkey continued down to the eighteenth century, though circumstances prevented the exercise of any permanent influence there, or the development of a distinctive communal life.

Two Marrano refugees in Turkey deserve special mention, since they were among the foremost figures of sixteenth-century diplomacy in the Near East. João Miguez was the son of the late body-physician of the King of Portugal, and nephew by marriage of the brothers Mendes, the famous bankers. On the death at Lisbon of Francisco Mendes, the head of the firm, his widow, Beatrice da Luna, had gone to Antwerp with her daughter, her sister, and her nephew, to join her brother-in-law, Diogo, who managed the powerful local branch. Their vast wealth and culture obtained them admittance to the highest circles in their new home. It is reported that the Queen Regent of the Netherlands solicited the hand of the fair Reyna for one of her court favorites. The mother replied outspokenly that she would rather see her daughter dead. This incredible refusal, coupled with the rising tide of suspicion against the Marranos in the Low Countries, made it advisable for the family to seek a safer environment.

Through Lyons and Venice they made their way to Constantinople. Here they threw off their disguise of Catholicism. Beatrice da Luna became known as Gracia Mendes, the most benevolent and the most adored Jewish woman of her day. João Miguez married his cousin, the lovely Reyna, and was henceforth called Joseph Nasi. His subsequent career is like a tale out of the Arabian Nights. He rose to high position at the Sublime Porte, so that for a time he was considered virtually the ruler of the Turkish Empire, then the most powerful in Europe. He was able to recuperate himself for the confiscation of his property in France by the seizure of one-third of every cargo despatched from that country to Egypt. His interest was solicited by every power in Europe. He was able to sway the election of a new ruler in Moldavia. He avenged himself on Spain by encouraging the revolt of the Netherlands. He repaid Venice for the indignities that his family had suffered at her hands by bringing about a declaration of war, in the course of which she lost the island of Cyprus. He was created Duke of Naxos and the Seven Islands. He ruled his Duchy through the medium of a deputy, Dr. Francisco Coronel, whose father Salomon, perhaps a descendant of the renegade Abraham Senior,[4] had been governor of Segovia. Meanwhile, Nasi remained generally in Constantinople enjoying an almost royal state. He is above all memorable in Jewish history for his remarkable attempt to re-create a Jewish center in Palestine in and around Tiberias, which city, then in ruins, was granted to him by his grateful master. For a few years before his death, which took place in 1579, his political influence was on the wane; but his coreligionists continued to

look up to him as a veritable Prince. No professing
Jew in recent history has ever attained such power.

Joseph Nasi was closely rivaled by Alvaro Mendes,
whose very name was long forgotten, but who exercised
a remarkable influence in his day. He was born in 1520
at Tavira, in Portugal. After making a considerable
fortune in India, he returned to Europe. Here his worth
was quickly recognized, and he was created by João III
a Knight of Santiago. For some time, he traveled about
from one place to another, being a familiar figure in
Paris, Florence, Venice, and elsewhere. Ultimately, he
followed the example of Joseph Nasi (with whom he had
long been in close touch), adopting as a Jew the name of
Solomon Aben-Ayish and settling in Constantinople.
Here he soon attained similar distinction. He became a
power at the Turkish court. He was one of the most
important figures in international diplomacy of the day.
He was one of the principal movers in the epoch-making
alliance between England and Turkey against Spain, was
in close touch with the great Lord Burleigh, and sent
agents almost like an independent potentate to treat with
Queen Elizabeth. As a reward for his services, the Sultan
created him Duke of Mitylene. He did not indeed
follow the example of Joseph Nasi in patronizing Hebrew
learning. Nevertheless, the grant of Tiberias was renewed to him, and he did his utmost to forward its
settlement. After his death, in old age, in 1603, his
devout and studious son Jacob, alias Francisco Aben-
Ayish, continued to live in the colony which his father
had maintained.[5]

Simultaneously, a considerable tide of emigration had
set in towards those parts of Italy which were not

under Spanish rule. A report of 1564 states that there
was no city in the Peninsula in which refugees from the
Inquisitions of Spain and Portugal were not to be found.
A scandalized Portuguese clergyman, Fernando Gois de
Loureiro, filled a whole volume with their names and
details of the amounts which they had taken with them
from the Peninsula. They prospered immensely since,
as titular Christians, their activities could not be limited.
However, after making their fortunes, they emigrated
to the Levant, where they threw off the disguise of
Christianity and kept the Grand Turk informed of
everything that was going on in Italy.

Not all, indeed, waited till they had left Italy in
order to declare themselves Jews. Many proclaimed
their adhesion to their ancestral faith without delay,
and went immediately to join the Jewish communities
of the places in which they settled. Even in Rome, such
figures were by no means uncommon. The main center
of attraction was however the coast-town of Ancona.
The seat of an ancient and renowned Jewish settlement,
it was at this time one of the most flourishing Italian
sea-ports; and its close relations with Turkey and the
Levant added to its other attractions. The fact that
the city was under the rule of the Holy See made no
difference, for the Renaissance Popes were notorious for
their tolerance. Marranos from Portugal had accordingly
begun to settle there under Clement VII (1523–1534);
they had received a special safe-conduct in 1547 from
Paul III, guaranteeing that, in case of any prosecution
for apostasy, they should be exclusively subject to the
papal jurisdiction. The local authorities meanwhile
promised that they should remain undisturbed for a

period of five years at least, and that any person against whom proceedings were at any time meditated should have freedom to depart. These articles were confirmed in 1552 by Julius III. Under these auspices, the Marrano settlement grew apace. It numbered something over one hundred adults. They controlled the maritime traffic of the town. A good deal of the commerce of the entire Papal States passed through their hands. Many of the great Jewish mercantile houses of the Levant maintained agencies amongst them. A synagogue was established, in which divine worship was conducted according to the traditional Portuguese rite.

Upon this prosperous little community, disaster suddenly fell from heaven, in one of the most appalling tragedies in Italian Jewish history until recently. In 1555, there ascended to the throne of St. Peter as Paul IV the fiery Cardinal Caraffa, in whom the most fanatical aspects of the Counter-Reformation seemed to be personified. Notwithstanding all the solemn promises of his predecessors, the Marranos of Ancona were among the first to suffer from his religious zeal. On April 30, 1556, he withdrew the letters of protection and ordered immediate proceedings to be taken against them. The unfortunate victims undertook to raise among themselves the sum of 50,000 ducats in order to secure a respite. But in vain — the Pope's order was no attempt at blackmail; and he remained implacable. It was of no use for them to deny, even under torture, the fact of their baptism; since it was notorious that for the past sixty years no declared Jew had been able to live in Portugal. The persecution was carried out remorselessly. Twenty-four men and one woman, who stood steadfast

to the end, were burned alive in successive "Acts of
Faith," in the spring of 1556, their martyrdom being
celebrated in several poignant elegies. Joseph Mosso, the
agent of Gracia Mendes, escaped the same fate by
suicide. Contemporaries were struck especially by the
heroism of the venerable Solomon Jachia, who proclaimed
his faith undauntedly from the scaffold. Twenty-six
others who professed penitence, and were reconciled,
were condemned to be sent to Malta to row in the
galleys as punishment for their apostasy. But by great
good fortune, they succeeded in making good their way
to freedom. Thirty others had escaped from prison
before trial in consequence of a heavy bribe paid to the
papal commissary.

Meanwhile, at the court of Constantinople, the noble
Gracia Mendes had been exerting her influence. Thanks
to this, on March 9, 1556, the Sultan had addressed a
haughty letter to the Pope, protesting against this inhu-
manity and insisting upon the release of any of the victims
who were his subjects. The city of Ancona, fearing the
total destruction of its Levantine trade, fervently supported the request. Accordingly, those of the survivors
who were domiciled in Turkey were released. The few
who remained fled, mainly to the neighboring Italian states.

An episode followed which was almost unique in
Jewish history. The Jews had only one weapon by which
they could retaliate for this savage outbreak — the
economic one. Doña Gracia Mendes, with characteristic
insight, was the first to realize this, and threw herself
heart and soul into the work of organizing it. An attempt
was made to bring about a complete boycott of the port
of Ancona, if not the Papal States as a whole, on the part

of the Jewish merchants who controlled the trade of the
Turkish Empire. Their agencies were to be transferred
to the neighboring port of Pesaro, where many of the
Marranos had been benevolently received by order of the
Duke of Urbino. The plan was enthusiastically espoused
by the communities of Constantinople, Salonica, and
Adrianople. However, that of Brusa hung back. Moreover, the native Jews of Ancona appealed pathetically
for a reconsideration of the decision arrived at, which,
they urged, would only result in ruining them and bringing reprisals upon their heads. The result was that the
attempt ended in utter failure. What was worse, the
Duke of Urbino, disappointed in the hope of transferring
the trade of Ancona to his own ports, expelled the
refugees from his dominions.

The great center of Marrano migration in Italy during
the next few decades was Ferrara. Here, it was possible
to count upon a benevolent reception from the enlightened Dukes of the house of Este. As early as 1538, we
find "Portuguese Jews" (about whose antecedents there
can be no doubt) settled there for the purpose of trade;
and, from the middle of the sixteenth century, the
privileges granted by the Popes to those of Ancona were
extended to them. Even after Paul IV had committed
his great act of treachery, they were protected. Many
of the refugees were received there; and the colony grew
apace. Numerous New Christians formally re-entered
Judaism in this city of refuge, before going on to settle
in the Levant. A flourishing "Portuguese" community
took its place by the side of those of the Italian and
German elements which had been settled there for many
generations. Literary life in the little colony was active;

and it was here, in the first decade of the second half
of the sixteenth century, that the first Spanish translations of the Bible and liturgy, as well as various independent works, were published for the benefit of those
Marranos who knew no Hebrew.

Meanwhile, scandalized Catholics or treacherous renegades, returning to Portugal after a stay in Italy, were
filled with outspoken condemnation of what they had
seen. In 1574, for example, a penitent New Christian
denounced by name to the Inquisitional Tribunal at
Lisbon over thirty Marrano householders who were living
openly at Ferrara as Jews. Four years later, the Inquisitor General caused to be drawn up, for presentation to
the Pope, a list of refugees from the district of Coimbra
alone who were to be found Judaizing in various parts
of Italy, particularly in the dominions of the house of
Este. The numbers were impressive, and it was impossible for the head of the Catholic Church to remain
indifferent. In consequence, pressure was brought upon
the reigning Duke, Alfonso II, who was forced to submit.
In 1581, vigorous steps were taken at Ferrara. Many
of the members of the Portuguese community were
thrown into prison, where they remained for over a year.
Three, worse offenders than the rest, were sent to Rome
for punishment, and, on Saturday, February 19, 1583,
were put to death at an Act of Faith on the Campo dei
Fiori. The only one who remained steadfast to the last
was Joseph Saralbo, alias Gabriel Henriques, a native of
Serpa, who prided himself that he had initiated no less
than eight hundred of his fellow-Marranos into the
Covenant of Abraham. As he passed through the streets
on his way to the place of execution, bareheaded and

almost naked, he urged his brethren in faith not to mourn
for him, as he was going gladly to meet immortality.
For many years after, his memory was revered as that
of a saint and a martyr.

The Marrano colony of Ferrara was thus finally
broken up. The main stream of migration, as far as Italy
was concerned, was henceforth directed to Venice. The
Marranos had already begun to settle here at an early
date, their expulsion being ordered by the scandalized
Senate as far back as 1497. After the establishment of
the Inquisition in Portugal they began to turn their
steps thither once again. Many of them went to join
their coreligionists in the Ghetto. A greater number
remained living among the ordinary population about
the city, still wearing a transparent mask of Christianity,
and proving strenuous competitors in trade. This aroused
great jealousy. In 1550 the question of their expulsion
again came up. It was generally believed that three
hundred at least would be allowed to remain, by reason
of the advantage which their activities brought to the
city. Unfortunately, the Emperor Charles V, with his
characteristic zeal for the faith, threw his influence into
the scales against them; and, in 1550, their expulsion
was decreed for the second time.

The relief to orthodoxy was only temporary. Almost
immediately afterwards, a few individuals again began
to settle furtively in the city, both in the Ghetto and
outside it, as the Inquisitional tribunals in Portugal were
informed with pained horror. Meanwhile, the policy
of the Government underwent a change. It began to
realize the material benefits which might accrue through
the activities of these immigrants — a fact which out-

weighed the spiritual considerations that had hitherto prevailed. Daniel Rodrigues, himself apparently a Marrano, had come forward with a plan to resuscitate the dwindling commerce of the Republic by creating a free port at Spalato, in Dalmatia. In pursuance of this, he was authorized to do what he could to persuade his fellow-Jews to transfer themselves there; and several New Christian families took advantage of the opportunity. At the same time, thanks to his intervention, Jews from Spain and Portugal were authorized to settle in the capital itself, for the purpose of trade, without any close inquiry being made into their antecedents. Indeed, the great Venetian theologian, Fra Paolo Sarpi, maintained that these Marranos could not be considered Christians, since their ancestors had been baptized by force. Hence, no proceedings could be brought against them by the Church if they threw off allegiance to their new religion, no matter after how many generations. In consequence, though a tribunal of the Holy Office existed at Venice and attempted to intervene in a number of cases, it was kept relatively innocuous.[6]

The new colony increased with the utmost rapidity. The tide of migration, diverted to Venice, gathered force with every year. Portuguese was heard everywhere about the narrow Ghetto courts, where the aristocratic names of the best families of the Peninsula became familiar. The curate of a neighboring parish asserted categorically in 1651 that there were many red-hatted Jews there, who had once been Christian priests in Portugal. The Inquisitional tribunals in the Peninsula were kept busy hearing the shocked denunciations made by returned visitors. Many illustrious figures in Jewish life had their first experience of Judaism in the Venetian Ghetto — physicians, philosophers, poets, scholars, and mystics. The members of the new colony were known as *"Ponentines"* or Westerners; and, in Venetian Jewry, they formed a distinct element by the side of the German and Levantine "nations" which already existed. The members of the "Ponentine" element were legally restricted to wholesale maritime trade, in which some prospered exceedingly. Within a few years, they attained the hegemony in local affairs, in importance though not in numbers. They paid as much in communal taxation as the two other elements combined. In consequence, they were represented on the Council of the community by sixty members, as against forty Germans (who were by far the most important numerically) and twelve Levantines. Their synagogue, originally constructed in 1584, and rebuilt later under the supervision of the great Longhena, was the greatest and most luxurious in the Ghetto, and served as the official place of worship on important occasions. The language officially employed in it, for sermons and announcements, was Spanish or Portuguese. Numerous works in these languages — literary, legal, and liturgical — were published at the local printing-presses. The coats-of-arms of hidalgo families from the Peninsula appeared upon the marble tomb-stones on the Lido, where the exclusive use of Hebrew became less general. The local rabbis were assailed with casuistic questions relative to the problems raised by these numerous demi-proselytes. Thus, the first of the permanent communities formed by the Marrano exiles came into being. For a long time, it enjoyed the hegemony in the Marrano world. Its printing-presses provided most of its newer literature. It was the main center of spiritual and intellectual activity. It sent forth teachers to guide the nascent congregations elsewhere, and furnished the model upon which their organization was based.[7]

The influx to Venice did not in every case come direct from Spain or Portugal. Frequently the exiles found temporary refuge on the way, at some place where they were free from danger, professing Judaism publicly only at a later stage. In about 1630, an episode took place which greatly shocked contemporary opinion. For some time past, there had been living at Florence an eminent Portuguese jurist named Antonio Dias Pinto, who had been invited to Pisa in 1609 by the Grand Duke to lecture on Canon Law, and had afterwards become a member of the ecclesiastical Court of Appeal (*Giudice della Ruota*) at Florence. After he had lived there for many years, fulfilling this semi-clerical function, he suddenly transferred himself to Venice and declared his allegiance to Judaism. In the same year, his example was followed by two other jurists practicing at Florence — Francisco Jorge and Duarte Pereira, the latter a judge of the supreme court. This triple defection caused great scandal, all the more so since Jews were canonically incapable of acting as judges. A special edict was accordingly necessary to confirm the validity of the decisions in which these renegades had participated! Duarte Pereira, who apparently assumed the name of Judah Lombroso, became a doughty protagonist for his new faith, writing important polemical works in its defence. Antonio Dias Pinto took up his residence under the protection of the Lion of S. Marco at Verona, where there had grown up a small Marrano colony. There he died about 1650.

These were by no means the only illustrious Marrano characters associated with Venice. There was Immanuel Aboab, great-grandson of the last Sage of Castile, who returned to Judaism in manhood but nevertheless became one of the foremost polemists in its favor; Andreas Falleiro, alias Jacob Aboab, a wealthy merchant and father of an illustrious line of rabbis; Jacob (Rodrigo) Mendes da Silva, formerly Historiographer Royal at the Court of Spain; the brothers Cardoso, both physicians, of whom one ended his days in the odor of sanctity as an apologist of Judaism and the other as a Messianic prophet in attendance upon the Pasha of Egypt; and very many others of equal importance, whose names will be mentioned later in a different connection. If the Ghetto of Venice in the seventeenth century was so colorful a place, and its intellectual standards were so high, the influence of the polished refugees from the Inquisitions of Spain and Portugal was by no means least of the contributory causes.

The prosperity brought by the Marrano settlers to the Venetian Republic was followed with eager eyes by other Italian rulers. When therefore Ferdinand II, Grand Duke of Tuscany, set himself to develop the commerce of his dominions by the establishment of Free Ports at Pisa and at Leghorn, he endeavored to attract persons of this class. The charter which he issued in 1593 to tempt merchant strangers contained one remarkable clause: "We desire moreover that, during the said time, no Inquisition, Visitation, Denunciation or Accusal shall be made against you or your families, *even though during the past they may have lived outside our dominions in the guise of Christians, or with the name of being such."* This was little less than an open invitation to the persecuted Marranos of Spain and Portugal to come to establish themselves in the new Free Ports. Pisa was at the time the more important of the two, being the seat of an ancient Jewish community of some note. Occasional Marranos had found their way thither during the past half-century, but they had not dared to throw off the disguise of Christianity, and generally made their way to Venice in order to be admitted into Judaism. Now, however, the influx began on a larger scale. Before long, the old Italian congregation had become entirely swamped by the new immigrants — linguistically, liturgically, and culturally. Meanwhile, the Grand Duke carried out his promise, and protected the immigrants from ecclesiastical persecution to the best of his ability.

The port of Pisa had passed its prime. Contrary to expectations, a far greater tide of emigration was directed towards the hitherto unimportant harbor of Leghorn. Through the influence of the new settlers, it was raised within a very few years to the position of one of the most important ports in Italy, and, indeed, in Europe as a whole. In a short time the new community outstripped the parent body in which its absolute control had been vested by the Charter of 1593. There was inevitable friction, until in 1614 its independence was at last established. It was not long before the *Kaal Kados de Liorne* had become in numbers, in wealth, and in culture one of the most important in Italy. The contribution which its members made to the wealth of the

Grand Duchy of Tuscany is inestimable. Their share in the commerce of the port was a dominant one. They initiated, and almost monopolized, the coral trade. The traffic in drugs and medicine was entirely in their hands. Their ships traded to every port in the Mediterranean. They introduced the manufacture of soap. They set up looms for the weaving of silk and woolen cloths. They established a company for maritime insurance. Their wealth was immense. They made enormous donations to the government. The feasts and spectacles with which they regaled the populace in honor of a royal visit were famous. On one occasion, they constructed a military hospital at their own expense. In the eighteenth century, no less than sixteen families possessed their coaches; and this, at a time when in the majority of Italy it was forbidden for a Jew to be seen riding in a carriage. In 1593, Leghorn was little more than a fishing village. Two centuries later, the Jewish population alone amounted to little short of 7,000.

As has been indicated, this extraordinary development was due to a very large extent to the influx and the influence of the Marranos from Spain and Portugal, who were the backbone of the community. Already by 1644, they numbered close upon one hundred well-to-do families; and, in the following years, further refugees continued to arrive — scholars, physicians, soldiers, and above all merchants, who added still further to the welfare of the growing port. Unlike their kinsmen at Venice and elsewhere, the Marrano settlers on their arrival had found no Jewish community in existence. They were therefore able to develop their own characteristic life in a manner unexampled at any other place in Italy. As at Pisa, no formal Ghetto was established, for that would have been contrary to the spirit of the concessions of 1593. Accordingly, the traditional *grandeza* of the hidalgo was abundantly retained. The official language of the community, down to the beginning of the nineteenth century, was Spanish. In daily life, Portuguese — the *lingua franca* of Mediterranean commerce — was generally used. In these languages, there flourished an independent cultural life, with its own literature and its characteristic intellectual institutions.

Only once was the security of the colony threatened. In May 1730, Jacob Guttieres Penha, a newly arrived immigrant from the Peninsula, was arrested by order of the local Inquisitional tribunal on a charge of apostasy. Great consternation was naturally felt in the community, hardly one of the leading families of which would have felt safe had this precedent been followed. Within a short while the central government realized the blunder that had been made and ordered the release of the prisoner. Thereafter, the pledge made in 1593 was never again in danger of being broken.

The control of the community was originally vested exclusively in the Spanish and Portuguese section. It was only in 1715 that a constitutional reform gave the remaining elements any voice whatsoever in communal politics; and even after that date the latter remained, socially and economically, in a position of unmistakable inferiority. Thus, the Marrano element was able to impose its own distinctive culture upon all the later arrivals, whether they were Levantine merchants from the Mediterranean ports, or refugees from distant Poland,

or even immigrants from the neighboring Italian towns.
All these, if they wished to settle at Leghorn, had to
obtain permission from the Jewish communal authorities,
who belonged exclusively to the dominant class. Subsequently, they found themselves constrained to conform
to the manner of life followed by the latter. Thus we
find the extraordinary spectacle of the natives of the
country having to adapt themselves to the standards of
the immigrants, to follow their customs, and even to
learn their language! Families of ancient Italian stock
had to spell their names in accordance with Portuguese
standards of orthography, and German settlers flaunted
Spanish inscriptions on their tombstones.

The method by which the community was governed
approached complete autonomy. In its final form, the
supreme authority was vested in a Council of sixty
members designated by the Grand Duke, whose seats
descended by primogeniture from father to son. Of this
number, one third sat in rotation each year to transact
the affairs of the community, the whole body being con-
voked only in matters of supreme importance. Three
"Censors," nominated biennially, supervised expenditure
and exercised ultimate control. There was complete
internal jurisdiction, in both civil and criminal cases, the
secular authorities being enjoined to enforce the sentences
of the Jewish courts. There was an elaborate system of
taxation, the proceeds of which covered all branches of
expenditure — political, religious, charitable, and educational. A model organization of societies embraced all
aspects of life, from dowering penniless brides to reading
penitential prayers. Numerous academies existed for the
study of the Law; and the name of Leghorn was famous

throughout the Mediterranean world as a seat of learning.

The Marrano settlement at Leghorn was no less distinguished than that of Venice. Quite a number of Spanish priests and friars made their way thither to embrace Judaism. On one occasion, a Spanish colonel who was expressing his contempt of the Jews a little too openly in a Leghorn coffee-house, found himself confronted by the cultured Dr. Jacob Fonseca, who to the general amusement demonstrated that the two of them were closely related, though his own blood was if anything the nobler. In 1658, informers denounced to the Lisbon Inquisition an illustrious group, including one Chaves, a captain in the Portuguese army; a couple of members of the Villareal family, kinsmen of the martyred states-man-poet of that name; Custodio Lobo, alias Moses Yesurun Ribero, a poet and controversialist of note; and two physicians, one of whom was Jacob Rosales, alias Immanuel Bocarro Frances — one of the most illustrious practitioners of his age. The latter, a friend of Galileo, was author of a number of important works on medicine and astronomy, and had been created a Count Palatine by the Emperor Ferdinand III in recognition of his services to scholarship. In conversation with his fellow-Portuguese in the Synagogue, he had admitted quite frankly that he was a Jew, though he held that the followers of the religion of Jesus would also be saved. This heretical expression of opinion was reported with horror at Lisbon, when, not long after, those to whom he had spoken returned thither and gave an account of their journey.

In western and northern Europe, the settlement of

the Marranos followed somewhat different lines. Those who had fled to Turkey and to Italy in the first part of the sixteenth century had been in the main persons of a more or less intense religious feeling, who seized the first possible opportunity to make their way to some spot where they might revert to the faith of their fathers with impunity. Those who were left in the Peninsula after this period were necessarily of somewhat feebler convictions. As we have seen, they had penetrated deeply into the commercial life of the two countries, much of the maritime trade of which rested in their hands. It was the era when Spain and Portugal had attained the zenith of their power, and when they regarded trade with the New World and with the Far East almost as a monopoly. Accordingly, in every city of northern Europe which lay on the newly developed routes of oceanic commerce, there was now a considerable Spanish and Portuguese mercantile colony. A very large proportion of this was necessarily composed of persons of New Christian descent. Some may have been led to emigrate from fear of falling into the hands of the Inquisition, the suspicions of which were inevitably attracted to them by reason of their origin. Nevertheless, the motives which brought about the formation of these settlements were essentially economic and not religious in character. It was notorious that their members were of doubtful orthodoxy, so much so, indeed, that throughout Europe, at this time, the terms "Portuguese" and "Jew" were regarded as almost synonymous. [8] Nevertheless, the religious spirit in many of them was weak. In most cases, the recent arrivals were content to have found a place where they could earn their living without fear of persecution. They retained the mask of Catholicism, complying punctiliously with all of its rites and ceremonies. At the most, they continued to maintain some sort of crypto-Jewish existence in the privacy of their own homes, just as they had done before leaving Spain or Portugal. The ultimate history of these colonies varied. Some faded away, or became absorbed in the surrounding population; the attempts at proselytization made amongst them by their more fervent kinsmen in letters from Venice or the Levant being in vain. Others maintained a dual existence for many generations, until finally they were able to adopt Judaism openly without any untoward results. Others, again, who had the good fortune to discover themselves in a more tolerant environment (generally in a Protestant country), were able to cut short the intervening period and to organize themselves into undisguised and open Jewish communities without great loss of time.

Once these communities were established, on the other hand, they attracted increasing numbers of persons endowed with a more steadfast spirit, whose main object in leaving the Peninsula was to be able to worship the God of their fathers in security. At one time, indeed, there was an elaborate organization to smuggle the New Christians to the safer regions of northern Europe. A certain friar named Martin Lopes, alias Martin de Santo Spirito, who distinguished himself in this direction, was long considered a thorn in the flesh of the Spanish government. One of the charges brought against the Mogadouro family, member after member of which perished in a prolonged martyrdom between 1672 and 1684, was that they had facilitated the flight of fellow-Marranos to France, being in consequence known as "Transporters of New Christians" (*passadores dos christãos-novos*).

In France, the Marrano settlement followed a characteristic course. The country was Catholic, and officially in sympathy with the policy which had been adopted in Spain and Portugal. It had expelled the Jews finally in 1394; there were therefore no congregations existing in the country to serve as precedent (as in Italy) for the treatment of any new arrivals. But at the same time the Inquisition was not active in France. Declared Jews were indeed unable to settle there. Marranos on the other hand might immigrate without interference so long as they continued to call themselves Christians; and there was no over-meticulous supervision of their conduct.

In 1474, Louis XI had accorded many privileges to the foreign merchants who came to settle in Bordeaux. Spaniards in particular availed themselves of the opportunity; and there were among them a large proportion of New Christians. After the period of the introduction of the Inquisition and the forced conversion in Portugal, their numbers increased. In 1550, their position was strengthened, Henry II issuing letters patent specifically granting the Portuguese New Christians rights of residence, naturalization, property, and traffic similar to those enjoyed by all other foreign merchants. This charter was confirmed in 1574, 1580, and 1604. In 1614, Louis XIII ordered that all Jews, disguised or otherwise, should leave France within one month. The New Christians of Bordeaux alone, though their secret was all but open, were not disturbed. Ten years later, the *jurats* of the city passed a resolution speaking in the highest terms of the loyal services which the "Portuguese merchants" had rendered to the city during the past forty years. After this date, their right of residence was never seriously questioned.

Elsewhere in southern France, conditions were very much the same. From about 1520, there were settlements at the foot of the Pyrenees, in the flourishing port of Bayonne, as well as in the neighboring towns of St.-Jean-de-Luz and Biarritz. In 1597, their number was recruited by the arrival of a few families expelled from Bordeaux at the instigation of their coreligionists, on the ground that they had not been established there for ten years. In 1602, Henry IV ordered their removal to some place further distant from the frontier; but it does not appear that this was generally carried into effect. Thus, a second center of Marrano settlement was formed besides that at Bordeaux.

The immigration took on very considerable proportions. By the beginning of the seventeenth century, it was calculated that from 800 to 1000 families were living in the frontier provinces. In 1632, the commissioner of the Inquisition at Pamplona despairingly reported that troops of Portuguese were passing into France, many of them persons of considerable wealth, with their litters and coaches.

As we have seen, Jews were not, officially, allowed to live in France. The new immigrants were thus unable to lay aside their disguise and to return formally to their ancestral religion, as was the case in Turkey, Venice, or Leghorn. They had to keep up the pretence of being Christians. On the other hand, now that the menace of the Inquisition was removed, they began to throw off

precaution and to revert more and more openly to their
ancestral faith and practices. Gradually, a properly
organized Jewish life began to grow up, with its academies, its rabbis (imported, in the first instance, from
abroad), its autocratic organization, its network of
charitable and religious institutions. Synagogues were
built, thronged for worship three times each day, and
frequently visited by curious strangers. Hardly any
disguise was kept up. It was obvious to all the world
that these Portuguese newcomers were Jews. They
were not, however, permitted to describe themselves as
such. They were officially designated as "New Christians" or "Portuguese Merchants"— though it was notorious what those appellations meant. They had their
own Portuguese priests and confessors (possibly as little
sincere as they were themselves) who administered the
Catholic sacraments to them as a matter of form. They
were married in the Church, in accordance with Catholic
rites, notwithstanding the fact that the Jewish wedding-
service was performed in elaborate detail under the
traditional canopy at home. They took their children to
be baptized, though the rite of circumcision was performed upon the boys by expert practitioners. They
had a burial-ground reserved for their use; but it was not,
officially, a Jewish one, that at Bordeaux being situated
in the courtyard of the convent of the Cordelite Friars,
who did not object to lending their protection to the
sham. Even when, at the close of the seventeenth or
the beginning of the eighteenth centuries, the "Portuguese Nation" purchased its own cemetery, from the inscriptions in which their real identity was made perfectly
obvious, the pretext was still kept up. In 1705, the

practice of having marriages celebrated in Church was abandoned, a declaration in the presence of the parish priest henceforth taking its place. The baptism of children was kept up for some years later. It was not until 1730 that the hollow formality which had prevailed for two centuries was abandoned and that the New Christians of southern France were at last officially recognized as Jews.

The most important numerically of the French Marrano communities continued to be at Bordeaux. Here, there were said to be as many as seven synagogues; and, down to the last decade of the eighteenth century, there was a perpetual stream of Marranos from Spain and Portugal who arrived there to be received into the covenant of Abraham. Second in importance was the K. K. Nefusot Yehudah (Holy Congregation "The Dispersal of Judah") of Bayonne. So qualified was the local tolerance that the Marranos were not allowed to establish themselves in the city itself, but were restricted to the suburb of St.-Esprit, just across the river. Here, a synagogue was built as early as 1660; and Jewish life has remained centered in this quarter till the present time. Bayonne was the center of a little group of communities—at Biarritz, Bidache, Peyrehorade, St.-Jean-de-Luz — over which it attempted to exercise an autocratic control. These smaller communities, too, had their own distinctive names. Thus that of Bidache was the K. K. Neveh Shaanan (Holy Congregation "Tranquil Abode"— a name obviously referring to the present freedom from Inquisitional persecution); that of Peyrehorade was called K. K. Beth El (Holy Congregation "The House of God").[9]

The local record had its more tragic pages. The existence of the community of St.-Jean-de-Luz was especially chequered. In March 1619, a New Christian woman of sixty, named Catharina Fernandes, newly arrived from Portugal, went to Church to receive the Holy Communion from one of the three Portuguese priests who at that time served the formal needs of their compatriots settled there. After having accepted the consecrated particle, she was observed to remove it surreptitiously from her mouth. She was immediately arrested; but the populace, infuriated, broke into the prison, dragged her out, and burned her alive. Public indignation was not satisfied until all New Christians had been expelled from the city. Many of them settled in the neighboring township of Biarritz; but a whole ship-load was so intimidated that they sailed to the freer atmosphere of northern Europe. It did not apparently take long for the little community to reëstablish itself. When in 1636 the Spaniards captured St.-Jean-de-Luz, the Inquisition seized the opportunity to pursue its revenge against the refugees; and the Admiral of Castile was ordered to arrest and send to the frontier all whom its agents might designate. Many Marranos from the south of France who had ventured back to their native land figured in the Spanish autos throughout the seventeenth and eighteenth centuries. Thus, at the famous Madrid holocaust on June 30, 1680, Luis Saraiva, alias Arraya, of Bordeaux perished gallantly at the stake; while five other persons from the same region were burned in effigy, and several more were reconciled.

The contribution of the Marrano settlers in southern France to local, and indeed to national, achievement was considerable. This was especially the case at Bordeaux, where the largest colony was situated. Already in the first half of the sixteenth century the Granholas, the Ran, the Tarrégua, the Millanges, the Costa, and especially the Gouvea families were prominent in every branch of local life; and there is little doubt that all were of New Christian origin. The mother of the great Montaigne was Antoinette de Loppes, or Lopez, a descendant of the family Pazagon which had once been prominent in the *judería* of Calatayud. Isaac La Péreyre, the jurist and theologian, one of the founders of higher criticism, was obviously of Marrano extraction, though himself a fervent Huguenot. They provided large numbers of eminent physicians, culminating in the eminent Jean-Baptiste de Silva, principal of the faculty of the University of Paris and medical attendant on Louis XV. Their contributions to economic activity were great. The ship-building house of Gradis was especially noteworthy for its public spirit. Its services at the time of the wars with England in the eighteenth century were incredibly large; and much of the weight of the Canadian campaigns rested on its shoulders. The most illustrious member of the colony was probably Jacob Rodrigues Pereira, inventor of the system for the instruction of deaf-mutes, who was brought from Portugal to Bordeaux in his infancy.

Elsewhere in France, especially in the south of the country, there were further Marrano centers, though none of them was able to develop (as was the case with Bordeaux and Bayonne) into a formal Jewish community. Such settlements were to be found at Toulouse, Montpellier, Lyons, La Rochelle, and even small places like

Tartas, where one of the most mourned Inquisitional martyrs had been born. At Nantes, in Brittany, there was from the close of the sixteenth century a considerable colony, viewed askance by the local merchants, but protected and encouraged by the wise policy of Henry IV. The settlement was broken up by the decree of expulsion issued against the Jews in 1615; though, even after this date, a few Marranos managed to find their way thither. At Rouen, there was a similar colony, headed by João Pinto Delgado, a poet of great repute in his day. It was alleged that the New Christians settled here monopolized the trade of the city and amassed enormous fortunes, after which they took the first opportunity to leave for some place where they might observe Judaism publicly. Meanwhile, they continued to act in public as devout Christians — so much so that when in 1613 an attempt was made to dislodge them, they had no difficulty in obtaining certificates of orthodoxy from the curés of the parishes in which they lived. From 1631, the Estates of Normandy became outspoken in their complaints against these unwelcome settlers. Nevertheless, no steps were taken against them; and the community might have managed to develop in the same manner as those of Bordeaux or Bayonne excepting for an internal quarrel which broke out in 1632. Delgado and his friends were denounced to the authorities as Judaizers. The little group was broken up. Half of its members sought safety in flight; the rest were transferred under arrest to Paris. Here, they brought counter-charges against their enemies, to precisely the same effect, backed up by further certificates testifying to their own impeccable orthodoxy. Finally, as the result of the payment of an enormous bribe, they were released. The Rouen colony never regained its previous prosperity; and not long afterwards, with the commercial decline of the port, it came to an end.

Some members of the Rouen community subsequently settled in Hamburg. Here (attracted by the commercial possibilities of the place, now one of the principal ports of Northern Europe), a considerable body of Portuguese Marranos had been established. ever since the close of the previous century. As early as 1577, the settlement was already of some importance. The city was a Protestant one, while the new immigrants were titularly Catholic; but it had become increasingly evident that they practiced Judaism in secret. In 1604, the Court of Aldermen (*Bürgerschaft*) complained to the Senate at the state of affairs, but nothing was done. By 1612, the community numbered some 125 adults, without counting children and servants. Their utility to the city was far from negligible. In the period 1604–7, they contributed 10,000 *reichsthalers* in extraordinary taxation to the civic treasury, besides the ordinary ducs which they shouldered with the other inhabitants. They first created, and subsequently monopolized, trade with the Peninsula. They were the sole importers of colonial products such as tobacco, cotton, and spices. When in 1619 the Bank of Hamburg was established, the Portuguese immigrants took a prominent part in it; and over forty of them figured on its earliest roll of shareholders. Meanwhile, the disguise of Christianity was being slowly laid aside. By 1610, there were already three small synagogues in the city. In the following year, three representatives of the "Portuguese Nation resident in this city of

Hamburg" purchased a piece of ground near the neighboring port of Altona — at that time under the rule of the King of Denmark — for use as a cemetery.

This increasing lack of caution naturally attracted attention. Accordingly, in 1611, a petition was presented to the Senate requesting the expulsion of these strangers from the city. It was decided to apply for a decision to the Lutheran academies at Frankfort and at Jena. The reply of these bodies was far from intransigent; for they recommended that the Jews should be received, under certain restrictions, in order that they might be won over to the love of the Gospel. In consequence, on November 7, 1612, the Senate at last formally authorized the settlement of the Jews in the city, on condition that they did not give scandal to the Christians by indulging in public worship. Further concessions were made in 1617 and 1623; and, in 1650, public worship was at last authorized. The result was seen two years later, when the three little synagogues which had hitherto carried on an unostentatious existence in the houses of the wealthier communal magnates were unified as the *K. K. Beth Israel* (Holy Congregation "House of Israel"), which henceforth represented the whole body of the Portuguese Jews in the city. Daughter communities had meanwhile been founded at Glückstadt (1622), Altona (1642), and Emden (1649).

The Hamburg colony included the inevitable men of mark. No less than five physicians are included in an informer's list of 1617. Among these the most illustrious was Rodrigo de Castro, of Lisbon (1550–1627), "the tyrannical doctor." In his native city, he had been of considerable service to the Great Armada before it sailed, in 1588; he was prominent for his devotion at the time of the plague which ravaged Hamburg in 1595 — the year following his arrival; and he may be reckoned the founder of the science of gynaecology, on which he wrote a classical work. He served as medical attendant to the sovereign Count of Hesse, the Bishop of Bremen, and the King of Denmark. Of his two sons, one, André de Castro, alias Daniel Nahmias, was body physician to the King of Denmark, and the other, Bendito de Castro, alias Baruch Nahmias, who played a prominent part in communal life, served in the same capacity to the famous Queen Christina of Sweden. Rodrigo de Castro's reconversion to Judaism had been due to the persuasions of another Hamburg physician, Enrique Rodrigues, alias Samuel Cohen, of Santa Comba (d. 1638), whose wife had herself suffered at the hands of the Inquisition. She was the daughter of Anrique Dias Millão, burned at Lisbon in 1609, all of whose family was settled at Hamburg. Samuel da Silva, of Oporto, another local physician, was a notable theological writer, who championed the doctrine of the immortality of the soul against Uriel Acosta. He was the father-in-law of Benjamin Musaphia (Dionysius), scientist, mystic, and lexicographer, physician-in-ordinary to Christian IV of Denmark, who was expelled from Hamburg in 1640 in consequence of a frank expression of his views on Christianity. Alvaro Diniz (Dionis), alias Samuel Jachia, who maintained one of the three local synagogues in his house, became Master of the Mint at Altona and Glück-stadt, and was the author of an abortive scheme to procure a settlement of Portuguese Jews in the kingdom of Bohemia. His descendants were the financial agents to the Dukes of Gottorp (Schleswig-Holstein) and to the Danish crown. The Abaz family (one of whom, Samuel Abaz, alias Jorge Diaz, was a notable figure in local literary and intellectual life) were ennobled by the Emperor Mathias. It would not be difficult to protract the list still further.

The foregoing does not give a complete idea of the vast extension of the area of Marrano settlement. The important colonies in London, Amsterdam, and the New World will be dealt with in detail in the succeeding chapters. Christian IV of Denmark issued, in 1622, Letters Patent guaranteeing protection to those who settled in his dominions and, though the commercial prospects were not sufficiently promising to attract them in large numbers, a few settled at Copenhagen, besides those who had spread from Hamburg to the neighboring ports. In the middle of the eighteenth century, an attempt was made to draw them to Sweden. Under the protection of the Dukes of Savoy, they settled at Nice and Villafranca. The house of Este, in the seventeenth century, attempted to attract them to Reggio. Scattered families were to be found at Corfu, Florence, Rome, Turin, Lucca, Genoa, Marseilles, Ostend and Vienna. Individuals made their way to Russia. Outposts were to be found, as will be seen, even as far afield as India.

The importance of these settlements was great, both in Jewish and in general life. In the economic sphere, they played an extremely significant part. From the beginning of the seventeenth century, these little colonies were to be found in every important commercial center of Europe, as well as in America and the Far East. They played a rôle which was altogether out of proportion to their numbers in the trade of Western Europe. The same language and the same essential culture prevailed among a larger or smaller circle in every port. It was possible for a man to go from Hamburg to Bordeaux, and from Bordeaux to Leghorn, without any violent sense of change. Correspondence could be conducted over half of the civilized world in the same tongue. Most of the important families were international, members being settled in each of the greatest centers. Thus "credit," in the literal sense, was a social reality, which automatically assisted commercial intercourse. Even with Spain and Portugal, economic relations were continued, though for obvious reasons assumed names were adopted for the purpose.[10] A commercial nexus was thus formed which has perhaps no parallel in history except the Hanseatic League of the Middle Ages. Certain branches of commerce were almost entirely in the hands of these Marrano settlements. They controlled the importation of precious stones into Europe, both from the East Indies and from the West. The coral industry was a Jewish, or rather a Marrano, monopoly. Trade in sugar, tobacco, and similar colonial commodities rested largely in their hands. From the middle of the seventeenth century, Jews of Spanish and Portuguese origin were prominent figures on the various European exchanges. They played an important part in the establishment of the great national banks. It was they above all whom Joseph Addison had in mind when he wrote, in his famous Essay on the Jews: "They are, indeed, so disseminated through all the trading parts of the world, that they are become the instruments by which the most distant nations converse with one another, and by which mankind are knit together in a general correspondence." The transference of the center of the world's commerce during the course of the seventeenth century from southern to northern Europe is not the least important of the achievements which the Inquisition helped to bring about.

In Jewish life, their importance was no less. They possessed, it is true, the faults of their qualities, to a very marked extent. They were conscious, and proud, of their external qualifications. Accordingly, they introduced with them into Judaism a certain sense of separatism and class-pride which had never been known before. They accentuated the superficial differences which existed between them and the *tudescos*, from Germany and Poland, or even the *italianos* and *berberiscos* whose antecedents were nearer to their own. They did their best to accentuate this superficial distinction even in gentile eyes. They regarded intermarriage with them as little better than apostasy. They excluded them as far as they were able from all synagogal dignities and office. In more than one instance, in their eagerness to safeguard their own position, they endeavored to deprive their less fortunate and less polished brethren of the political privileges which they had won. Nevertheless, in spite of themselves, the ultimate results of their influence were diametrically opposed to their more narrow views.

As compared with the generality of the inhabitants of those countries in which they settled, they were essentially persons merely of a different faith. They were not, like their coreligionists, members of a different people, a different culture, a different world. Intellectually, they stood on a level with any other burghers. They dressed in the same manner. They spoke as pure a language. They were by no means deficient in the social graces. Hence, the social emancipation of the Marranos returned to Judaism was complete from the start. They had to be accepted as equals, and, from this point of vantage, the movement for political emancipation could be begun.

In many places, too, the Marranos were pioneers. Before their reversion to their ancestral faith they had been accepted in Protestant London, Amsterdam, or Hamburg as foreigners. It was impossible to exclude them simply because they turned out to be not Papists, but Jews. Once a Jewish settlement was authorized, however, it was not possible to exclude the Germans and the Poles, less attractive though they might be superficially. Hence, in Holland, Hamburg, and in England the settlement of the uncouth Ashkenazi Jews from Eastern Europe, long excluded, followed automatically upon the reception of these aristocratic fore runners. The Marranos were thus the pioneers of Jewish settlement in half the civilized world.[11]

Within the community, too, their influence was considerable. They were, as will be seen, the pioneers of the vernacular literature of the Jews. They set the example for abandoning the traditional Jewish costume and the hybrid Jewish dialect. In synagogal worship, they first adopted secular standards of decorum and harmony. The members of the Marrano Diaspora may be termed, without exaggeration, the first modern Jews.

CHAPTER IX

THE DUTCH JERUSALEM

THE settlement of the Marranos in the Low Countries, contrary to the general impression, goes back to a comparatively early date. From the beginning of the sixteenth century, the region had been dynastically associated with Spain. Antwerp was moreover, at this time, the greatest port of northern Europe. It was therefore inevitable that it should have offered considerable attraction to the New Christians of Spain and Portugal, who found there both commercial opportunity and freedom from persecution. Hence they began to settle in the city at least as early as 1512. With the approach of persecution in Portugal, the stream of migration increased. As we have seen, recent converts were forbidden to leave that country without special license. If the object of the journey were Turkey or some other Moslem country, where the opportunity would certainly be taken to revert to Judaism, the requisite permission would unquestionably be refused. Hence an increasing number of the refugees used a round-about route, obtaining permission to proceed to the untainted parts to the north, from where they made their way overland to Salonica or some other haven of refuge. Thus the emigration directed to Antwerp increased; and in 1526, new arrivals were empowered to remain in the city for a period not exceeding thirty days.

Besides those who passed through the city en route

for Turkey, others remained as permanent settlers. The
most important member of the New Christian colony
was Diogo Mendes, who managed the Antwerp branch
of the great Bank founded by his family in Lisbon,
which now enjoyed the coveted pepper monopoly. In
1532, drastic action was taken against the group. Mendes
and twelve others were arrested, and put on trial for
Judaizing. The case was ultimately allowed to lapse, on
the payment of heavy fines; this being partly due to the
intervention of Henry VIII of England, who made use
of the House of Mendes as his financial agents. Petty
minor annoyances continued. All the same, in 1537, the
Emperor Charles V formally permitted New Christians
to settle in Antwerp, with full rights. This license seems
to have been utilized to the full, the advent of the
Inquisition in Portugal stimulating the emigration from
the country. In 1540, whole shiploads, to avoid suspicion, made their way thither by way of Madeira. One
convoy, comprising one hundred persons, was arrested in
Zealand on their arrival. Ultimately, they were released,
since no definite ground could be found for proceeding
against them.

Henceforth, as was inevitable, conditions became less
favorable. The entrance of Judaizing New Christians
into the Low Countries was strictly forbidden. Simultaneously, proceedings were taken against the fugitives
throughout the Spanish dominions in Europe. At Milan,
as we have seen, a commission was appointed to inquire
into the question.[1] When the news reached Antwerp,
Diogo Mendes hurriedly called together a meeting to
consider what action should be taken. It was resolved to
instruct his agent in Lombardy to exert himself to the

utmost to help the prisoners and to procure their release. A relief fund was immediately raised among those present, a draft for two thousand ducats being despatched by special courier to Milan.

The Antwerp colony was for the moment left undisturbed. Nevertheless, conditions there became more and more difficult. About 1542, Diogo Mendes died. Shortly afterwards, his sister-in-law, Beatrice da Luna, alias Gracia Mendes, fled from the country under dramatic circumstances, with all her family, who were to attain such distinction. An edict was issued in 1549 expelling from the Low Countries all New Christians arrived from Portugal during the last five years. The Burgomasters of Antwerp strenuously resisted, going so far as to refuse to append their signatures. In the end, their opposition was overruled. The regulation was repeated on May 30, 1550, after which it was rigorously enforced. Even now, the New Christians of older establishment, as well as those who were of Spanish origin, were allowed to remain. They seem to have been somewhat less attached to Jewish tradition than those of a previous generation. Many of them, indeed, brought up in ignorance of Judaism, apparently leaned towards the Reformed Church, which was rapidly gaining ground. Thus, for example, a certain Marco Perez was at the head of the Calvinist consistory at Antwerp. It was even alleged that the Marranos in Flanders were deliberately introducing Lutheran literature into Spain.

From 1565, a fresh immigration began, which increased after the union of Portugal with Spain in 1580. The new arrivals were not transients, but permanent settlers, of a somewhat different type from those who had preceded

them. Removed from immediate dread of the Holy
Office, the members of the colony began to some extent
to throw off the mask of secrecy. It was reported that
many of them were circumcised, and that they had
established a synagogue. In 1585, the Lisbon Inquisition received a detailed denunciation of a couple of dozen
refugees Judaizing at Antwerp, whither they had brought
two "rabbis" from Italy to act as their spiritual guides.
All the Portuguese families residing there, with three
exceptions, it was asserted, were Judaizers. In the same
year, the Duke of Alva ordered the arrest of a number
of secret Jews who were said to be residing at Arnhem
and elsewhere. Whether this was carried out or not, it
was no permanent deterrent.

The settlement of the Jews in the Netherlands was not,
therefore, a sudden or a miraculous phenomenon. When,
with the establishment of the independence of the United
Provinces, Amsterdam ousted Antwerp from its previous
unquestioned supremacy, it was natural that an increasing number of those merchants who thought fit to leave
Spain and Portugal should have established themselves
there. This, of course, became the case more than ever
after 1648, when the Treaty of Westphalia closed the
navigation of the Scheldt and reduced Antwerp to the
position of comparative unimportance which lasted for
the next two centuries. The overthrow of the Roman
Catholic Church in the revolted provinces may have
given rise to hopes that more humane treatment might
be expected there in future; but this was not the sole
cause of the settlement which now began.

An ancient legend, which need not be discounted in
all its details, gives a most romantic origin for the

Amsterdam community. In the year 1593, we are told, a brother and sister, Manuel Lopez Pereira and Maria Nuñez (whose parents had suffered from the persecutions of the Inquisition), set sail from Portugal with their uncle, Miguel Lopez, and a large party of Marranos, in the hope of finding· a place of refuge in the freer lands to the north. The vessel was captured on its journey by an English ship, and brought to port. An English noble, fascinated by Maria's rare beauty, solicited her hand. · Queen Elizabeth, hearing the story, expressed a desire to see the fair prisoner. Captivated by her loveliness, like everyone else, she drove about London with her in the same coach, and gave orders for the vessel and all its passengers to be set at liberty. In spite of this, Maria would not accept the tempting offer which she had received. "Leaving all the pomp of England for the sake of Judaism" (as the old record puts it), she pursued her way with her companions to Amsterdam. Here, in 1598, they were joined by her mother and other members of the family. Later in the same year, whe was married to one of her fellow fugitives. This, as it appears, was the first wedding to take place in the Amsterdam community; and it was celebrated by a stately dance, in which twenty-four cousins of the bridal pair took part.[2]

There was thus far no manifestation of communal or religious life. Another venerable legend tells how this came into being. Early in the following century, another party of Marranos who had left the Peninsula with all their household property, in search of a place of refuge, put in at the port of Emden. Walking about the city, they saw over a doorway some letters which they suspected to be Hebrew. They managed to get in touch with the occupant of the house, who was a certain Moses Uri Levi. They begged him to receive them into the Jewish religion. He refused, on the ground that it was too dangerous a step, but he promised that, if they went to Amsterdam, he would follow them and do as they desired. He kept his promise punctually. Ten men and four children, who formed the kernel of a new community, were circumcised; and services were regularly held in the house of the Morroccan envoy, Samuel Palache, who happened to be a Jew.

The activities of these recent arrivals from the Peninsula, titularly Christians as they were, could not escape attention for long. It seemed obvious that they were holding Catholic services — at that time forbidden — and perhaps even conspiring against the newly-established government. On the Day of Atonement, the unwonted attendance resulted in drastic steps being taken. The whole party was arrested, and dragged off for examination. They were as yet entirely ignorant of Dutch, and their difficulty in expressing themselves increased the suspicion against them. Fortunately, one of the leaders of the little group — Manuel Rodrigues Vega, alias Jacob Tirado, who had recently been circumcised notwithstanding his advanced age — happened to be thoroughly familiar with Latin, and had the happy idea of expressing himself in that language. He made it clear that the assembly was not one of Papists, but of followers of a religion persecuted by the Inquisition even more ferociously than Protestantism; and he pointed out the great advantages which might accrue to the city if the New Christians of the Peninsula were encouraged to establish themselves in it. His appeal, whether to humanity or to interest, was convincing. The prisoners were released; the Atonement service was finished in peace; and the position of the refugees was henceforth regularized. Not long after, under the auspices of Jacob Tirado, a Jewish congregation was formally founded, being named after him *K. K. Beth Ja'acob* ("Holy Congregation, The House of Jacob"). As their first rabbi, they brought the Salonican scholar, Joseph Pardo, from Venice, the traditions of which community became firmly embedded in that of the "Venice of the north."

The colony grew with astonishing rapidity. In 1608 the immigrants from North Africa who were grouped about Samuel Palache established their own synagogue, *K. K. Neveh Shalom* ("Abode of Peace"), choosing first Judah Vega, from Constantinople, and then Isaac Uziel of Fez as their rabbi. The unbending sternness of this scholar drove some members of the community, headed by one David Osorio, to secede and form yet a third congregation, *K. K. Beth Israel* ("House of Israel"), in 1619. In 1638, the petty differences between the three were composed, and they were welded into one single community, named like that of Venice *K. K. Talmud Torah* ("Study of the Law"). In 1675, a stately new synagogue, which is still one of the architectural monuments of the city, was constructed to accommodate the growing congregation. In 1602, a plot of land for use as a cemetery had been secured at Groede. Fourteen years later, that at Ouderkerk, which is still in use, was opened. In 1615, after a report had been drawn up by the great jurist, Hugo Grotius, the Jewish settlement was formally authorized by the civil power, without any restrictions

of importance save that intermarriage with Christians
and attacks on the dominant religion were forbidden.
Every city was empowered to regulate the Jewish settlement at will. Minor communities were formed in the
course of time at The Hague, Rotterdam, Maarsen, and
one or two other places. That of Amsterdam, however,
remained unquestionably supreme.

That picturesque city was now at the height of its
fame. Its harbor was filled with shipping, which unloaded
the merchandise of every quarter of the world into its
warehouses. Its wealth increased with phenomenal
rapidity. Considerations of material advantage were
reinforced by the reputation for tolerance which Holland
had recently acquired. Almost weekly, some fresh New
Christian immigrant arrived from the Peninsula — sometimes, a more or less apathetic merchant, who had emigrated in order to benefit himself, but seized the opportunity to declare his adherence to Judaism now that he
might do so with impunity; sometimes, refugees fleeing
from the rigors of the Inquisition, and eager to return
to the religion of their fathers. Occasionally, a whole
shipload came together. When the New Christians were
expelled from Nantes, in 1615, it was to Amsterdam that
the greater number of them transferred themselves. In
1617, seventy-three persons arrived from St.-Jean-de-Luz
— in consequence, no doubt, of some local persecution.
Many of those who had been released in consequence of
the General Pardon of 1605 in Portugal seized the first
opportunity to migrate to the new land of refuge. With
the intensification of persecution after 1630, immigration
began on an even larger scale. Merchants and others,
who had hitherto been established as crypto-Jews in

rapidly decaying Antwerp, transferred themselves in large numbers to the rival port, where they threw off all disguise and joined the community. In 1617, over one hundred Marrano householders settled in Amsterdam were denounced by name by a returned informer to the Lisbon Inquisition. By the middle of the century, the community counted over four hundred families. Before its close, the total had risen to something like four thousand souls.

It was no insignificant body. They controlled a great part of the maritime commerce of the town with the Peninsula, the East Indies, and the West. They established important industries. They introduced with them vast capital. Ultimately, they controlled 25 per cent of the shares of the famous East India Company.[3] The wealth of some was legendary. The house of one, David Pinto, was so ornately adorned that the civic authorities were forced to intervene; but still its splendor remained such as to tempt the populace to sack it. The dowry which this same individual gave to his daughter was immense. On one occasion, at a wedding in the community, the combined wealth of forty of the guests exceeded 40,000,000 florins. It is difficult to say to what extent this influx actually contributed to the well-being of the city. It may be stated however as a fact that the greatest period of Dutch prosperity coincided with the period of the Marrano immigration and activity. In the nexus of the Marrano settlements, the primacy had definitely passed, together with her mercantile supremacy, from the City of the Lagoons to the City of Canals.

Hardly any rank or calling was left unrepresented in

the stream of migration. There were scholars, professors, priests, friars, physicians, manufacturers, merchants, soldiers, poets, statesmen. Simão Pires Solis, who had suffered for the so-called "outrage" of Santa Engracia at Lisbon in 1630, had a brother called Henrique Solis— a Franciscan friar, noted both for his learning and for his eloquence as a preacher. Dismayed or disgusted at his brother's fate, he made his way to Amsterdam, where he adopted the name of Eleazar de Solis, married, followed the career of medicine, and became a pillar of the community. His effigy was burned in an auto-da-fè held at Lisbon on Sunday, March 11, 1640, but the fact did not seriously inconvenience him. When in 1596 the English fleet under the Earl of Essex sacked Cadiz, among the captives was the Moroccan Resident at that port, a certain Alonso Nuñez Herrera, who boasted that he was a descendant of Gonsalvo de Cordova, the *Gran Capitan*. After some little difficulty, he was ransomed, but, instead of returning to Spain, he retired to Amsterdam, where he entered official Judaism and spent an exemplary old age, under the name of Abraham Cohen Herrera, in the compilation of Cabalistical treatises.[4] Thomas de Pinedo, of Trancoso, was reckoned one of the most promising pupils of the Jesuits in Madrid. However, to their disgust, he settled in Amsterdam, adopted the name of Isaac, and established a reputation as one of the foremost classical scholars and philologists of his time. The seventy-five year old martyr, Jorge Mendez de Castro (alias Abraham Athias), who was burned alive "for the sanctification of the Name" at Cordova in 1665, had a son Joseph, who was already established at Amsterdam. Here he attained such distinction as a printer, more especially of beautiful editions of the Bible, that he was awarded a medal and a gold chain by the States General. Fra Vincente de Rocamora, born at Valencia about 1600, had been a Dominican friar famous for his piety and eloquence. To this he owed his appointment as Confessor to the Infanta Maria of Spain, subsequently Empress of Austria, who thought highly of him. In 1643, he disappeared from Spain. He is next heard of, under the name of Isaac, studying medicine in Amsterdam, and playing a prominent part in the general life of the community. Enrique Enriquez de Paz, alias Antonio Enriquez Gomez, was one of the doughtiest competitors of Calderon for the favors of the theater-going public of Madrid, where several of his twenty-odd comedies were produced and rapturously received. He was in addition a gallant soldier, holding the rank of Captain and being created in recognition of his services a Knight of the Order of San Miguel. Accompanied by his son, Diego Enriquez Basurto, who also made himself a name in the annals of Spanish literature, he made his way, first to France, and then to Holland, where he openly joined the community. His flight could not of course be kept secret. He was tried by the Inquisition of Seville, which executed symbolic punishment upon him at a public auto on April 13, 1660. Some time afterwards, a fellow Marrano, whose presence at the grisly spectacle had prompted him to follow the poet to Amsterdam, met him in the street. "Ah! Señor Gomez!" he exclaimed, excitedly. "I saw your effigy burning on the pyre at Seville." "They are welcome to it," replied the poet phlegmatically.

The community boasted a model organization. The

power of the *Parnasim*, the elected Wardens, was autocratic, as offenders like Benedict Spinoza or Uriel Acosta learned to their cost. It seemed, almost, as though something of the spirit which prevailed in the Peninsula had entered into their soul, so that they endeavored to set up a miniature Inquisitional tribunal of their own. There were, besides, no less than one hundred minor organizations, which covered every branch of communal activity — benevolent, educational, religious, even literary. On the banks of the Amstel, about the Jodenbreestraat, it seemed that a miniature Lisbon or Madrid had arisen. Spanish and Portuguese remained the official tongues of the community, and were everywhere heard about the streets. Books in those languages poured in an incessant stream out of the printing presses — literary, liturgical, historical, philosophical, ethical, scientific. Literary academies existed where poets of considerable reputation met to criticize one another's latest productions.

Jewish studies were of course not neglected. The public school of the Portuguese community, with its extraordinarily modern system and organization, was considered a model foundation, and turned out many men of mark in both the Jewish and the non-Jewish world. The superior academy, *Etz Ḥayim*, was famous for the acute academic responsa published monthly by its alumni. There were many further associations for the purpose of study, such as the *Yeshiba de los Pintos*, established by the immensely wealthy Pinto family, which they transferred with themselves from Rotterdam. Out of these institutions, many native-born or native-trained rabbis issued to lead the Spanish and Portuguese

communities in the New World and the Old, such as
Isaac Aboab da Fonseca, Moses Zacuto, Menasseh ben
Israel, Solomon d'Oliveira, Daniel and David Cohen
d'Azevedo, Joshua da Silva, and very many others.
In 1627, Menasseh ben Israel established the first local
Hebrew printing press, thus setting a tradition which
was to make Amsterdam for the next two hundred years
the center of the Jewish book-trade.

For the newly arrived refugee from the Peninsula,
the transition to his new life was an easy one, save
for the contrast in climate. He might employ the
same physician, the same attorney, the same poetaster,
the same bookseller, the same tradesman, the same
broker, the same bravo, and even the same priest of
whose services he had made use at home. In their place
of refuge, many rose to positions of importance — not
merely as financiers and captains of industry, but even
as diplomats. Some of them were even elevated to the
nobility by various European monarchs. In the congregational cemetery at Ouderkerk, sonorous Spanish and
Portuguese inscriptions, surmounted by elaborate coats
of arms with knightly helms or nobiliary coronets, testi-
fied to the hidalgo origin which so many members of
the community boasted. Rembrandt van Rijn, living
in the midst of them in the Jodenbreestraat, found in
these picturesque fugitives an ideal subject for his active
brush.

The coming of the Marranos to Holland was of more
than local importance. Jewish communities similar to
those in the neighboring regions of Germany had existed
in the Low Countries in the Middle Ages. Expulsion
and massacre had however done their work; and the

final traces of the medieval settlement had disappeared
with the banishment of three last families from Wagen-
ingen in 1572. With the formal authorization of the
Marrano settlement, the continued exclusion of professing Jews, however inferior they might be in fortune or
in superficial graces, became impossible. Hence a separate immigration began to set in from Germany. A
community gradually grew up. Public service after their
own traditional rite was first held on the New Year
of 1635. The new settlement multiplied. After the
Chmielnicki massacres in Poland in 1648 and the following year, the refugees at Amsterdam formed yet a third
grouping, which maintained a separate existence until
1673. Ultimately, this, the "Ashkenazi" community,
came to outnumber the "Sephardi," composed of the
descendants of the Marrano pioneers. The latter nevertheless maintained its superiority in wealth and general
influence for some time to come.

It is extraordinary to what extent the communities of
Amsterdam and the other Marrano centers were affected
by the pseudo-Messianic mania in the middle of the
seventeenth century, associated with the name of Sabbatai Zevi. It might have been imagined that, cultured
men of the world as they were, they would have realized
from the beginning how hopelessly fantastic it was. In
fact this was far from being the case. A strong streak of
mysticism ran through them. By virtue of their recent
sufferings, they imagined that the final deliverance must
be imminent. Moreover, they were predisposed to sym-
pathize with any such movement in consequence of the
facts of their previous life, when their cardinal principle
of faith had been that the Messiah was still to come.

Accordingly, a wave of enthusiasm ran in that fatal year 1666 through the whole of the Marrano world, where the imposter found his most steadfast supporters. In the Peninsula, as we have seen, there was a general attempt at flight to join him. A Marrano physician, who had escaped to the Levant and had been amongst the first to swear allegiance to the Pretender, received as his reward investiture to the throne of his native Portugal. In London, recent arrivals from Spain and Portugal were waited upon by the leaders of the community, who informed them gravely that the time had now come to proclaim their allegiance to Judaism. In Hamburg, youths wearing wide green sashes — the livery of their Master — danced madly in the synagogue, led by men of distinction like Bendito de Castro, the physician to the Queen of Sweden, or Manoel Texeira, the great capitalist. On the bourses, large sums were wagered that their hero's claims would be officially recognized within a very short period.

But it was in Amsterdam that the mania reached its height. Rabbis, like Isaac Aboab da Fonseca and Raphael Moses Aguilar, were carried away in the stream of enthusiasm. The philosopher and physician Benjamin Musaphia, despite his rationalistic tendencies, became a devoted adherent. Even Benedict Spinoza watched the movement with interest. An official letter was sent, subscribed by a couple of dozen of the leading members of the community, whose signatures would have been good on Exchange for an almost unlimited amount, assuring the pseudo-Messiah of their devotion. The immensely wealthy philanthropist and author, Abraham Israel Pereira, alias Thomas Rodrigues Pereira, who had not long since fled from Spain to escape the unwelcome attentions of the Inquisition, set out for the Levant to join his hero. The printing presses were kept busy turning out devotional works, in Hebrew and in Spanish, for use in the many services, private and public, by which it was hoped to hasten the great consummation. Even after the pseudo-Messiah had apostatized and died, his cause was kept alive by one of his many Marrano adherents, Abraham (Miguel) Cardoso (brother of the philosopher and apologist, Isaac Cardoso). It is not perhaps far wrong to trace the beginning of the decline of the Amsterdam community to this terrible disillusionment. Nevertheless, down to the second half of the eighteenth century, it continued one of the principal centers of attraction to the fugitive Marranos, and an island of Iberian culture in the Teutonic north. Spiritually, it remained down to the tragic year 1940 the center of the far-flung group of Marrano communities; and throughout this period, it still deserved the title which the enthusiasm, the learning, and the industry of the original settlers had won for it soon after their arrival — the Dutch Jerusalem.

CHAPTER X

RESETTLEMENT IN ENGLAND

THE last great community of Western Europe to be formed by the Marrano refugees was that of London. It was long considered that this was due to the providential intervention of one man, Menasseh ben Israel, at the time of the Protectorate. Recent research has however made it plain that this is not quite correct. On the one hand, the intervention of Menasseh ben Israel, though epoch-making, was not decisive. On the other, the formal establishment of the Jewish community was merely an episode in a long Marrano connection, dating back for over a century.

The Jews had been banished from England in 1290; and from that date down to the end of the Middle Ages, none had been officially allowed to live in the country. Nevertheless, there is evidence that after the Expulsion from Spain, in 1492, some of the refugees came to London, with bills of exchange on the local Spanish merchants. Apparently, a few Marranos similarly sought shelter here. This "infesting scourge," as it was described (though the numbers in question must have been extremely small), continued till 1498. Then, at the time of the negotiations for a marriage between his son Arthur and Catherine of Aragon, Henry VII promised the Spanish envoys that he would prosecute without mercy any Jew or heretic whom they might point out in his dominions.

After the forced conversion in Portugal, the New Christian element began to figure more prominently in the growing mercantile colony in England. Traces of them are not to be found until 1521, but the settlement probably began even earlier. The great Marrano mercantile and financial house of Mendes had established its Antwerp branch in 1512; its operations, carried on largely by New Christian agents, speedily spread across the North Sea; and it ultimately became the agent for the loan transactions of the English treasury. On her way to Antwerp in 1535, Beatrice da Luna, better known as Gracia Mendes, paid a short visit to England with her whole family, including the young João Miguez, later famous as the Duke of Naxos.

The Marrano community which she found in England was not by any means an insignificant one. It comprised at this period no less than thirty-seven householders. Organized religious life was not absent. Services were regularly held at the house of one Alves Lopes, to whom newly arrived fugitives would come for assistance and advice. Christopher Fernandes, one of Diogo Mendes' local agents, would send to intercept the Portuguese spice-ships touching at Southampton and Plymouth, and warn any Marranos who might be on board if danger awaited them in Flanders. There were several physicians — Master Diogo, Master Antonio, Manuel Fernandes, and Dionysius Rodriguez; the last-named, who was to die as a professing Jew at Ferrara, had formerly been in the service of the Queen of Portugal. Another prominent member of the community was a kinsman of the Mendes family named Antonio de la Roña, apparently a man of some erudition, since he is described as a "master of Jewish theology." It was his practice to help refugee Marranos to realize their property, providing them with bills of exchange on Antwerp. When in 1540 proceedings were taken at Milan against the fugitives, he was summoned to Antwerp to the meeting at which were discussed the steps to be taken to meet the situation; and he subscribed to the emergency fund one hundred ducats — partly in English crown pieces. The crisis was, in fact, even more serious than was realized at the time. One Gaspar Lopes, a cousin and agent of Diogo Mendes, on whose behalf he had resided in England for some time, was arrested by the Milan commission and turned informer. In consequence of this, and of other indications elicited in the course of proceedings in Flanders, the secret of the little London community was laid bare. The Spanish authorities communicated what they had discovered to the English government. On February 4, 1542, the Privy Council ordered the arrest of certain Merchant Strangers "suspected to be Jews" and the sequestration of their property. Ultimately, they were restored to liberty at the request of the Queen Regent of the Netherlands, who gave her personal assurance that they were good Christians. Her information turned out to be based upon pious hope rather than established fact, and possibly proceedings were again initiated against them. In any case, the little community seems to have dwindled henceforth. A majority of its members made their way in due course to Antwerp, while one or two straggled as far as Ferrara. For a time, the London group was very small in number.

It was not long before the settlement was resumed; the total exclusion of such furtive refugees for any long

period of time was impossible. The Añes family, which
hailed from Valladolid in Spain, had not been disturbed
by the upheaval of 1542; for they had been settled in
London ever since 1512, and were after so long a period
of residence hardly to be included in the category of
Merchant Strangers. The same applied to the family
of Simon Ruiz, with whom they had intermarried. By
the close of the reign of Edward VI (1553), we find
diminutive Marrano communities settled, not only in
London, but also at Bristol, which maintained a considerable trade with the Peninsula. Among the residents
in the latter place was Pero Vaz, a young surgeon
(nephew of the great Amatus Lusitanus), and a physician
named Henrique Nuñes. The latter, with his wife
Beatriz Fernandes, acted as the leader of the community.
Services were regularly held at their house; they periodically received from London the dates of the festivals;
they were in touch with the latest Jewish literature, reading avidly Usque's *Consolaçam ás Tribulaçoës de Israel*,
recently published at Ferrara.[1] It is on record that
Beatriz Fernandes baked unleavened bread for Passover,
and was careful, on her journeys between London and
Bristol, not to touch food which had been cooked in pans
defiled by forbidden flesh. Of the community of London
at this period, we have less information; but it comprised
at least eight householders.

No doubt, the Marranos of this period had posed as
Calvinist refugees from the Continent. Hence, with
the reaction under "Bloody" Queen Mary against the
Reformation, no safe course remained for them but to
leave the country. Henrique Nuñes with his family
retired to France in 1555, and probably other members

of the two communities followed his example; though, once again, a small residuum remained behind.

In the remarkable period of English expansion which coincided with the reign of Queen Elizabeth, the foreign mercantile colony in London naturally increased. Among these there was, as always, a considerable number of New Christians from the Peninsula; encouraged, perhaps, by the greater possibilities of tolerance which were heralded by the victory of Protestantism. Thus the Marrano community developed. It numbered at this time approximately one hundred souls. At its head was Dr. Hector Nuñes, who had been the leading spirit already in the reign of Mary. Though a physician, he also engaged in trade. His wide-spread connections were of considerable benefit to the Government, particularly as regards Spanish affairs. He enjoyed the complete confidence of both of Elizabeth's great ministers, Burleigh and Walsingham, and actually brought the latter the first news of the arrival of the Great Armada at Lisbon on its way to the English channel. The most important family in the community, after that of Hector Nuñes, was that of Jorge Añes, or Ames, which (as we have seen) had been settled in London ever since 1512, though possibly they had returned to Portugal in the meanwhile. Dunstan Ames, Purveyor to the royal Court, traded extensively with Spain, and was in addition the financial agent in London to Dom Antonio, Prior of Crato, Pretender to the throne of Portugal. Dunstan's eldest daughter, Sarah, was the wife of Dr. Roderigo Lopez, the Queen's physician. The latter was connected by marriage with Alvaro Mendes, Duke of Mitylene, who was at this time in continuous diplomatic intercourse with the English Court. The degree of religious observance in the little community is obscure. But it is certain that they were Jewish by virtue of something more than descent. At the beginning of the reign of Mary, Hector Nuñes and Simon Ruiz (Dunstan Ames' father-in-law) had provided the crypto-Jews in Bristol with calendars and literature for their guidance; and it is hardly likely that their attachment to Judaism decreased in the subsequent period. They collected funds among themselves for the maintenance of the secret synagogue at Antwerp. At one period, at least, in 1592, when an envoy of Alvaro Mendes' was in England, proper services were held at his house; and the crypto-Jews of the capital seized the opportunity to attend.

From the time of the defeat of the Armada, the Marrano community in England began to decline. The reason was partly political. Hector Nuñes and Roderigo Lopez had broken with the Prior of Crato, whose pretensions to the crown of Portugal they had previously championed, and began to work for peace with Spain. This brought them into opposition to the war party, headed by the Earl of Essex. The latter trumped up a charge against Lopez of implication in a plot to poison his royal mistress; and, after a partisan trial, he was executed, on June 7, 1594. This episode aroused a miniature anti-Semitic storm in England, reflected in Shakespeare's *Merchant of Venice*. The heyday of the Marrano community was over. Hector Nuñes had died in 1591; Dunstan Ames followed him to the grave in 1594. Of the latter's family, some remained in the country, where they became assimilated with the general population; others made their way to the Levant,

where English travelers in after-years were surprised to
encounter, openly professing Judaism, men and women
born in London. The disturbed relations with Spain in
the following years, coupled with the rapid decline in
English prestige at the beginning of the following century,
no doubt adversely affected the settlement of the New
Christians, who now found a powerful counter-attraction
in the community of Amsterdam. Finally, in 1609,
the Portuguese merchants living in London who were
suspected of Judaizing were expelled from the country,
having called the attention of the authorities to their
existence by an internecine quarrel. It was necessary
to wait for a further half-century before a settlement
was officially authorized.

As the seventeenth century advanced, the expansion of
international commercial activity and organization
resulted in the formation of a further settlement of
Spanish and Portuguese merchants in England. A good
number of them, as usual, were New Christians; especially
so, after the year 1630, when the recrudescence of persecution in Portugal drove hundreds into exile. Moreover,
the formation of open communities in the other great
commercial centers of northern Europe, such as Amsterdam and Hamburg, which stood in close commercial
relations with London, made it inevitable that their
agents, correspondents, or rivals, should settle here also.
An impetus seems to have been given to the process in
1632, when, as we have seen, the Marrano colony at
Rouen was temporarily broken up. Some of its members
apparently sought refuge in England. Among them was
Antonio Fernando Carvajal, a native of Fundão, who
had previously lived for some time in the Canary Islands.

It did not take him long to establish his position in his new home. Speedily, he became known as one of the most prominent merchants in the City. He possessed his own vessels, which traded in a variety of commodities with the East and West Indies, South America, and the Levant; he imported bullion on a large scale; and during the Civil War, he acted as Grain Contractor for the Parliament. When in 1649 war broke out with Portugal, the Council of State expressly exempted his goods from seizure, and he was given special facilities for the continuance of his trading activities. The political intelligence which he obtained at this period from his business correspondents overseas was found immensely useful by the government. In 1655, he and his two sons were endenizened as English subjects. Another prominent Marrano resident in London was Simon de Caceres, who made himself useful at the time of the conquest of Jamaica, advised the government concerning the trade with Barbados, and presented Cromwell a memorandum in which he actually suggested the conquest of Chile by a Jewish force. Others of their associates were notable merchants, controlling a good part of the trade of the City. They were all living, however, as Catholics, attending Mass regularly in the chapel of the French or Sardinian ambassador. Such Jewish sympathies as they had were sedulously concealed.

There were in England at this period, in the heyday of the Protectorate, two independent philo-Semitic tendencies. Firstly, there was a religious element. Puritanism had represented a return to the Bible, and above all a return to the Old Testament. Many of its adherents had carried this to its logical extreme. We find persons prosecuted in England for holding Judaistic doctrines, and English proselytes admitted to the Jewish community at Amsterdam. One sect of the Puritans suggested the alteration of the Christian Sabbath to the seventh day. Others championed total abstention from blood. These literalistic biblical tendencies naturally brought about a more favorable frame of mind towards the Jews, as the People of the Old Testament. With this was intermingled the hope that the Jews, so long blind to Popish or Episcopal blandishments, might be unable to withstand the attractions of the new and purer form of Christianity, once they had the opportunity of becoming acquainted with it at close quarters. This was the attitude of agitators like Sir E. Spencer or Leonard Busher, the Brownist. On the other hand, a more disinterested standpoint was taken up by Sir Edward Nicholas, Roger Williams, and others. In 1649, two Puritans settled at Amsterdam, Johanna Cartwright and her son Ebenezer, boldly presented a petition to the government asking point-blank for the recall of the Jews to England. The proposal was well received; and, although consideration of it was indefinitely deferred, it assisted in preparing a favorable atmosphere.

Another, more practical, point of view was represented by some of the more responsible statesmen, with Oliver Cromwell himself at their head. The latter was naturally inclined to favor the Jews by reason of his religious attitude, based as it was largely upon the Old Testament. He was not indeed in sympathy with the extreme sectaries, whose desire for "Judaistic" practices he condemned and opposed without qualification. But, on the other hand, his naturally tolerant nature was antagonistic to any religious persecution which could not be justified on political grounds. His idealism was, moreover, reinforced by a strong practical tendency. He was quick to realize the material advantages which the Jews could bring to England, as they had done to Holland and other countries. In the mercantile revival which he was endeavoring to foster, the Spanish and Portuguese merchants, with their far-flung international connections, could play an important part, assisting to establish London as a principal center of European commerce. Conversely, the capital which was not brought by them to England was more than likely to go to Amsterdam, thus strengthening England's most serious commercial rival. In a manner, Cromwell's patronage of the Resettlement was merely an episode in the Anglo-Dutch rivalry which was one of the distinctive features of the middle years of the seventeenth century.

Events in England had their repercussion in Amsterdam. Here, the Puritan mystics found a kindred spirit in Menasseh ben Israel, alias Manoel Dias Soeiro, who, notwithstanding the fact that he had been born outside the pale of Judaism, had made himself a name as one of the most illustrious rabbis of his age. Savants and statesmen both at home and abroad had been in the habit of consulting him on matters of Jewish scholarship. He had thus become a representative figure in gentile eyes, and had no hesitation in approaching those in authority on behalf of his people as a whole. He was a master of Latin, at that time still an international tongue, and thus had no difficulty in expressing himself in any circle. A curious episode set his mind on England. A Marrano traveler named Antonio de Montezinos, alias Aaron

Levi Montezinos, who had recently returned from America, claimed that about 1642 he had discovered near Quito, in Equador, certain natives belonging to the lost Hebrew tribes of Reuben and of Levi, who practiced various Jewish ceremonies and were even acquainted with the traditional confession of faith, the *Shema'*. On his return to Holland, he embodied his account in an affidavit executed under oath before the authorities of the Amsterdam community. The report aroused a good deal of attention throughout Europe. Menasseh ben Israel himself gave a full account of it in 1650 in a little Messianic treatise in Spanish and in Latin, which he called *The Hope of Israel*.

Slowly, he began to realize what appeared to him to be the less immediate implications of the report. The Prophet Daniel had intimated (12.7) that the final Redemption would begin only when the scattering of the Jewish people was complete. On the other hand, the Book of Deuteronomy plainly stated (28.64) that the dispersion was to be universal, "from one end of the earth even unto the other." Hebrews had now been found in America; they were missing only in Great Britain. Moreover, the classical name for England, in medieval Jewish literature, was "the end of the earth"— an over-literal translation of the French *Angleterre*. It was plain that, if only they were introduced into the British Isles, the utter Dispersion prophesied could be completed, and the great Messianic Deliverance would begin. Filled with these thoughts, Menasseh had dedicated the Latin edition of his recent work to the English Parliament, whose "favour and good-will" he solicited for the scattered Jewish nation. In the following year, he

opened up formal conversations with the mission to
Holland, headed by Oliver St. John. The results must
have been satisfactory; for in October 1651 Menasseh
sent the Council of State a formal petition for the read-
mittance of the Jews. This was considered in London on
the day after the passing of the Navigation Act, which
dealt so shrewd a blow against Dutch commerce; a coincidence which is not without its significance. An influential committee, of which Cromwell was a member, was
appointed to consider the question; and two passports,
couched in flattering terms, were sent over to enable the
Dutch Rabbi to come over to treat in person. At this
stage, war, inevitable for some time past, broke out
between England and Holland; and Menasseh's family
persuaded him to remain at home. When peace was
concluded, he was too ill to travel. Accordingly, he
empowered his friend, Manuel Martinez Dormido, to
appear in his stead.[2]

The latter's had been a typically adventurous Marrano
career. He had been born in Andalusia, where he had
been life-treasurer of the royal revenues and had held
the rank of Alderman. Falling under the suspicion of the
Inquisition, he had been arrested, together with his wife
and sister, and had remained in prison for five years
(1627–1632). On his release, he had gone to Bordeaux,
and thence to Amsterdam. Here he threw off all disguise
and became a member of the community, being known
henceforth by the name of David Abrabanel Dormido.
He was accompanied to London by Menasseh's son,
the young Samuel Soeiro. On November 3, 1654, they
appeared before Cromwell with a petition. The Protector
received it benevolently; but it was rejected by the

Council of State. Samuel Soeiro returned to Amsterdam to lay the matter before his father. The latter, though not yet fully recovered from his illness, was now no longer to be restrained; and, in September 1655, he arrived in London. Here he was joined by a few Jews from other parts of Europe, such as Raphael Supino, of Leghorn. Immediately on his arrival, he presented to the Lord Protector his *Humble Addresses*, which he had brought with him from Amsterdam; following it up with a further formal petition in which he requested in moving language the authorization of the resettlement of the Jews.

To consider the various aspects of this question, Cromwell convened a Conference of various notables — statesmen, lawyers, and theologians. They met at Whitehall on December 4, 7, 12, 14, and 18, 1655. The lawyers gave it as their opinion that there was no statute which excluded the Jews from the country. Theological and mercantile interests, on the other hand, were either opposed to their readmission, or would countenance it only with such restrictions as to rob it of all attractiveness. By the close of the fifth session, Cromwell was convinced that the outcome would disappoint his expectations and be contrary to the best interests of the country. He therefore dissolved the conference, after a speech of extraordinary vigor, before it came to any definite conclusion.

It was now expected that he would make use of his prerogative and assent to Menasseh's petition on his own authority. Month after month dragged on, and it became evident that this was not to be the case. Instead of formally authorizing the resettlement of the Jews, he preferred to 'connive' at it; to allow those persons already in the country, or who cared to follow them, to remain undisturbed, without making any official declaration on the subject. The little group of Marrano merchants in London gave up hopes of anything more definite. In the following Spring (March 24, 1655/6) they presented a further petition to Cromwell asking simply that they might "meete at owr said private devotions in our Particular houses without feere of Molestation" and establish a cemetery "in such place out of the cittye as wee shall thincke convenient."

This was granted in due course. At the same time, the property of Antonio Rodrigues Robles, which had been seized on the outbreak of war with Spain, was restored to him in consequence of his plea that he was not a Spaniard, but a Jew — a member of the people which was undergoing such suffering at the hands of the Spanish Inquisition. A small number of fresh arrivals "with intent to live in London" trickled in during 1656, and were admitted by the authorities. In December 1656, a house was rented for use as a synagogue. A couple of months later, a piece of ground for use as a cemetery was acquired. Moses Israel Athias, a cousin of Carvajal, was brought over from Hamburg to act as the spiritual guide of the nascent community. The London Marranos had thrown off the mask. Their position was indeed still highly informal. The Resettlement had not been authorized — it had been 'connived' at. It was a typical English compromise — inconsistent, illogical, but unexpectedly satisfactory as a working arrangement. The high millenary hopes with which Menasseh ben Israel had come to London were disap- .

pointed. This furtive procedure was not what he had dreamed of, nor could it be counted as completing the Dispersion of Israel. He returned, broken-hearted, to Holland, dying almost immediately after his arrival. His mission, as it seemed, had ended in utter failure.

Though he did not live to see it, what had happened was providential. Menasseh had succeeded in creating the favorable atmosphere, as a result of which the Marranos were able to throw off their disguise. If nothing formal had been done, it was (as matters turned out) all to the good. At the Restoration of Charles II, when almost the whole body of the legislation of the Commonwealth was automatically repealed, there was nothing to undo. The Jews were hence able to continue living informally in London without disturbance, just as they had done before. Moreover, some Amsterdam Jews had been in close relations with Charles II while he was in exile, and had liberally supported him with money. He was thus favorably inclined towards their London coreligionists. Hence an agitation for the expulsion of the Jews, fostered by Thomas Violet and embodied in a petition of the corporation of London, had no effect. When in 1664, the Earl of Berkshire and Peter Ricaut made an attempt to blackmail them, a formal charter of protection was easily obtained from the Crown. Henceforth, the community was properly and legally authorized. Before long it took its place, by the side of the congregations of Venice, Amsterdam, Hamburg, and Leghorn (with all of which it continued to maintain close connections), as one of the most important components of the Marrano Diaspora. The distinctive name adopted was *K. K. Sha'ar ha-Shamayim* — Holy

Congregation "The Gate of Heaven"— an accurate characterization of the light in which the community appeared in the eyes of many Marranos who had there their first experience of official Judaism. After another petty disturbance, freedom of worship was guaranteed in 1673, and again, under similar circumstances, in 1685. Henceforth, the position of the Jew in England was unquestioned.

The informality of the Resettlement had an important consequence. By reason of its somewhat equivocal and unofficial nature, it was impossible to make for the control of the settlement any special provisions, such as even Menasseh ben Israel himself had assumed to be a matter of course. Thus, alone almost in the whole of Europe, the new Anglo-Jewish community was treated juridically from the first on terms of virtual equality with the generality of the population. Its condition compared favorably even with that of Amsterdam. Disabilities were few, and on the whole unimportant. The separate, and ipso facto excessive, taxation of the Jew, elsewhere invariable, never obtained any footing, though it was once or twice proposed. Thus the strangely casual nature of the Resettlement in England, so disappointing to the prime mover in the matter, ultimately had a markedly beneficial effect, which spread far beyond the British Isles.

The next hundred years witnessed a rapid expansion. Fresh immigrants were continually arriving — either direct from the Peninsula, or by way of Bordeaux, Amsterdam or Leghorn. Remarriages of couples *vindos do Portugal* or 'arrived from Portugal' as it was recorded in the synagogue registers, were common. After the

Revolution of 1688, there was a considerable influx from Holland, the wealthy Portuguese Jews of which country had assisted to finance the triumphant expedition of William of Orange. In 1701, a synagogue was erected in Bevis Marks; the first specially constructed for the purpose since the Jews had been expelled from England in 1290. Meanwhile, the small Marrano settlement which had existed in Dublin since about 1660 had developed, by the end of the century, into a diminutive congregation, which flourished for some decades.

The London community included many men of mark. Its earliest spiritual leaders included men like Jacob Sasportas, Joshua da Silva, Solomon Ayllon, and David Nieto. The latter, who belonged to a family of Marranos settled in Italy, was among the most eminent scholars of his age, and produced several works of importance. Among his successors were Moses Gomes da Mesquita and Moses Cohen d'Azevedo, both of Amsterdam, whose highly characteristic names indicate their Marrano origin. Other notable Marranos who resided in London included Dr. Fernando Mendes, physician to Queen Catherine of Braganza; Jacob (Henrique) de Castro Sarmento, physician and scientist, who was a leading member of the community in the course of a romantic peregrination which he began as a Catholic and ended in an Anglican churchyard; Isaac Sequeira Samuda, the former's contemporary and fellow-practitioner, a Fellow of the Royal Society; Diego Lopez Pereira, first Baron D'Aguilar; and many others. Of members of the community of Marrano descent, of the first or second generation, may be mentioned Anthony (Moses) da Costa, a famous financier, though not (as was long asserted) a governor of the Bank of England; his kinsman Emmanuel Mendes da Costa, the eminent conchologist, Secretary of the Royal Society; Solomon da Costa Athias, founder of the Hebrew collection of the British Museum; Sir Solomon de Medina, who was in charge of the commissariat during Marlborough's campaigns; Isaac Pereira, Commissary General to the forces in Ireland at the time of the Battle of the Boyne; and many another. One of the Henriques family (it is said) first projected the Bank of England. As in Amsterdam and elsewhere, Spanish or Portuguese remained the official tongue of the community long after direct immigration from the Peninsula had ceased; and several works of importance in those languages — philosophical, liturgical, or literary — were printed in London.

In the middle of the eighteenth century, the *K. K. Sha'ar ha-Shamayim* was at the height of its influence. Its members were prominent in the city of London. Among their coreligionists, of whatever provenance, they were supreme. They had begun to move about in English society on terms of virtual equality. Assimilation had already made great strides. The repeal in 1753, in consequence of a popular agitation, of the famous "Jew Bill," which would greatly have facilitated naturalization, was a general and deep disappointment. A wave of desertion began, which robbed the community of many of its most gifted sons. Simultaneously, the Marrano emigration from the Peninsula was slackening, notwithstanding a momentary increase after the great Lisbon Earthquake of 1755. The community was becoming progressively diluted by the arrival of different elements, from Italy, the Levant, or Africa, previously contemptuously referred to as *Italianos* or *Berberiscos*, and long excluded from any share in the synagogal government. When Gibraltar was besieged by the Spanish in 1786, a large number of refugees arrived from that place together, revitalizing the congregation, but at the same time permanently modifying its composition.

Meanwhile, the "Sephardi" community had lost its previous unquestioned supremacy in the country. As in Amsterdam and elsewhere, the less prepossessing, and less pliable, "Ashkenazi" Jews from Central and Eastern Europe had taken advantage of the privileges somewhat surreptitiously won by their more courtly coreligionists. A congregation was formed no later than the year 1690; a permanent synagogue was constructed thirty years later. By the middle of the century, they were superior to the Spanish and Portuguese community in numbers, if not in wealth and general influence; and they continued to make rapid strides. The Marrano element is now insignificant in the general Jewish population of London. It is no longer supreme even in the venerable congregation, still hale and flourishing, which was founded under the auspices of Cromwell and Menasseh ben Israel. Nevertheless, with those first romantic settlers must always lie the credit of the establishment of the Anglo-Jewish community, which, but for their efforts, might have been delayed for many a long decade.

CHAPTER XI

THE MARRANOS IN THE NEW WORLD

"In the same month in which Their Majesties issued the edict that all Jews should be driven out of the kingdom and its territories — in that same month they gave me the order to undertake with sufficient men my expedition of discovery to the Indies." With this significant passage, Christopher Columbus began his account of the expedition which led to the discovery of the New World. He might have added, had he thought it worth-while, that he actually set sail within a day or two of the departure of the last of the Jewish exiles, and that the vessels which conveyed them were lying in the roadstead of Seville in close proximity to his own little squadron.

The connection between the Jews and the discovery of America was not, however, merely a question of fortuitous coincidence. That epoch-making expedition of 1492 was as a matter of fact very largely a Jewish, or rather a Marrano, enterprise. There are grounds for believing that Columbus was himself a member of a New Christian family. It is, indeed, highly ironical that the patriotic attempts made today to claim him as a Spaniard are mostly based upon an assumption that he was a furtive member of the race which Spain was even then chasing from her shores. Less hypothetical is the case of others who participated in the great expedition. It was made possible by a loan which Luis de Santángel, Chancellor and Comptroller of the royal household, a great-grandson

271

of Noah Chinillo, advanced (though not out of his own purse) to his royal master and mistress. He was, as a matter of fact, the first person to listen to Columbus' dreams seriously, and it is highly doubtful whether the Queen would have displayed any interest but for his intervention. Gabriel Sanchez, the High Treasurer of Aragon, who was another of the explorer's most fervent patrons, was of full Jewish blood, being a son of a *converso* couple, and a nephew of Alazar Ussuf, of Saragossa. It was to these two that Columbus addressed the famous letter first announcing the news of his discoveries. Among Columbus's other patrons was Alfonso de la Caballeria, member of a famous Marrano family, Vice Chancellor of Aragon. The only one of the high officials intimately concerned with the genesis of the expedition belonging to an Old Christian house was the royal secretary, Juan de Coloma, whose wife was however descended from the Jewish clan of De la Caballeria.

The personnel of the expedition was very similar in composition. There was Alonso de la Calle, whose very name denoted that he was born in the Jewish quarter. Rodrigo Sanches, a relative of the High Treasurer, joined the party as Superintendent at the personal request of the Queen. One Marco was the ship-surgeon; Mestre Bernal, who had been reconciled in 1490 for Judaizing, served as physician; and Luis de Torres, who accompanied the expedition as interpreter, was baptized just before sailing. The latter was, as a matter of fact, the first European to set foot in the new land (which had been first sighted by the Marrano sailor, Rodrigo de Triana), and is worth recording also as the first to make use of tobacco. [Recent research necessitates a modifica-

tion of this statement. Only Torres was assuredly of
Jewish origin.] Those who had favored the enterprise naturally reaped some of the rewards. The first
royal grant to export grain and horses to America
was made in favor of Luis de Santángel, who may
thus be reckoned the founder of two great American
industries.[1]

The Marranos (possibly, in part, in order to escape
the attentions of the Inquisition) were quick to realize
the possibilities of the New World and to transfer themselves thither as colonists. Thus Luis de Torres, the
interpreter to the expedition, received large grants of
land in Cuba, where he died. Many others of his race
followed him. Attempts were repeatedly made in after-
years to prevent New Christians and those penanced by
the Inquisition, as also their descendants, from emigrat-
ing to the Indies. This was at the best difficult to enforce;
while suspension was occasionally secured for financial
considerations. Thus in 1509, in the composition arrived
at in Seville between the *conversos* and the Crown,
it was specifically stipulated that, in return for a payment of 20,000 ducats, the former were at liberty to go
to the colonies for the purpose of trade for periods not
exceeding two years. In 1518, Charles V, with characteristic zeal for the faith, ordered the royal officers at
Seville to prevent them from embarking. After a prolonged struggle, they gained their point, and were again
allowed to leave freely. Among the *conquistadores* who
accompanied Cortes to the conquest of Mexico, there
was at least one Marrano — Hernando Alonso, a smith
by trade, of whom we have a picturesque glimpse,
"hammering nails into the brigantines which served to

recapture the city of Mexico," taking a personal share in the assault, and subsequently swaggering about in a belt of refined gold which he had exacted from the natives.

The nightmare of the Inquisition was not long in following the Marranos to the new home, the discovery of which had owed so much to their energy and enterprise. As early as 1515, a Marrano, Pedro de Leon, was brought back with his family from Hispañola to face his trial at Seville. Four years later, Apostolic Inquisitors for the American colonies were appointed by the Supreme Tribunal in Spain. Among the earliest batch of victims was Hernando Alonso, the *conquistador*, who was burned at the stake with another Judaizer in 1528, at the first auto held in the New World, a third person being reconciled at the same time. In 1539, a New Christian named Francisco Millan was penanced for the same offence. On the whole, the main preoccupation of the Inquisitors in America at this period was with Lutheran heretics rather than with Judaizers. The reason is not difficult to find. In 1537, Paul III had issued a Bull forbidding any apostate from going to the Indies, and six years later Prince Philip ordered the expulsion of any *conversos* found resident there, or their children. Thus the native Spanish Judaizers, who were now rapidly losing ground in the Peninsula, were prevented from obtaining a footing. Within a very short time, however, a fresh and more vital influx began.

The beginning of the persecution in Portugal drove large numbers of the *conversos* to migrate. In view of the difficulty of finding a refuge anywhere in Europe, their thoughts naturally turned to the New World. It was a land of golden opportunity, where the inhabitants

of the less prosperous parts of the Peninsula might hope
to make their fortunes. Moreover, in this virgin field
of settlement, where they were entirely unknown, they
might hope to begin a new life, free from suspicion and
from persecution. Judaizers thus spread in increasing
numbers throughout the Spanish Main. They were
especially numerous in Mexico, where a group existed
in almost every town. They maintained connections with
every part of the Old World, even as far afield as Italy,
Amsterdam, and Salonica. In many ways they seem to
have been better informed of Jewish lore and practice
than their brethren in the Peninsula. They entered into
almost every field of economic activity. In Peru (and
the description was true also of the other provinces) they
became by the beginning of the sixteenth century the
masters of the colonial commerce. All imports and
exports "from brocade to sackcloth, and from diamonds
to cumin-seed" passed through their hands. Castilians
complained that it was impossible for them to succeed
in business without a Portuguese partner. It was
alleged against them that they purchased with fictitious credits the cargoes of whole fleets, which they
divided amongst themselves, thus rendering capital unnecessary; in other words, that they evolved an economic
system in advance of their age. The articles in question
were distributed throughout the country by their agents,
who were likewise Portuguese. In 1634, they negotiated
for the farming of the royal revenue.

So rapidly did they grow in influence and number that,
before the sixteenth century was over, it was considered
necessary to make special provision against them. Thus
in 1571, Philip II secured the establishment in the city

of Mexico of an independent Inquisitional tribunal, on the model of those which flourished in the Peninsula, for the purpose of "freeing the land, which has become contaminated by Jews and heretics, especially of the Portuguese nation." On February 28, 1574, the first auto under these auspices took place, with great pomp. At this, but one New Christian appeared, and that for a minor offence only. It was in 1577 that the first Judaizer suffered. Thereafter, the number rapidly grew.

One family, of Portuguese origin, was particularly prominent among the martyrs of this period. The father, Francisco Rodríguez Mattos, was described as a rabbi and dogmatizer, or teacher, of the Jewish religion. He had died before punishment could be executed on him. He was accordingly burned in effigy, as also was his son, who had escaped trial by flight. His four cultured daughters (of whom the youngest, a girl of seventeen, was reported to know all the Psalms of David by heart and to be able to repeat the Prayer of Esther and other hymns backwards) were all reconciled. The most illustrious member of the group was their uncle, Luis de Carvajal, Governor of the Province of New Leon, who had rendered considerable service to the state. For the crime of having failed to denounce his sisters, he was prosecuted, deprived of his office, and died in prison. Before long the family was found to have relapsed into their Judaistic practices. There was now no possibility of escape; more especially since the ruthless Fray Alonso de Peralta (against whom proceedings were subsequently brought for misconduct in office) had in the meantime been appointed Inquisitor. In a great auto held in 1596, the governor's nephew, another Luis, was burned, with his mother and three of his sisters. At the same time, four other persons were relaxed in person for Judaizing, ten relaxed in effigy, and twenty-two reconciled. All told, forty-one persons out of the sixty-six who appeared on this occasion were Marranos. One of the younger Carvajal's surviving sisters, who escaped on this occasion, was burned for relapse on March 26, 1601, when another was reconciled.

During the previous quarter of a century, no fewer than 879 trials had taken place, activity being thus nearly as great as that of the far-famed tribunal of Toledo. The work of extermination was done so well that for the next forty years, up to 1642, less than thirty further Judaizers were punished, of whom some twenty were reconciled, one relaxed in person and six in effigy. When in 1605 the General Pardon for Judaizers of Portuguese extraction reached Mexico, there was only one in the Inquisitional dungeons to be liberated. Elsewhere in the New World, the same falling-off was to be observed. Thus in Peru, where a tribunal had been opened in 1570 (a year before that of Mexico), the number of Marrano victims had been small until 1595. At the great auto held at Lima on December 17 in that year, ten Judaizers figured, four of them being relaxed, of whom one — Francisco Rodriguez — was burned alive. On December 10, 1600, fourteen Portuguese Judaizers were punished, two being relaxed in person and one in effigy. The auto of March 13, 1605, exhibited sixteen Judaizers reconciled, six burned in effigy and three in person. Thereafter, there was a very considerable falling-off, though there were slight recrudescences in 1608 and 1612. The Tribunal of New Granada, founded in 1610 with its seat at Cartagena, was less concerned with Judaizers, and only attained its maximum activity after the first quarter of the seventeenth century was finished. Thus, at the auto of June 17, 1626, seven Judaizers suffered among the twenty-two penitents; one of them, Juan Vincente, being relaxed. All told, in its two centuries of existence, something like fifty Judaizers figured in a total number of condemnations comprising 767 persons, and pronounced at approximately fifty-four autos. The majority of the sentences inflicted were however comparatively light, only five persons all told being burned. To the Philippine Islands, too, the Marranos had penetrated, persons being sent thence to Mexico for trial. Here, similarly, there are no traces of any such cases for nearly half a century after 1601.

A chance episode made it clear, with startling rapidity, that this diminution of activity was not due to any lack of material, and that the Marranos were stronger in the New World than they had ever been before. One day, in August 1634, a jealous trader at Lima appeared before the Inquisitional tribunal to denounce Antonio Cordero, the local factor of a merchant from Seville, on the ground that he had been unwilling to make a sale on Saturday, besides refusing to eat a rasher of bacon for his breakfast. A secret inquiry was made into the matter; and, in the following April, the accused person was secretly removed to prison in a sedan-chair. Under torture, he made admissions which implicated his employer and a couple of other persons. The latter in turn were forced to denounce many other accomplices. To accommodate the fresh prisoners expected, fresh cells were erected. Then, on August 11, between 12:30 and 2 o'clock, seventeen arrests were made, among the most prominent citizens and merchants of the city. But the work was not by any means complete. Up to May 16, eighty-one arrests had been carried out, and evidence collected against as many more suspects. Property to a vast value was confiscated. The impression created in the city, from the first day, we are told, was like that of the Day of Judgment; for the majority of the trade of the city was concentrated in the hands of those implicated. A wide-spread commercial crisis ensued, culminating in the failure of the Bank.

The fruits were seen in a great auto held on January 23, 1639, at which about sixty Judaizers figured. Of these, seven abjured *de vehementi*, forty-four were reconciled, after being sentenced to punishments of varying severity, and eleven persons were relaxed. Seven of the latter were burned alive, as pertinacious and impenitent heretics — true martyrs to their faith. The most prominent of them was the heroic Francisco Maldonado da Silva, alias Eli Nazàreno, who had been languishing in prison for thirteen years.[2] All of the others were members of the *Complicidad Grande*, as the crypto-Jewish connection at Lima was henceforth called. Foremost amongst them was Manuel Bautista Perez, the wealthiest merchant of the city and a great patron of literature. He was known among his fellow-Portuguese as the *Capitan Grande*; and it was at his house that they had been accustomed to come together for prayer. Besides these, the effigy of one person who had committed suicide during trial was condemned to the flames. Another prisoner, a mere boy, had become mad as a result of his sufferings. On the next day the populace enjoyed the spectacle of the public scourging through the streets of twenty-nine of those reconciled, men and women, naked from the waist up. In the autos of the following years, the remnants of the *Complicidad Grande* were dealt with. The last victim was Manuel Henriquez, who was burned as late as 1664, in company with the effigy of Dona Murcia de Luna, who had died under torture. This exemplary display of severity (coupled with a menace of total expulsion in 1646, evaded only through an ample payment) finally exterminated the offence of Judaizing in the province for many years to come. The next case — a light one — occurred as long after as 1720. The last victim burned at the stake by the Peruvian Inquisition was a reputed Judaizer, the beautiful and romantic intriguer Ana de Castro, who suffered on December 23, 1736 — apparently, in consequence of private enmity. In the following year, at an *auto particular*, Juan Antonio Pereira was punished for the same crime. Though the Inquisition in Peru continued a sporadic activity for another three quarters of a century, and even had a few accusations of Judaizing brought before it, on trivial grounds, no further prosecutions of this nature figure in its records.

The *Complicidad Grande* had its repercussions at Cartagena, where several persons implicated in the confessions extorted at Lima were arrested and put on trial. Of these, eight were reconciled. There were indeed no relaxations, but the confiscations which resulted were so considerable as to put the Tribunal in the possession of enormous funds. Thereafter, it was comparatively inactive as far as Judaizers were concerned; though in 1715 it reconciled the disreputable renegade ex-friar and ex-pirate, José (Abraham) Diaz Pimienta, who five years later, after a relapse, was burned at Seville.

More drastic by far was the upheaval in Mexico. Here, it had taken some time for the possibilities which had been opened up to be realized. However, in July 1642, Gabriel de Granada, a child of thirteen against whom suspicions had been aroused, was arrested. He was ruthlessly examined, and thus forced to make admissions which implicated no less than 108 persons in all, including his own mother and the whole of his family. The province was found to be filled with Judaizing heretics, who clung to their ancestral religion with unusual fidelity. They were in contact with their co-religionists as far afield as Italy and Turkey; and large numbers of the males amongst them were circumcised. The vast majority of them were emigrants from Portugal, some direct and some via Spain. The little community enjoyed a certain degree of organization. Miguel Trinoco acted as their sacristan and religious factotum, distributing the unleavened bread amongst them before the Passover. Services were held at fairly regular intervals at the house of Captain Simon Vaez Sevilla (whose whole family had suffered bitterly at the hands of the Inquisition) and his wife, Juana Enriquez.[3] The latter was the daughter of Blanca Enriquez, an eager Judaizer, who had initiated all of her family and circle into the Jewish faith, and whose bones were afterwards exhumed and burned. In order to announce when a service was to be held, it was the custom for them to send a negro slave in party-colored clothes to play a tambour in those streets where their fellow-Marranos lived. At Guadalajara, the house of Manuel de Mello served as the religious center.

The whole of this circle was implicated in the confessions wrung out of Gabriel de Granada. Wholesale arrests were immediately carried out, this *complicidad* forming the solitary subject of conversation in the city. Meanwhile, an embargo was placed upon the emigration of any Portuguese from the province without special license. At the first signs of danger, a meeting was held by the Marranos in the house of Simon Vaez Sevilla to decide upon the best course of action. The general consensus of opinion was that in case of arrest all should deny the whole charge steadfastly, this being the safest means to prevent the implication of other persons; as one of those present remarked, his arms were strong enough to withstand torture. Meanwhile, fasting and penitence were resorted to in order to incline the God of Israel to save His children from the present persecution and strengthen the hearts of those in prison, so that they should not display any weakness.

The Inquisition set to work with its usual thoroughness and its usual deliberation. In 1646, a total of thirty-eight Judaizers were reconciled, bringing a very considerable profit to the coffers of the Holy Office. Twenty-one followed in the next year. In 1648, there were two autos, in one of which eight Judaizers were penanced, eight reconciled, twenty-one burned in effigy and one in person; in the other, twenty-one Judaizers figured, though no burnings took place. The climax of the Mexican Inquisition was reached in the terrible *Auto General* of April 11, 1649 — the greatest known outside the Peninsula. Out of 109 persons who appeared, all but one were Judaizers. Of these, fifty-seven persons were relaxed in effigy and thirteen in person. Twelve indeed professed repentance, and so secured the preliminary grace of garroting. The only person burned alive was thus Tomás Treviño of

Sobremonte, a member of a family of martyrs, who met his death heroically.[4] The spectacle was a magnificent one. We are informed how there was a double row of coaches all along the route of the procession, their occupants remaining in them all night so as to make sure of their positions. So many of the inhabitants of the surrounding places streamed into the city in order to be present that it seemed as though all the countryside, for a hundred leagues round or more, had been depopulated.

This terrible lesson went far to check Marranism in the province. In the following period, Judaizers occupied a less and less prominent position in the preoccupations of the Inquisition. Thus, in the auto of 1659, only four figured amongst the thirty-two victims;[5] and in later years the proportion was even lower. In 1712, a solitary Judaizer was reconciled. As late as 1788, one Raphael Gil Rodriguez, a cleric in Holy Orders, was sentenced to relaxation for the same offence. He however professed repentance at the last moment, and was reconciled instead. Thus, by the close of the first half of the seventeenth century, it may be said that in the Spanish dominions of the New World crypto-Judaism had been almost completely suppressed.[6]

A very considerable stream of Marrano emigration was meanwhile being directed to the Portuguese colony of Brazil. This was not entirely spontaneous in origin. From 1548, one of the penalties imposed by the tribunals of the mother-country upon convicted but "penitent" heretics was that of deportation — generally across the Atlantic. Hence Brazil became filled with New Christians, of doubtful orthodoxy. Indeed, even before this date, the settlement had been considerable. The colony thus harbored an increasingly high proportion of secret Jews. They comprised many persons of great wealth, some being worth from 60,000 to 100,000 *cruzados*. They controlled a great part of the commerce of the country. In Bahia (S. Salvador) nearly all the physicians were New Christians, who were said to prescribe pork to their patients in order to lessen the suspicions against themselves. It is stated that the sugar-cane was first introduced into Brazil from the island of Madeira by Portuguese Marranos. They were thus instrumental in the inauguration of one of the most important local industries, in which they continued to engage on a large scale.

The Inquisition was never formally introduced into Brazil, which continued to be subject in this respect to the mother country. The New Christian settlement had become so considerable by 1579 that Inquisitorial powers were conferred on the Bishop of Salvador. All prisoners, however, had to be sent to Europe for trial. Great "visitations" were held under these auspices in 1591–5 and 1618. In the latter year (in consequence of the revelations made during the proceedings against the New Christian merchants of Oporto) an Edict of Faith was published at Rio de Janeiro by an Inquisitor specially despatched from Lisbon. This resulted in extensive arrests, coupled with confiscations to the value of 200,000 pesos. Despite the governmental precautions large numbers of terrified Judaizers sought refuge on Spanish territory, where the local Inquisitors were kept busily occupied for a time. At Lima, the fugitives provided the material for the great auto on December 21, 1625, at which ten Judaizers were reconciled, and four relaxed, two of them in person.

This outburst of Inquisitorial activity in their new

home drove the Marranos of Brazil into disaffection. When in the second decade of the seventeenth century the Dutch began their attempt to conquer the country, the local New Christians eagerly espoused their cause. Naturally, it was also warmly favored by those Marranos recently admitted to Amsterdam, who realized the great economic opportunities which they might enjoy in the event of success. Thus, the war resolved itself almost into a struggle between the Spanish and Portuguese on the one hand and an alliance between the Marranos and the Dutch on the other. Francisco Ribeiro, a Portuguese captain with Jewish relatives in Holland, was intimately concerned with the earliest intrigues. Two Jews, Nuño Alvarez Franco and Manuel Fernandez Drago, planned the capture of Bahia by the Dutch in 1623. The taking of Pernambuco was said to be the work of certain Amsterdam Jews, the principal of whom was Antonio Vaez Henriquez, alias Moses Cohen. The latter, who arranged the plans and accompanied the expedition, subsequently settled at Seville, where he was suspected of acting as a spy in the Dutch interest. Another Jew of Amsterdam, Francisco de Campos, was said to be responsible for the capture of the island of Fernando de Noronha; yet another, David Peixotto, was alleged to be in the command of a fleet of eighteen sail which fitted out at a later period for the relief of Pernambuco; and it was said that on the way he proposed to make a raid on the Portuguese coast and to penetrate as far as Coimbra, where the palace of the Inquisition was to be burned and the prisoners released. Other Marranos were believed to maintain an extensive espionage service in the Peninsula. The Dutch themselves, in forming their West India Company in 1622 in furtherance of the scheme of conquest, counted confessedly upon the support of the native New Christians; while the fugitives in Holland invested eagerly (though, at the outset, modestly) in the shares. It was therefore natural that, in those places which were captured by the Dutch, the Marranos seized the first opportunity to declare their true identity. Thus, when Bahia was taken, the Dutch commander immediately issued a proclamation guaranteeing protection and religious liberty to all who would submit. However, in 1625 the city was recaptured; and although the terms of surrender provided for the safety of the inhabitants, five renegade New Christians who placed over-much trust in the agreement lost their lives.[7]

The Dutch rule was of longer duration in the city of Recife, or Pernambuco, which was captured in 1630. The local Marranos immediately threw off all disguise; and they were reinforced by numerous immigrants from Holland. In 1640, the Jewish inhabitants were said to be more numerous than the Christians. Their trade exceeded that of any other section of the population; and their sugar-mills and stately houses were among the sights of the city. In 1642, a large party arrived direct from Amsterdam, bringing with them two young scholars to minister to their spiritual needs—Isaac Aboab da Fonseca, "the first American Rabbi," born of New Christian parentage at Castrodaire in Portugal; and Raphael Moses de Aguilar, who was to act as reader or *Hazzan*. A community was organized, after the model of that in Amsterdam, under the name of *K. K. Zur Israel* (Holy Congregation "The Rock of Israel"),[8] with the usual subsidiary institutions. The backbone of the congregation was formed of persons who had returned locally to Judaism. In 1648, when the *Ascamot* or communal regulations were revised, four persons "well-acquainted with Judaism" had to be co-opted to assist in the work. Even Menasseh ben Israel, the great Dutch Jewish scholar, was proposing at this period to go to Recife, and interrupted the printing of his *Conciliador* to dedicate the part dealing with the Book of Kings to the leading men of the local congregation.

Other Marrano settlements were to be found elsewhere in the colony. In Tamarica, Jacob Lagarto officiated as Rabbi. At Paraiba, Captain Moses Peixotto was the leading spirit.

The war for the reconquest of Brazil was pursued with additional vigor after the restoration in Portugal of the House of Braganza, and the shaking off of the Spanish yoke. One of the arguments made to the new government in order to incite them to begin a fresh campaign was the scandalous spectacle of the synagogues which had been opened publicly by renegades in those places under Dutch rule. It is a somewhat ironical consideration that the new campaign was directly financed, though much against their will, by the New Christians in Portugal. In 1649, King João IV introduced certain reforms into the Inquisitional procedure, restoring property recently confiscated and abolishing sequestration in case of arrest. In return for this short-lived concession (which, in the event, did not survive the reign of the ruler who made it), the New Christian merchants organized a trading company, the *Companhia do Brazil*, which was to provide thirty-six men-of-war to serve as convoys for their merchantmen.

It was this fleet, backed up by the enormous resources of the affluent Marrano, Duarte da Silva, which proved the decisive factor in the campaign. It was, in effect, a struggle between the Marranos of Portugal and their brethren who had escaped beyond the seas. The latter on their side supported the Dutch regime to the utmost limit of their ability. They raised large subscriptions for the benefit of the treasury. The wealthy Abraham Cohen Henriques made himself prominent by his indiscriminate beneficence. Isaac Aboab da Fonseca proclaimed days of prayer and fasting, and stimulated his brethren to further efforts in fiery addresses from the pulpit. In the two sieges of Recife, the Jews fought desperately, many being killed in action or dying of starvation. On the first occasion when relief came, the congregation celebrated the event by a service of thanksgiving; and Aboab recorded the tribulations through which they had passed in a lengthy Hebrew poem — the first specimen of Jewish literature to be composed in America. But a second siege followed; and, despite all exertions, the city was forced to capitulate (1654). In the terms of surrender the captors granted an amnesty "in all wherein they could promise it." Nevertheless, the continuance of the community was now out of the question. Large numbers returned to Amsterdam —among them Jacob de Andrade Velosinho, then an infant, but subsequently to distinguish himself for the ability with which he opposed Spinoza. He was thus the first Jewish author of American birth. Others of the refugees were scattered throughout the New World.⁹

The reconquest of Brazil by the Portuguese and the consequent break-up of the local communities of Marranos returned to Judaism under Dutch protection was an episode of the highest importance in Jewish history, a majority of the older American communities owing their origin to the minor dispersion which that catastrophe brought about. In those places which were not under the intolerant rule of Spain or Portugal, little open colonies of Marranos of Portuguese descent now came to be established, formed in the first instance by refugees, but subsequently reinforced from Europe. In Jamaica, where the Inquisition had never obtained a footing, large numbers of "Portugals," as they were called, were to be found even before the English conquest in 1655. The pilot upon whom Penn and Venables relied in their attack, Captain Campoe Sabbatha, is said to have been a Marrano; another, Acosta, superintended the commissariat for the English troops and negotiated the terms of capitulation; while Simon de Caceres, "the chauvinist Jew," in London, contemporaneously furnished much valuable information. Ultimately there were open communities at Kingston, Spanish Town, Falmouth, and Lacovia; and the majority of the Jewish community of Jamaica even today is of Marrano descent.

In the island of Barbados, the oldest English colony, the earliest known arrivals were refugees from Brazil. They included Abraham de Mercado, who had previously been an elder of the dispersed congregation of Recife, and his son, David Raphael de Mercado; both doctors of medicine. On April 20, 1655, these two were officially permitted to settle on the island; and they were speedily followed by others. In the following year, on August 12, 1656, the Jews were granted full enjoyment of the "privileges of Laws and Statutes of ye Commonwealth of

England and of this Island, relating to foreigners and
strangers." At one time, there were two communities on
the island, the *K. K. Nidhe Israel* ("Dispersal of Israel")
at Bridgetown, and the *K. K. Semah David* ("Branch
of David") at Speightstown.[10] Spiritual leaders were
forthcoming from Europe: for example, Abraham Gabay
Izidro, a native of Spain, where, with his wife, he had
been imprisoned for some time by the Inquisition (he had
been circumcised in London and studied at Amsterdam).
He died in London in 1755. Other Marranos who found
refuge in the island included members of the Chaves
and Vargas families, of Covilhã in Portugal. The community on the island is now entirely extinct; but a little
synagogue and a cemetery, filled with inscriptions in
Portuguese, remained at Bridgetown to recall its existence and the tradition to which it was heir.

Conditions were very similar in the other West Indian
islands.   In Martinique, an open community of ex-
Marranos was formed during the Dutch regime. This
was allowed to continue after the French conquest in
1654.   In 1655, the sugar industry on a large scale was
established in the island by Benjamin da Costa, a refugee
from Brazil, who went there accompanied by a large
number of his coreligionists with their slaves.   In 1685,
with the promulgation of the *Code Noir*, the Jews were
expelled.   Under British rule, there was, at the close of
the seventeenth century, a community of a similar nature
at Nevis.   Another existed at the island of Tobago.   In
Curaçao, at the very outset of Dutch rule, in 1634, we
encounter an alleged Jew named Coheño whose linguistic ability gained him appointment as Captain
of the Indies.   Eighteen years later, the Dutch West

Indian Company granted a considerable tract of land along the coast to Joseph Nuñez da Fonseca (alias David Nasi) to establish a settlement of his coreligionists. The colonists were under the lead of João Ilhão (Jan Illan), a Portuguese long settled in Brazil, where he had been denounced for Judaizing. When in 1654 Pernambuco was recaptured, the colony was very considerably reinforced: and in 1659 twelve families were formally permitted to settle in the town of Nassau. Fresh settlers afterwards came from Amsterdam, or else in some cases direct from Portugal. The local congregation, which still flourishes, was at one time among the most important in the Marrano Diaspora.

To Cayenne, Jews of Portuguese origin had penetrated at the middle of the century, being reinforced by the refugees from Brazil a few years later. In 1660, a whole party (including Daniel Levi de Barrios, the Marrano poet) left Leghorn to settle there. They nearly perished on the way owing to lack of drinking water, and several ultimately turned back. Shortly after the arrival of the party, the colony was ceded to France; and, despite a clause which guaranteed them freedom of worship, the Jewish community was dispersed. A majority removed to the English colony of Surinam. This was ceded to the Dutch in 1667. The wealthy Jews living there now formed the subject of an unusual international dispute, the English desiring to remove with them to Jamaica all who desired, while the Dutch were anxious to retain them at all costs, owing to their great importance to the welfare of the colony. Under the Dutch rule, the Jewish settlement continued to flourish, becoming one of the most remarkable of its sort in the world. After the reconquest of Brazil, their numbers had been immensely recruited by the fugitives, this being the nearest place of refuge. Besides the congregation at Paramaribo, on the sea-coast, which still exists, there were a number of flourishing settlements grouped about the "Savannah of the Jews" (Joden Savanne) up the river, where a splendid synagogue was built in 1685. Here, they enjoyed a remarkable degree of autonomy. Their status in the colony was very high. It goes without saying that their commercial importance was considerable. They were largely interested in agriculture, and were the first persons to cultivate the sugar-cane. When, in 1689, Surinam was attacked by the French fleet, the Jews under Samuel Nasi fought bravely in the defence. On a second attack, in 1712, the defence was led by Captain Isaac Pinto. The Jews of the Joden Savanne were also foremost in the suppression of the successive negro revolts, from 1690 to 1722: these as a matter of fact were largely directed against them, as being the greatest slave-holders of the region. These disturbances, together with the inroads of the climate, led ultimately to the abandonment of the settlement, of which nothing but the ruin now remains. However, as late as 1796 proposals were circulated for the establishment here of a seminary for the youth. The importance of Paramaribo, on the other hand, has continued to the present day. Towards the end of the eighteenth century, some Portuguese sailors who were chased by a French privateer and put in at Surinam were amazed to find themselves greeted by the Jews in their native tongue; and on their return to their own country the government hastened to attempt to establish relations with this forgotten outpost.

Events on the mainland of North America followed much the same course. In 1654, a ship-load of twenty-three refugees from Brazil arrived at New Amsterdam. They were not, indeed, the earliest settlers, a German or Polish Jew named Jacob, son of Samson (Jacob Barsimson), having preceded them by a few months. They were shortly afterwards followed by another contingent of Portuguese Jews coming from Holland. The new arrivals received a surly reception from Governor Peter Stuyvesant, who ordered them to leave. Fortunately, before he could take action, letters arrived from the Governor of the Dutch West India Company, dated April 26, 1655, intimating that it was inequitable for those who had taken so important a share in its undertakings and had lost so much in the Brazilian disaster, to be excluded from its possessions. They were therefore authorized to remain, "provided that the poor amongst them shall not become a burden to the community, but be supported by their own nation." A congregation, named the *K. K. Shearith Israel* ("Remnant of Israel"), which still flourishes, was founded immediately afterwards. It was thus as an indirect consequence of the Portuguese reconquest of Pernambuco that the greatest Jewish community of all time was founded.

From New York, the settlements of the Marrano communities spread. Some of the earliest arrivals, discouraged by the reception which they had received from Stuyvesant, migrated to Newport, Rhode Island, where the congregation, *K. K. Yeshu'ath Israel* ("Salvation of Israel") perhaps originated in 1658. They were reinforced from many quarters. A small contingent arrived from Curaçao in 1690, and, in the eighteenth century, the

community enjoyed a brief halcyon period.   Jacob
Rodrigues Rivera, who came to Newport direct from
Portugal in 1745, was the first person to introduce the
manufacture of spermaceti to America.   Aaron Lopez
was the wealthiest merchant of the port in the pre-Revo-
lutionary era, owning as many as thirty vessels.   After
the Lisbon earthquake of 1755, a number of Marranos,
whose consciences had been stirred by the disaster, are
said to have arrived to swell the community, which however fell into complete decadence with the decline of the
port after the Revolution.   Towards the close of the last
century, the Jewish connection with Newport was revived.
Hence the dignified synagogue constructed in 1763 by
the Marrano refugees, which still stands, is regularly
used for worship, although the families originally assoc -
ated with it have without exception either emigrated or
died out.

In Georgia, a group of Jewish immigrants, who had
sailed under the auspices of the Spanish and Portuguese
community of London, arrived in 1733, within a month
of the first settlers, and on the actual day of the formal
partition of the land of the colony.   They were received
in a kindly manner; and a community was founded at
Savannah.   Among the most prominent members was
Dr. Samuel Ribeiro Nuñez, who had been a Court Physician at Lisbon, had suffered at the hands of the Inquisition, and had himself smuggled out of the country on
an English brigantine in the middle of a dinner which
he had given to allay suspicion.   Another member of the
settlement was Abraham de Leon, who introduced into
the colony the culture of grapes, having been a wine-
grower in Portugal.   The first child born in the colony

was a Jew, Isaac Minis, the son of one of the immigrant families. The community is in existence to this day, though it may have been suspended for a time during the Revolution; while some of the very families that founded the congregation in Savannah still live there. Other similar communities were set up in the course of the eighteenth century in Charleston and Philadelphia. The first Jewish resident in Maryland who is known to us by name is João (Jacob) Lumbrozo, "ye Jew Doctor," a Portuguese Marrano who was arrested in 1658 for some unwary remarks which he had let slip in the course of a religious discussion.

Thus, of the half-dozen Jewish congregations established in the United States before the War of Independence, practically all had been founded by Marranos returned to Judaism, or else by their immediate descendants; though this original stock had been diluted to a considerable degree, even at this early date, by persons of German or Polish origin. As in the Old World, Spanish or Portuguese remained the official language of the community for many years, long after the use of the vernacular had become universal in private life. Thus, the circle of Marrano communities was complete from the Indian Ocean to the furthest shores of the Atlantic, and from the immemorial East to the newest Republic of the West.[11]

CHAPTER XII

SOME MARRANO WORTHIES

IN no branch of history, perhaps, does the record of individuals possess quite such fascination or importance as is the case in connection with the Marranos. No degree of rationalization of their romantic record can diminish this. The underlying phenomenon is not by any means difficult to understand. The forced assimilation to the general population of a large body of Jews at the close of the middle ages allowed the natural talents of the latter to assert themselves and afforded opportunities for instantaneous advancement perhaps unexampled in any other period of history. Freed from tne dead weight of the disabilities from which they had previously suffered, the neophytes rose irresistibly to the top, like a cork suddenly released below the surface of the water. The process was discernible from the very beginning. Already in the fifteenth century, the Marranos had begun to push their way forward, whether as poets, statesmen, Churchmen, explorers, or pioneers in any other branch of human endeavor. At a later period, in Portugal, the Jewish leaven was even more universal. Trade and commerce lay very largely in Marrano hands. Their blood permeated a large part even of the nobility. Natural aptitude was responsible for the fact that the most eminent physicians were of Jewish descent. The Marranos were important in literature, in science, in the universities, in the army, even in the Church.

A list of those who may be identified, whether by reason of their ultimate flight or of their persecution, is nothing less than dazzling. Yet a majority indubitably escaped discovery, and, if they resisted the temptations to emigrate, maintained a crypto-Jewish existence to the end. What eminent figures are comprised in this category must remain a matter of conjecture.[1]

The exiles continued this magnificent tradition in their new homes throughout Europe. In consequence, there grew up in Amsterdam, Hamburg, London, and elsewhere an intellectual life as brilliant as any city in the Peninsula could boast, and no less distinctively Iberian in character. Coupled with their personal distinction there was the romance inherent in the career of almost every one of the refugees, enhanced in many cases by the amazing contrast between their former and their present circumstances. There was no branch of human activity which they did not touch and adorn. In the few following pages account will be taken only of a small selection of the eminent figures who actively proved their Jewish sympathies.

Of many, there has been occasion already to speak in detail. A mere recapitulation of their names is eloquent. In medicine, there was Juan Rodrigo, alias Amatus Lusitanus, of the old family of Habib, one of the greatest practitioners and theorists of his age, who escaped from Ancona in 1556, and subsequently practiced his art in Salonica; Felipe Rodrigues, alias Elijah Montalto, physician to Marie de Medicis who received special dispensation to make use of his services; and Rodrigo de Castro, creator of gynaecology. To these we may add Manoel Alvares, alias Abraham Zacuto

(Zacutus Lusitanus), a friend of Menasseh ben Israel, whose reputation was second to none in his day; Joseph Bueno, who attended the Prince of Orange in his last illness; his son, Ephraim, the friend of Rembrandt; Ezekiel (Pedro) de Castro, who settled at Verona as a professing Jew, and published there some important scientific works; and many more, the enumeration of whom would fill pages.

In politics, there were João Miguez, Duke of Naxos, and Alvaro Mendes, Duke of Mitylene, both of whom exercised enormous power at the Turkish court; and Daniel Rodriguez, creator of the Free Port of Spalato. In literature, there were characters like Didaco Pyrrho, of Evora (Flavius Eborensis), who lived successively in Flanders, Switzerland, Ancona, and Ragusa, and was one of the outstanding Latin poets of the sixteenth century; Antonio Enriquez Gomez, the famous playwright; and several more. Philosophy was represented by Uriel Acosta; theology by Thomas de Pinedo; science by the Count Palatine, Immanuel Bocarro Frances, the friend of Galileo. Many were those who had attained distinction even in Holy Orders, like Vicente de Rocamora or Eleazar de Solis. A surprisingly large number studied on their return to Judaism with such a will that they became renowned rabbinic scholars: witness Jacob Zemah, apparently a lecturer in law in the Peninsula, who escaped to Palestine, embraced the medical profession, and became known as one of the most abstruse mystics of his day. Such lists of names could be continued almost indefinitely. It is a better plan to take in greater detail a few concrete instances. The plain, unadorned fact will outdo fiction in interest, though not in credibility.

At the great auto held at Seville in 1660, one of the thirty persons burned in effigy — almost all for Judaizing — was Doctor Melchor (Balthazar) de Orobio, a native of Braganza in Portugal. He was a person of considerable distinction, having been Professor of Medicine in the University of Seville,[1a] and subsequently physician to the Duke of Medina Celi. Some years before, he had been denounced to the Inquisition by a servant accused of theft. In consequence, he had been thrown into prison, where he remained, undergoing terrible sufferings for three years. In the end, he had been reconciled, and this illustrious figure in intellectual life had to go about for some time wearing the *sambenito*. It is no wonder that he seized the first opportunity to flee the country. In France, he found a safer environment, and began a new life. His abilities rapidly won him appointment as Professor of Medicine at the University of Toulouse, together with the honor of Medical Attendant and Privy-Counselor to His Christian Majesty. He had not yet declared his allegiance to Judaism, though his sympathies were sufficiently notorious at this period to secure his condemnation and figurative burning by the Seville Tribunal, as we have seen above. About 1666, he took the final step, going to Amsterdam and declaring himself a Jew, under the name of Isaac Orobio de Castro. Henceforth, he was one of the leading figures of the community, and naturally considered among its greatest ornaments. His was the inspiration in all manifestations of literary and intellectual life. Above all, he threw himself with all his heart into the work of defending and vindicating his new faith, to which he devoted all his extensive learning and his trained intellect. He opposed Spinoza on the one hand and the Catholic theologians on the other. He crushed, with a minimum of effort, Juan (Daniel) de Prado, a fellow-Marrano and a fellow-physician, who dared to criticise Jewish tradition. He discussed Christianity with the Dutch preacher, Philip van Limborch, one of the foremost critics of the Inquisition, who embodied their conversation in a Latin work. His vindication of the Jewish interpretation of the fifty-third chapter of Isaiah is still classical. His death, in 1687, deprived Amsterdam Jewry of one of its outstanding characters.

Rodrigo Mendes da Silva, whom Thomas de Pinedo criticised for knowing nothing of classical literature, or of Hebrew, was a native of Celorico in Portugal, and was one of the most prolific writers of his day. He was the author of vast numbers of historical works, which earned him the name of the Spanish Livy and the post of Historiographer Royal to the King of Spain, as well as a seat on the Privy Council. Late in life, however, he retired to Italy, leaving behind him a library to the value of 20,000 ducats. He is next heard of at Venice, where he became circumcised, assuming the name of Jacob; and, to the amusement of some spiteful contemporaries, he married a girl of eighteen. Not unnaturally, the veteran historian found some difficulty in accommodating himself in his old age to a completely different manner of life. It was remarked that he was seldom seen in synagogue, and never wore phylacteries. By force of habit, he continued to raise his hat at the mention of the names of Jesus and Mary, and regularly kissed the robe of any Christian priest with whom he spoke. His freedom of opinion, too, gave rise to considerable talk. He held very modern views about the Bible, denying in particular the historicity of the Book of Esther. He was a confessed sceptic, being reported to doubt even the immortality of the soul. Nevertheless, the fact that he continued to live as a red-hatted Jew in the oppressive atmosphere of the Ghetto, rather than occupy the place which belonged to him of right in the intellectual life of the outside world, shows unequivocally in what direction his sympathies lay.

One of the most illustrious of all Marrano families was that of Sampaio. Dom Francisco de Sampaio, alias Francisco de Mello, was a gentleman of the Portuguese royal household; his wife, Doña Antonia de Silva Texeira, was lady-in-waiting to the Queen. Their second son was Diego Texeira de Sampaio. The father died in battle in 1609, and in 1643, Don Diego left the Peninsula and settled in Antwerp, where he acted as Consul and Paymaster-General for the Spanish Government. Here his first wife died, and he renewed an earlier romance by marrying Doña Anna d'Andrade, who by her descent from Tomas Rodrigues da Veiga,[2] was related to half the nobility of Portugal. So strong was the call of the Jewish blood in her that she persuaded her husband to remove to Hamburg. Here, on Good Friday, 1647, he submitted to circumcision, together with his two sons, notwithstanding the fact that he was approaching the age of seventy. Henceforth he was known as Abraham Senior Texeira, his wife assuming the name of Sarah.

This episode naturally caused great scandal in Catholic circles. The Imperial government demanded that the

apostate should be arrested and put on trial. The Minister
of Hamburg at the court of Vienna, however, indicated
that this display of religious zeal was inspired mainly
by a desire to lay hands on Texeira's fortune, valued at
300,000 crowns. Accordingly, the Senate energetically
opposed the demand. Thus Don Abraham was able to
pass undisturbed the not inconsiderable span of life
which was left to him. He adopted the cause of his new
religion zealously. He contributed lavishly to the
construction of the new synagogue, obtained considerable
privileges for the community of Glückstadt, founded a
couple of important benevolent institutions, and for
some years served as president of the congregation.
His share in the general civic life was equally notable.
He supplied the copper roofing for the Church of St.
Michael, refusing all payment. He was universally
known as "The Rich Jew." He maintained a princely
household. His carriage was luxuriously upholstered in
velvet, and he never stirred abroad without a whole
retinue of servants. When therefore in 1654 Queen
Christina of Sweden visited Hamburg, she took up her
residence in the house of the aristocratic old Marrano,
whom the Spanish envoy cordially recommended to her.
In recognition of this, she appointed him her financial
agent and diplomatic representative in Hamburg. This
office he filled with distinction from 1655 to his death
in 1666. He was then succeeded in it by his son, Isaac
Hayim (Manoel) Senior Texeira (1625-1705), who had
embraced Judaism at the same time as his father. The
son held the office for twenty-one years, to the complete
satisfaction of his royal mistress, who more than once
stayed at his house and highly valued his advice. Late

in life he removed to Amsterdam, where he died in 1705. His descendants, some of whom were known by the name of Texeira de Mattos, remained prominent in Jewish and general life.

A more remarkable phenomenon perhaps was that of Jews acting in the capacity of diplomatic agents for the countries from which they had fled, and where they would have been burned had they dared to venture back. Sir William Temple, the famous English writer and diplomat, for a long time ambassador at The Hague, expressed his wonder both at the Spaniards for making such appointments and at the Jews for accepting them. A typical instance was that of Duarte Nuñes da Costa (d'Acosta), alias Jacob Curiel. He belonged to a notable Portuguese house, being the nephew of Fray Francisco de Vittoria, Archbishop of Mexico.[3] Born at Lisbon in 1587, he transferred himself first to Pisa, then to Florence, and in 1618 to Amsterdam. Ultimately, he settled in Hamburg. He had proved highly useful to Dom Duarte de Braganza, the brother of the king of Portugal. In consequence, when the latter established diplomatic relations with Hamburg, in about 1640, Duarte Nuñes da Costa was the first *chargé d'affaires*, being in consequence raised to the nobility. He was succeeded in this office by his son, Manoel Nuñes da Costa, or Solomon Curiel (d. 1679); and other members of the family continued to occupy it until its extinction in 1795. Duarte's elder son, Geronimo Nuñes da Costa, alias Moses Curiel, filled a similar post in Holland, which remained hereditary in his family until the middle of the eighteenth century.

The Belmonte family was no less illustrious. It was

allied with half of the noblest families of the Peninsula.
Baron Manuel de Belmonte, known in the community
as Isaac Nuñez Belmonte, acted from 1664 as Agent-
General for the King of Spain in the Netherlands, and
from 1674 to his death in·1704 as Resident. In 1693,
he was created Count Palatine by the Holy Roman
Emperor, in recognition of his great public services.
This eminent diplomat was at the same time a loyal
Jew. He founded at Amsterdam two famous literary
societies; and, on the martyrdom of Abraham Nuñez
Bernal, he composed a touching elegy in his memory.
He was succeeded in his high diplomatic office by his
nephew, Baron Francisco de Ximenes Belmonte, whose
son Emmanuel continued to hold it after his death.
Another member of the family, distantly related to
them, was Jacob de Abraham de Belmonte, grandson
of the poet Jacob Israel Belmonte, who altered his name
into the Dutch equivalent of Franz van Schoonenberg
and (presumably after embracing Protestantism) entered the Dutch diplomatic service. In this capacity,
he served as *chargé d'affaires* successively in Madrid
and Lisbon (where he died in 1717), and was one of the
architects of the Grand Alliance. His aid was partly
instrumental in the acquisition of the English throne by
William of Orange.

This by no means exhausts the list of Jews who
attained similar distinction, in the diplomatic service
or as financial agents for foreign potentates. In Hamburg,
Daniel and Jacob Abensur (descendants of the martyred
Anrique Dias Millão) acted in succession as Residents
for the King of Poland, at the close of the seventeenth
and beginning of the eighteenth centuries; while, about

1650, Gabriel Gomez was agent of the King of Denmark. In Tuscany, in 1746, the King of Portugal was represented by Joseph d'Oliveira. Joseph Jesurun Lobo was Spanish Consul in Zealand at the close of the seventeenth century, and Joseph Manoel de Acosta filled the same post fifty years later. Jacob Cohen (son of the Abraham Cohen Henriques who had made a name for himself in Brazil[4]) was Agent at Amsterdam for Prince Maurice of Nassau. David Bueno de Mesquita acted as Resident for the Margrave of Brandenburg, besides being entrusted with a number of diplomatic missions by the Sultan of Morocco. In 1684, Miguel Osorio was appointed representative in Holland for the Queen of Sweden. David Salom d'Azevedo and various other members of his family successively represented the court of Algiers. That questionable character, Agostino Coronel (Chacon), one of the founders of the Anglo-Jewish community, was Portuguese Agent in London, negotiating the match with Catherine of Braganza through which the British obtained their first footing in India.

Their diplomatic interests were largely responsible for the fact that many of the Marranos, even after their return to Judaism, entered into the ranks of the nobility In Holland, the Barons de Belmonte were prominent. In gratitude for his financial assistance at the time of the Restoration, Charles II of England raised Agostino Coronel Chacon to the knighthood; while Solomon de Medina received a similar honor for his services as Commissary in the wars at the end of the seventeenth century. Antonio (Isaac) Lopez Suasso, of the Hague, was raised by Charles II of Spain to the dignity of Baron of Avernas de Gras in return for services rendered.

His son's devotion to the House of Orange contributed largely to the success of William III's expedition to England in 1688. It is recounted that he advanced the enormous sum of 2,000,000 crowns free of interest, refusing even a receipt, saying: "If your expedition is successful, you will repay me; if not, I will lose in either case."

The antecedents of the Marquisate of Montfort deserve special mention. Mention has already been made, on more than one occasion, of Duarte da Silva. Born in Lisbon in 1596, of middle-class New Christian parentage, he became one of the most opulent Portuguese merchants of his day. He had agencies at Antwerp, Rouen, Rome, Venice, London, and Leghorn. From the New World, he imported merchandise on a vast scale. He was in close relations with the Portuguese court, to which he advanced large sums. He provided ships, supplies, and munitions during the struggle with Holland for the possession of Brazil, the final retention of which province by Portugal was due in some measure to his assistance. More than once, he had been denounced by his personal enemies to the Inquisition as a Judaizer, without any proceedings being taken. In 1647, however, he was implicated in the confessions wrung from the children of his kinswoman, Brites Henriques, who was martyred in that year. The news of his impending arrest reached his ears, and he managed to keep in hiding until he could set his affairs (not all, apparently, of a business nature) in order. Ultimately, he gave himself up; but his action had exposed him to a second charge — that of violating the secrecy of the Inquisition, as well as that of Judaizing. The news of his arrest caused great commotion in Lisbon. It was bruited abroad that the Inquisitors were in the pay of Spain, and that they had acted as they did in order to undermine the credit of the country. In Amsterdam, the exchange on Lisbon slumped by 5%.

The trial dragged on for five years. In the end, on December 1, 1652 — in the same auto-da-fè at which Manuel Fernandez Villareal lost his life — Duarte da Silva appeared as a penitent; apparently escaping a worse fate through the intervention of the Court. It was not long before he regained his former position. When in 1662 Catherine of Braganza went to England as the bride of Charles II, she took Duarte da Silva with her to administer her dowry. Now that he was safe out of the country, he put forward certain proposals for the amelioration of the position of the New Christians in Portugal, for which he professed himself willing to pay heavily. Samuel Pepys knew him, and appreciated his comfits. Even now, he did not formally profess allegiance to Judaism. When his mission was ended, he retired to Antwerp, where he died in 1688. His sons, however, found the call of their ancestral religion stronger than their father had done. One of them, Diogo, went to Hamburg, where he assumed the name of Isaac da Silva Solis, became a pillar of the community, and was prevented only by the prejudices of the burghers from constructing in his house a synagogue which was alleged to threaten the outlook from a neighboring Church. Francisco, another son, who had been reconciled at the auto of December 1, 1652, and accompanied his father to London, was destined to a more refulgent career. He became a Knight of the Military Order of Christ, as well as Counselor and Treasurer General to Queen Catherine. In the Low Countries, he entered into the Spanish service and was responsible for the defeat of the Duc de Créqui's attempt to relieve Treves in 1673. In reward for his services, he was raised by the Emperor in 1682 to the dignity of Marquis de Montfort. His son, Fernando, the second Marquis, returned publicly to Judaism, assuming like his uncle the name of Isaac da Silva Solis.

Duarte da Silva was naturally not the only great capitalist to figure in Marrano history. Let us take a couple of more typical cases. José da Costa Villareal was *Proveditore General*, or Comptroller General, to the armies of the King of Portugal. In 1726, a charge of Judaizing was brought against him, and it came to his ears that his arrest was about to be ordered. As it happened, a great fire broke out in Lisbon. Profiting by the confusion, he embarked for England on one of his ships which happened to be in harbor, together with as much of his property as he could collect and seventeen members of his family, including his aged parents. The total value of the fortune which they thus brought with them was said to exceed £300,000. Immediately on their arrival in London, the family openly declared their adhesion to Judaism. The males underwent circumcision, led by the old father, then in his seventy-fourth year. All assumed Hebrew names to replace those which they had been given at baptism; and those who had wives saw to it that their marriages were resolemnized in synagogue. As a thank-offering for their escape, large sums were given to charity; and a school for Jewish girls, which still exists under the name of the Villareal School, was endowed.

Diego Lopez Pereira was one of the outstanding Portu-

guese financiers of his age. He farmed the tobacco revenue with conspicuous success, and established branches
of his banking house in London and Amsterdam. During
the course of the War of the Spanish Succession, he made
the acquaintance of the Austrian Archduke Charles, one
of the rival claimants to the throne. When the Archduke
became Emperor, he summoned Pereira to Vienna to
administer the tobacco revenue. He accepted only on
condition that he and his whole household would enjoy
complete religious freedom. Hardly had he arrived in
Austria, when he declared his allegiance to Judaism, adopting the name of Moses. In Vienna, he played a prominent
part. The Emperor Charles created him Baron d'Aguilar;
Maria Theresa made him a privy counselor; and he was
responsible for the rebuilding of the imperial palace at
Schönbrun. He espoused the cause of his own people
enthusiastically, founding the so-called "Turkish" community in the capital, and proving a constant champion
for his brothers in faith at any time when persecution
threatened. Ultimately, according to report, the Spanish
government demanded the extradition of this fabulously
wealthy renegade for trial by the Holy Office. This
determined him to leave Vienna; and he settled in London, with his fourteen children and his immense retinue
of servants and slaves. He died, in the then fashionable
thoroughfare of Bishopsgate, in 1759. His son, Ephraim
Lopez Pereira, succeeded to his title and his fortune.
The latter's claim to fame was a very different one.
After living in great style for some years, the loss of an
estate of 15,000 acres in America made him apprehensive
of utter ruin. He accordingly went to the other extreme,
becoming notorious for his parsimony. His miserliness

verged on mania. He gave up his town mansion and his three country houses; and his one remaining establishment, at Islington near London, became known as "Starvation Farm," from the ridiculously scanty food provided for the cattle. For all this, when he died, in 1802, a fortune estimated at £200,000 was found secreted about the house.

The variety of the pageant of Marrano life perhaps reaches its climax with Daniel da Fonseca, a member of a well-known family of martyrs. His grandfather had been burned at the stake by the Inquisition; his father had escaped the same fate only by flight. The little son, whom he had been forced to leave behind him in Portugal, was brought up as a priest. This did not prevent him from adhering to Judaism in stealth. The secret reached the ears of the Inquisition, and like his father he had to flee for his life. He studied medicine in France, and then made his way to Constantinople, where he openly embraced Judaism. His medical skill soon carved him out a position in the Turkish capital. He obtained the confidence of many high officials. He showed himself an accomplished diplomat, consistently espousing the cause of France and thereby earning the hearty dislike of the Court of Austria. He was appointed a physician to the French embassy, in which he occupied the position of confidential adviser. Subsequently, he became medical attendant to Prince Nicholas Mavrocordato at Bucharest. On his return to Constantinople, he became body-physician to the Sultan, continuing to occupy this office till 1730; and he was of great assistance to Charles XII of Sweden in his intrigues at the Sublime Porte against Russia and Poland. Finally he settled in Paris, where he intermingled with the highest society of his age and earned the respect of Voltaire, who regarded him as the only philosopher of his nation. It was a far cry from the sacerdotal career to which he had been brought up.

To what unexpected spots individual Marranos penetrated is remarkable. The last of the series of eminent physicians who came from the district of Castello Branco in Portugal, which had included Amatus Lusitanus and Elijah Montalto, was Antonio Ribeiro Sanchez, who was born at Penamacor in 1699. In his twenty-eighth year, he was denounced to the Inquisition by reason of his family connections and fled to join his uncle, Diogo Nuñes Ribeiro,[5] in London. Here, profoundly impressed by a passage relative to circumcision which he read in Saint Augustine's *City of God*, he formally entered the Jewish community. Subsequently, he was assisted to study at Leyden by his wealthy English coreligionists; and he showed such promise that he was recommended to the Empress Anna of Russia as her court physician. He remained in practice in St. Petersburg from 1731 to 1747, under several reigns, saving the future Catherine II from a dangerous illness and being made a Counselor of State by the Empress Elizabeth. At length, the secret of his Jewish origin leaked out, though for some time he had been out of sympathy with his coreligionists, and had even written against them. He was therefore dismissed and retired to Paris, where he ruined both his health and his finances by working gratuitously among the poor. His writings (in one of which he gives a graphic description of the consequences of the Inquisitional tortures, which he had witnessed with his own eyes) are of the greatest scientific importance. He was the first person to acquaint wider circles with the medicinal value of the Russian vapor baths; and he was a pioneer in educational reform. Moreover, despite his estrangement from Judaism, he wrote an important memorial advocating the amelioration of the condition of the Portuguese New Christians and the restriction of the power of the Holy Office.[6]

The subsequent history of some of the Marrano families is in itself a study of high interest. Amply endowed with all social graces, and blessed in many cases with an abundant measure of the goods of this world, they mixed from the first on conditions of virtual equality with other citizens in their lands of refuge. A generation or two of tolerance sometimes achieved what centuries of persecution had failed to do, and finally assimilated their descendants to the dominant culture and religion. Intermarriage similarly began at an early date. Thus, particularly in the Protestant countries in the north, Marrano blood runs in the veins of many of the proudest and most noble houses. In England, indeed, hardly a single family of the older aristocracy is free from some such admixture or alliance.

Let us take a fairly typical family story. Paul de Pina belonged to a good New Christian family of Lisbon. In 1599, he left for Italy, with the intention of entering some religious order. On the way he passed through Leghorn. Here there was living at the time the erudite Felipe Rodrigues, alias Elijah Montalto, who was subsequently to become famous as a Jewish polemist and as physician to the Court of France. To him, the youth brought a letter of introduction from his kinsman, Diego Gomez Lobato, a convinced Judaizer. It was conceived in the following terms: "Our cousin, Paul de Pina, is going to

Rome to become a monk. You will oblige me by putting him on the right road." Montalto (a born controversialist, as proved in his various writings) was quick to grasp the meaning of this intentionally equivocal message. He executed the commission so effectively that Pina returned to Lisbon a devoted adherent to the religion of his fathers. With Gomez Lobato, he emigrated to Brazil. Thence, after a short time, they went to Amsterdam, where both embraced Judaism. De Pina was henceforth known as Reuel Jessurun; the other, who preserved the tradition that he was of priestly descent, adopted the name of Abraham Cohen Lobato. It is noteworthy that the unusual name of Reuel is still common in the Cohen Lobato family.

Reuel Jessurun was henceforth an active worker in the Amsterdam community. He became a prominent member of the earliest congregation, *K. K. Beth Ja'acob*; was one of the persons responsible for drawing up the first regulations of the burial-ground; and is recorded among the earliest presidents of the *Talmud Torah*, the famous educational establishment of Amsterdam Jewry. His considerable literary gifts were henceforth devoted to his own people. In 1624, he composed in Portuguese his famous *Dialogo de los Montes*, consisting of a poetical discussion between the seven principal mountains of Palestine in honor of the faith of Israel. This was performed in the Amsterdam synagogue on Pentecost by a number of youths: Isaac Cohen Lobato — probably a son of Diego Gomez Lobato — taking the part of Mount Zion. The work was published only in 1767, being dedicated to David de Aaron Jessurun, presumably a descendant of the author.

Reuel Jessurun had a daughter, Sarah. She became the wife of Moses Gideon Abudiente, of Lisbon, who had embraced Judaism at Amsterdam and subsequently migrated to Hamburg. Here he became known as a grammarian, poet, and theologian, a couple of his works having been published in his lifetime. Their son, named Reuel after his grandfather, settled first in Boston, then in the West Indies, and finally in London, where he was known as Rowland Gideon. Here, in 1699, was born his son Sampson. The latter inherited some of the literary gifts of his ancestors, contributing a graceful commendatory poem in English to one of the local publications. But he devoted his main attention to more mundane matters. Entering the West India trade, he prospered exceedingly. Within a few years he was recognized as one of the wealthiest merchants in the city of London, and the most active of the twelve "Jew Brokers" then officially authorized. At the time of the "South Sea Bubble" he was one of the few persons in the country to keep his head; and he is said to have advised Walpole in the steps taken at this time to cope with the crisis and to restore public credit. During the Jacobite Rebellion in favor of the Young Pretender in 1745, he threw his influence whole-heartedly on the side of the Hanoverian dynasty, and was largely responsible for the maintenance of the financial stability of the Treasury. In this and the following years, he raised loans for the government to the total value of millions of pounds sterling. He was popularly thought to be the person responsible for the abortive Jewish Naturalization Bill of 1753. Its failure and repeal convinced him of the impossibility of establishing his position as an

English gentleman while still a Jew. Accordingly, he resigned his membership of the synagogue (to which he continued to contribute clandestinely): already his children were being brought up as Christians. On his death in 1762, he left over half a million pounds. In his will was found to be included a legacy of £1,000 to the Spanish and Portuguese community, conditional upon his being buried in the congregational cemetery. It was accepted; and, in the synagogue which he once attended, the soul of Sampson Gideon is still commemorated annually upon the eve of the Day of Atonement.

Sampson Gideon's eldest son, called after his father, was baptized in childhood, educated at Eton, created a baronet while still at school, and finally married the daughter of Chief Justice Sir John Eardley Wilmot, whose name he assumed. In 1789 he was raised to the peerage under the title of Baron Eardley. His father's dream of founding a landed family, for which he had given up so much, was not destined to be fulfilled, as all of Lord Eardley's sons predeceased him. However, one of his daughters married Lord Saye and Sele, her son succeeding to the title. Another became the wife of Colonel Childers of the Light Dragoons. One of the latter's granddaughters married Lord Auckland; while among the other descendants of the match was H. C. E. Childers, Gladstone's Chancellor of the Exchequer. It is interesting to speculate what amount of the latter's financial ability he owed to his ancestor, Sampson Gideon Abudiente, the famous "Jew Broker" of his age. On his death, the headship of the family devolved upon Miss Rowlanda Childers, whose first name recalls the biblical Reuel which her ancestor, Paul de Pina, assumed when, under the influence of Elijah Montalto, he embraced Judaism.[7]

One more instance, less dramatic though no less characteristic. The Bernal family was one of some importance in Marrano annals. Mestre Bernal, as we have seen, was physician to Christopher Columbus on his epoch-making voyage; Abraham Nuñez Bernal, and Isaac (Marco) de Almeyda Bernal, burned by the Spanish Inquisition in 1655, had been among the outstanding martyrs of the seventeenth century, their kinsman Jacob Bernal editing the memorial volume published in Amsterdam in their honor. One branch of the family emigrated to London. Here in 1744, Jacob Israel Bernal was elected *Gabbai*, or treasurer of the community. In the following year, he desired to marry a *tudesca* — a member of the despised German and Polish community. The idea of the contamination of his hidalgo blood in this manner shocked his fellow-officials. He had to resign his position, and consent was given for the wedding ceremony only under the most humiliating conditions. Henceforth, his connection with the community was less intimate; and it was not remarkable that his son, Jacob Israel Bernal, married out of the faith and left the community. The latter's son, Ralph Bernal, was famous as an art-collector, and was a prominent member of Parliament for a third of the nineteenth century. His son, in turn, married the daughter of an Irish landowner, whose name he adopted in addition to his own; and, as Mr. Bernal Osborne, was distinguished in Victorian society as a wit. Grace, his daughter, became the Duchess of St. Albans. Thus the blood of the Inquisitional martyrs, and of the despised *tudesca*, and of Charles Stuart, and of Nell Gwynne, became united in one of the foremost families of the British aristocracy.

Many are the family legends still current among the descendants of the old Marrano families, in the New World and in the Old, of hairbreadth escapes from the Inquisition and extraordinary subsequent episodes. It is not to be imagined that all are literally true; but they contain at least a substratum of fact, and recall to a superlative degree the romance of Marrano history. The Gomez family, of Bordeaux and New York, told how they were descended from a Spanish aristocrat, who stood in high favor with the king. The latter, hearing that the Inquisition was contemplating his favorite's arrest as a Judaizer, warned him with the enigmatical phrase: "Gomez, the onions begin to smell." Gomez thereupon took the precaution of sending his family and much of his property to France; but he himself underwent imprisonment for fourteen years before he could follow them into safety. The Da Silva Solis family, which subsequently made its mark in American life, used to recount how an ancestress of theirs was immured in a convent by her cruel stepmother, in order to secure the family titles and estates to her own children. The girl managed to make her escape, and fled to Amsterdam. Here she became converted to Judaism, and married a Da Silva Solis, who had befriended her on her first arrival. Some years later, a representative of the Spanish government is said to have waited upon a descendant of this romantic match in London and to have offered him restitution of the high dignities and titles which the family had previously enjoyed if he would revert to Catholicism. On encountering a point-blank refusal, the astonished grandee exclaimed: "Do not be foolish; you are refusing one of the greatest dignities in Europe." The other replied, with quiet dignity: "Not for the whole of Europe would I change my faith — nor would my little son here, either;" and he placed his hand on the head of a small boy playing about the room, who used to recount the tale to his grandchildren in after years. Abraham Mendes Seixas (grandfather of Gershom Mendes Seixas, "the patriot Jewish minister of the American revolution") was said in family legend to have been smuggled out of his house, when the familiars of the Inquisition came to arrest him, under a pile of washing in a large pannier, which a family retainer of gigantic strength carried on his back on board an English ship.[8]

The intellectual importance of the Marrano fugitives from the Peninsula was not confined to the first generation. It is, indeed, difficult to point to any branch of human activity in which their descendants did not win distinction. Benjamin Disraeli, Earl of Beaconsfield, used to recount how the founder of his family was a Marrano refugee, who adopted his distinctive name in gratitude to the God of Israel for his escape. This appears to have been a typical piece of hyperbole on the part of the great statesman; but the fact remains that, in the female line, he was descended from the great New Christian houses of Aboab, Cardoso and Villareal. Benedict Spinoza belonged to a Marrano family established in Holland no more than a single generation. Cesare Lombroso, the founder of the science of criminology, appears to have been descended from a family of similar

origin settled at Verona. To these names may be added
those of General Juan (Isaac) de Sola, of Curaçao, a
notable soldier of the War of Liberation in Venezuela;
Benjamin Peixotto, the American diplomat; David
Ricardo and Nassau Senior, the eminent economists;
Olinde Rodrigues, the companion of St. Simon and one of
the fathers of modern Socialism; Georges de Porto-Riche,
the eminent French dramatist; David Belasco and Arthur
Wing Pinero, his English counterpart; Charles Fustado
and Isidore de Lara, both eminent musicians; Henrietta
Hertz (*née* de Lemos), the German beauty and leader
of a salon; Joseph Samuda, builder of the first armor-
plated warships used in the British Navy; Texeira de
Mattos, the English litterateur, and Isaac da Costa, the
Dutch poet; American patriots like Daniel (Francis) Salvador, scalped in Carolina, or Major Benjamin Nones;
actors like Jacob de Castro and actresses like Teresa
Furtado; financiers and philanthropists like the French
house of Péreire and the English house of Mocatta;
jurists like the American Benjamin N. Cardozo; even
heroes of the prize-ring, like the brothers Belasco and
Daniel Mendoza. The foregoing are only a few names
which come to the mind at random; but the list could
be extended almost indefinitely.

As for the Marrano influence in the intellectual life
of the Peninsula, it is not so easy to tell. On the one
hand, there can be few families in whose veins there
runs no Jewish blood at all; on the other, except in those
cases where the facts were made clear by condemnation
or by flight, there is no means of identifying those whose
Marrano affiliations were closer. Nevertheless, there can

be no doubt that the element is very strong indeed. Guerra Junqueiro, the most eminent Portuguese poet of recent times, was known to be of New Christian descent, and looked like one of Rembrandt's Rabbis. Camillo de Castello Branco, the Portuguese Scott, showed in his writings that he had strong pro-Jewish sympathies; but it is only recently that it has been discovered that he was of Jewish blood. As recently as 1924, a Portuguese writer published a work in which he endeavored to demonstrate that all the prominent figures in the country, in any line of activity, with whose opinions he disagreed (and there were not many who did not fall into this category), belonged to New Christian families. As far as Spain goes, recollections are less distinct. It has however been stated that both the Premier, the Minister of Justice and the Minister of the Interior, in the revolutionary government of 1931, were of Jewish descent.

It is customary to speak of the Expulsion of the Jews as having proved a fatal blow to Spanish greatness. This, of course, is an indubitable exaggeration. The most glorious age of Spanish history — the era of the Conquest of America, of the *Conquistadores*, of the Great Captain, of Velasquez, of Cervantes — came when there were no professing Jews left in the country. Similarly, in Portugal, the period when the great colonial Empire was built up, when Manoelline architecture flourished, when Gil Vincente and Camões penned their immortal works, was subsequent to the forced conversion of 1497. It remains a matter for speculation what proportion of those to whom was due the greatness of the two countries had Jewish blood in their veins, how far that Jewish blood contributed to their achievements, and how much greater progress might have been realized had the Jews, as a body, been able to collaborate in it. Notwithstanding all this, it must be recognized that the decline of Spain and Portugal began a considerable time after the Expulsion from the two countries. On the other hand, when it took place, it was with a rapidity and a thoroughness perhaps unexampled in history. For this, the Inquisition cannot be held blameless. It was prompted by truly religious, though assuredly mistaken, motives. It was not without its better, and even beneficent, side. Nevertheless, through many generations, it was systematically engaged in crushing out that freedom of thought without which no civilization can progress and no country hold its own. Its method of activity was calculated to cause frequent commercial upheavals and to undermine the sense of stability essential for economic welfare. In addition, it set itself to carry on a vendetta against one class of the population — the New Christians — peculiarly possessed of the intellectual qualities which make for progress. Thousands of them were burned; tens of thousands were forced to emigrate; a greater proportion still were led to stifle their natural inclinations. Over a period of centuries, it systematically deprived the Peninsula of some of its best intellects. Under such circumstances, progress is inconceivable. The wonder is, perhaps, that the Spanish and Portuguese kingdoms were able to maintain a semblance of their former greatness for so long.

CHAPTER XIII

THE LITERATURE OF THE MARRANOS*

Up to a certain extent, the Marranos may be considered the originators of vernacular literature among the Jews. Of course, throughout medieval Europe, as in the classical world, the language of the country had universally been spoken in the home, but it had undergone certain inevitable dialectical modifications. Moreover, for literary compositions, the Hebrew tongue had been preferred; it monopolized attention in the schools; and, when it was necessary to write the language of the country for the benefit of the less erudite, it was universally transliterated into Hebrew characters. Thus a whole literature arose in Judeo-German, Judeo-Spanish, and even Judeo-French and Judeo-Italian.[1] The incongruity of these dialects became even more striking when (as in the two former cases) those speaking them were driven into exile, continuing to cherish them in places far distant from their original homes and among peoples of a completely different culture. With the forcible conversion of the Marranos, a different situation arose. A fresh generation grew to manhood, educated in the fullest cultural tradition of the Peninsula, and entirely ignorant of the tongue of their fathers. When they escaped to countries of greater tolerance, where they were able to

* I wish to record my thanks to Professor Alexander Marx for revising this chapter in the light of his vast bibliographical knowledge.

322

return publicly to Judaism, they began to study the traditional language of prayer from the beginning. In the meanwhile, they had to have recourse to translations. Sometimes, even, the old phenomenon was reversed, and the Hebrew liturgy was transliterated into Latin characters for their benefit, this being the case in at least one complete manuscript now extant as well as many scattered fragments.

From generation to generation, in the fogs of London, the marshes of Holland, or even the wastes of Manhattan, knowledge of the Spanish and Portuguese tongues was piously handed down. The former, spoken by the descendants of the exiles of 1492 in the Levant, the source and home of traditional lore, was regarded as something more of a sacred tongue, as well as being more polished; and it was used, besides, as the international medium of communication with itinerant scholars or merchants. The latter, the mother-language of the majority of the fugitives, tended to be used to a greater extent in private life and for less formal purposes. Down to the beginning of the nineteenth century, by which time these languages had become fully as unfamiliar as Hebrew itself, all communal business was conducted in the one or the other: the minutes of the governing body were written, its regulations were published, proclamations were made, sermons were delivered. It was only in 1735 that English began to figure on the curriculum of the public school of the London community; while at least at Amsterdam, Portuguese remained a principal item on the syllabus until the nineteenth century was well advanced. Even down to the present day, in the Sephardic synagogues of London and New York, Amsterdam and Bordeaux, little snatches of Spanish and Portuguese remain embedded in the service to remind the congregation of the land from which the founders of the community originated and the vicissitudes through which they passed.

The earliest home of Marrano literature was Ferrara. Here, the first press for the production of Spanish and Portuguese works for the use of Jews was set up, at the beginning of the second half of the sixteenth century. In the course of the next decade, several translations as well as one or two original works appeared here. Towards the end of the century, the center removed to Venice, at that time the home of Hebrew publishing, which retained the supremacy for a short period. After the settlement of the Marranos in the Netherlands, the hegemony passed thither. In 1612 appeared the first Spanish work to be published at Amsterdam. This city was henceforth the seat of publication of this sort of literature, producing many hundreds of volumes, over a period of more than two centuries. Hamburg, Leghorn, and, later, London were minor centers; while a few works appeared at Frankfort, Florence, the Hague, Pisa, Bayonne, etc. One or two similarly were printed amongst the vast mass in Ladino (or Spanish in Hebrew characters) in the Levant, at Smyrna or at Salonica. Works by Marrano authors, without any specific Jewish character, were also published in Naples, Antwerp, Rouen, and elsewhere. It is not surprising, in these circumstances, that occasionally the authors had to apologize for the printing errors which had crept into their works, owing to the fact that the composition was done by persons imperfectly acquainted with the language.

Thus the environment for this exotic literature was maintained. It was not, to be sure, confined to religious or liturgical use. Forcibly assimilated as they were to European standards, and counting in their ranks litterateurs of the utmost eminence, the intellectual horizons of the Marranos were by no means bounded by the traditional "four cubits" of rabbinic lore. Accordingly, in the colonies of the new Diaspora, there flourished a literary life hardly inferior in brilliance or in comprehensiveness to that of Lisbon or of Madrid itself. Poetry and drama, history and science, theology and philosophy, were cultivated with sublime impartiality. Among the productions were some of more than ordinary literary merit. One of the earliest of all was that stately prose-poem by Samuel Usque, *Consolaçam ás Tribulaçoës de Israel*, published at Ferrara in 1553. This magnificent work, one of our main sources for the history of the period, reaches its climax in a tirade against the Portuguese Inquisition, from which the author was himself a fugitive. It is now regarded as a classic of Portuguese literature of the period, and studied as such in the schools of the country from which the author had been forced to flee for his life.

Naturally, the first requirement of the Marranos was a translation of the Bible. This was therefore among the earliest products of the Ferrara press, where one based upon the old traditional rendering current among Spanish Jews, literal to a degree, appeared in the same year as the work just mentioned. It was published in two editions, virtually identical. The one, intended for Christian eyes, was dedicated to the Duke of Ferrara, bore the date 1553, and purported to have been produced

by Duarte Pinel at the expense of Jeronimo de Vargas.
The other, which was for the Jews, was inscribed to
Dona Gracia Mendes, contained a list of the *Haftarot*
(Prophetical lessons), gave the year according to the era
of the Creation, and furnished the editor and publisher
with their Jewish names, Abraham Usque and Yom-
Tob Athias, instead of the Marrano counterparts. This
edition became classical. It was repeatedly republished,
in full or in separate books, for many years to come.
Frequent re-issues appeared at Amsterdam; and subsequent revised editions were invariably based upon it. It
was from the Ferrara Bible that successive generations
of the Marranos re-learned their Judaism.

The earliest printed translation of the prayer book into
any language published in Latin characters was similarly
that issued by Yom-Tob Athias at Ferrara in 1552
and the following years, being the first of a long series.
Among the subsequent editions may be mentioned one
which was published furtively in 1584 with the imprint
Maguntia (Mayence), but was probably printed actually
at Dordrecht, and was no doubt intended to serve the
needs of the crypto-Jewish community at Antwerp;
another edited by Menasseh ben Israel, which enjoyed
considerable vogue; and finally, a new version by Isaac
Nieto, spiritual leader of the community of London.
At the time of the Pseudo-Messianic movement of 1666,
associated with the name of Sabbatai Zevi, large numbers
of special compilations in Spanish as well as in Hebrew
poured from the press. In the case of these liturgical
or biblical translations, it was exceptional for the text
to be accompanied by the Hebrew original. This was not
due merely to typographical exigencies; for in some of

the earliest Venice editions the difficulties were overcome. The reason was quite different. They were intended essentially for the Marranos who had been brought up in ignorance of the traditional language of prayer. On their first arrival, a Hebrew text would have been useless; afterwards, it was hoped, the Spanish one would be superfluous. The only compromise made was to transliterate passages from certain of the more important prayers or hymns into Latin characters, so that even the most ignorant could join with the congregation at these points.

For a prolonged period, it was considered little less than sacrilege to render the Hebrew prayer book into the actual vernacular of the country, as distinct from the Spanish hallowed by long association. Thus, the first published Dutch translation dates from late in the eighteenth century, nearly two centuries after the settlement of the first Marranos in Amsterdam. The earliest English version, published by Isaac Pinto in 1761-1766, appeared in distant New York, since (according to report) the *Mahamad* would not allow so undignified a production to appear in England.[2]

These liturgical and biblical translations, being of a sacred or semi-sacred character, and following moreover very closely upon the model set by their prototypes, were all in Spanish. For other publications, not of so essentially traditional a nature, Portuguese was used to an increasing extent. In the one language or the other, works appeared in a never-ending stream from the presses of London, Amsterdam, or Leghorn until the nineteenth century was well advanced: sermons, ethical treatises, handbooks of Jewish law and practice, calendars, polemical compositions, Purim-plays, dramas, epics, elegies, complimentary addresses, synagogal laws, regulations of various organizations, and all manner of other literature. There were Jewish publishers, and Jewish booksellers, whose main interest was in Spanish works. As late as 1821, the regulations of the Society for Dowering the Brides at Leghorn were re-issued in Portuguese — the last work, possibly, of the whole long series. Among the interminable series of published sermons, a complete list of which would fill a whole volume, particular interest is attached to one preached at Amsterdam by Samuel Mendes de Solla, later Rabbi at Curaçâo, to celebrate the safe arrival from Spain of his mother and two brothers. The little work contains a 'Eulogy' of *Haham* David Israel Athias, who had with his family made a similar escape from the clutches of the Inquisition.

A branch of literature which flourished especially amongst the Marranos was that of polemics. Each of them, it may be said, had known an acute internal conflict before he decided to abandon Catholicism in favor of Judaism. It was inevitable that they should have attempted in many cases to set down the arguments which had determined them, in the hopes of influencing others to take the same step, or of confuting their opponents. They were moreover familiar with Catholic literature — more so, in many cases, than they were with the traditional Jewish lore. They thus possessed all the necessary intellectual equipment; and in the free atmosphere they were able to write what they pleased without any misgivings. Hence a whole literature grew up, calculated to persuade wavering Marranos or to vanquish Christian objections.[3] Immanuel Aboab wrote his erudite *Nomologia*, a vindication of Jewish tradition. Elijah Montalto composed an acute examination of the Messianic prophecies in the fifty-third chapter of Isaiah. Saul Levi Mortara, the latter's pupil and former factotum, wrote *The Providence of God with Israel*, as well as a defence of the Talmud. Isaac Orobio de Castro, as we have seen, produced a whole series of works in defence of his new faith. Lorenzo Escudero of Cordova (apparently an Old Christian, who adopted Judaism under the name of Abraham Guer or Peregrino, and whose political activity in the Peninsula was a thorn in the flesh of the Spanish government) composed the *Strength of Judaism and Confusion of the Stranger*, subsequently translated into Hebrew. David Nieto, Rabbi in London, skillfully championed the Oral Law. Isaac, or Fernando, Cardoso, formerly Court Physician to Philip IV at Madrid, and equally distinguished as a scientist and as a philosopher, who had settled as a professing Jew at Verona, was the author of *The Excellencies of the Hebrews* — one of the most impressive apologies for Judaism and the Jews that has ever been written. This is only a very small selection out of the large literature on the subject which exists.[4]

Inevitably, the literature of the Marranos bore strongly the imprint of their sufferings. The poems and sermons on the victims of the Inquisition were sometimes printed, as permanent records. In 1626, David Abenatar Melo, who had lived at Madrid and had passed several years in the dungeons of the Holy Office, published at Frankfort a translation of the Psalms into Spanish verse. He dedicated it to "The Blessed God and the Holy Company of Israel and Judah, scattered through the world:" and the prologue contains a detailed account of his sufferings. The work itself is more of a paraphrase than a translation, and no opportunity is lost of introducing allusions to current events. Thus that well-known verse of the thirtieth psalm, "O Lord, Thou hast brought up my soul from the grave; Thou hast kept me alive, that I should not go down to the pit," is rendered: —

> "Doomed in the depths to dwell
> Of the Inquisition's Hell,
> At those fierce lions' hard arbitrement,
> Thou hast redeemèd me,
> Healed all my misery,
> For Thou didst see how deeply I repent"[5]

Another well-known poet, whose work similarly echoes his sufferings, was Daniel Israel Lopez Laguna. Born in Portugal in the second half of the seventeenth century, he was taken while still in his youth to France, where he lived at Peyrehorade. Subsequently, he returned to the Peninsula, in order to study at some Spanish university. Like Abenatar, he fell under the suspicions of the Inquisition, and was imprisoned for a considerable time. On his release, he settled in Jamaica, where he publicly professed Judaism. His life-work was a translation of the Psalms of David into Spanish, in a variety of metrical forms. This he had planned while in prison, and it occupied twenty-three years of his life. It was printed in London in 1720, under the title *Espejo Fiel de Vidas* ("Faithful Mirror of Life"), at the expense of the affluent Mordecai Nuñes de Almeida. A score of local litterateurs of either sex wrote commendatory verses, in Hebrew, Latin, Spanish, or Portuguese, and even English, which are prefaced to the work and demonstrate the vitality of local intellectual life. Like Abenatar's version, this is replete with current allusions. Thus Psalm 10.2 ("The wicked in his pride doth persecute the poor") becomes: —

> "The wicked prosper: and their terrors fall
> Upon the just, arraignèd in the Hall
> Of that sad Court, which dastards 'Holy' call."

David Nieto, the erudite Rabbi of London, in his masterly polemic on behalf of Jewish tradition, the *Matteh Dan* (which he published in both Hebrew and Spanish), goes out of his way to include the following reference to contemporary conditions (Book IV, § 164):—

"... Come and see the advantage enjoyed by the Saint who renders up his soul for the sanctification of the Divine Name, serving God with all his soul —'even though He takes away his soul': and, although he may suffer terrible tortures at his death, he yet accepts them with joy and contentment ... Thus, at the present day, is the case with our brethren and kinsfolk in Spain and Portugal. For they know that, besides receiving thereby pardon for their sins, their souls are left pure like those of angels and of seraphs, and they will enjoy perpetually infinite good and rejoicing ... Can this be called Evil, and Death? or Good, and Life?"

There was on the other hand nothing essentially Jewish, or even essentially religious, about some of the publications which appeared in the centers of the Marrano Diaspora, except as regards the public to which they catered. Frequently, complimentary verses appeared in honor of some political celebrity or some European potentate, in whom Jewish sympathies were entirely lacking. Solomon Usque (Salusque Lusitano), who lived in Italy in the second half of the sixteenth century, a kinsman of the author of the *Consolaçam ás Tribulaçoẽs de Israel*, translated Petrarch into polished Spanish verse and wrote a play based upon the story of Esther as well as Italian poetry. One of the Meldola family published a Portuguese grammar and book of commercial correspondence. As late as 1816, a Portuguese reading book was issued for the use of the school of the Amsterdam community. In 1726, a collection of Spanish comedies, mainly on biblical subjects but in barely a single case by a Jewish author, was published at Amsterdam, being dedicated to Don Manuel Ximenes, Baron de Belmonte. Similarly, in 1688, a volume of old Spanish *romances* or ballads saw the light in the same place. The oldest Jewish newspaper on record is the *Gazeta de Amsterdam*, which appeared from 1675 to 1690 in Spanish for the benefit of the refugees in the Low Countries, though news of Jewish interest was conspicuous in it by its absence. It is impossible to give any account of the innumerable medical works by Marrano physicians which appeared throughout this period (largely in Latin, but occasionally in Spanish), some of which became standard works of reference.

Besides the works published by the Marranos after their return to Judaism, mainly in northern Europe, there were a few which lay on the border-line, being written in exile subsequent to their escape from the Peninsula, though before formal reversion to their ancestral faith. Many of these indicated the state of mind

in which they were written by their choice of subject.
Thus João (Moses) Pinto Delgado, the leader of the
crypto-Jewish community at Rouen, issued in that city
in 1627 an exquisite poetical version of the books of
Esther, Ruth, and Lamentations, dedicated to the Cardinal Richelieu but showing clear indications of the
religious tendencies of the author. Similarly, Miguel de
Silveyra, an encyclopedic scholar, and relative of Thomas
de Pinedo, gave scant indication of his inclination to
Judaism save in his somewhat ambiguous poem *The
Maccabee*, published at Naples in 1638. Many of the
works of the famous playwright, Antonio Enriquez
Gomez (Enrique Enriquez de Paz), were printed at
Rouen and elsewhere after he had left Spain: among
them, an epic on Samson (Rouen, 1656) is worthy of
mention. His son, Diego Enriquez Basurto, published in
the same place in 1649 a poem based upon the book of
Job, which he dedicated to the Queen Mother.[6]

The Poet Laureate of the Amsterdam community was
Miguel, or Daniel Levi, de Barrios. His career, apart
from his writings, deserves a moment's attention. He
was born about 1625 at Montilla in Spain of Portuguese
parents who had emigrated in order to avoid the persecutions of the Inquisition. Ultimately, the whole family
left the Peninsula — the parents for Algiers, and the son
for Italy. Here he resided successively at Nice and at
Leghorn, where an aunt persuaded him to declare his
allegiance to Judaism. Shortly after, he married his kinswoman, Deborah Vaez. In 1660, the young couple joined
the colonizing expedition to America which sailed from
Leghorn on July 20. Their sufferings during the journey
through lack of drinking-water have been eloquently

described by the poet in one of his works. Shortly after his arrival at Tobago, his young wife died. Barrios, broken-hearted, returned to Europe. He now seems to have concealed the fact of his recent conversion. Going to Brussels, he entered the Spanish service, and rose to the rank of Captain. He had ample opportunity to indulge his poetical gifts. He wrote several comedies, and verses galore, dedicated to any person of eminence with whom he might have been brought into contact. To this period belongs his *Flor de Apolo* (Brussels, 1663) and his *Coro de las Musas* (Brussels, 1672) — a series of poems in honor of the principal cities and princes of Europe, preceded by a panegyric of Charles II of England. During all this time, his Jewish interests do not seem to have been marked, though he paid periodic visits to Amsterdam, where he married his second wife and where his son Simon (subsequently to be distinguished likewise as a poet) was born. He was however profoundly influenced by the mystical tendencies set loose as a result of the activities of the impostor, Sabbatai Zevi. In 1674 he left the Spanish service and settled at Amsterdam. For a time, he seems to have become mentally unbalanced, confidently expecting the coming of the Messiah on the approaching New Year's Day, and submitting himself to fantastic austerities to promote that happy consummation. After his disillusionment, he continued to live in Holland, earning a scanty living by writing eulogistic verses on all of the communal magnates. Besides his major works, he published a very considerable number of smaller effusions. Hardly a single death or marriage took place in any of the more important families that was not either celebrated or deplored by his facile pen, which was suitably, if not always adequately, rewarded. He described, in prose and in verse, the glories of the Amsterdam community — its academies, its institutions, its charities, its scholars, its litterateurs. He directed three Epistles to the Holy Congregation of London. He composed a Royal History of Great Britain — in the same year, unfortunately for the author, as the Glorious Revolution which drove out the Stuarts, for whom it was intended. He celebrated Inquisitional victims in pathetic verses. And, when he died, lines from his own pen marked the spot where he was laid to rest.

Apart from De Barrios, the army provided a surprisingly large quota of authors. Nicolas de Oliver y Fullana was a native of Majorca, of considerable erudition, who had embraced a military career. He wrote in three languages, was a competent poetaster, interested himself largely in cosmographical works, and rose to the rank of Sergeant Major in Catalonia. Ultimately he was transferred to Flanders, rising to the rank of Colonel and serving with distinction in the wars against France. At this period, he declared himself a Jew and was circumcised, assuming the name of Daniel Judah; and he married as his second wife the gifted Marrano poetess, Isabella de Correa. He continued his scientific interests, collaborated in editing one of the great atlases of the period, and was appointed Cosmographer Royal by the King of Spain. At one time, another distinguished Marrano acted as his adjutant; this was Captain Joseph Semah Arias, who translated Josephus' *Contra Apionem* into Spanish and published it under the auspices of the Jewish community. Captain Moses Cohen Peixotto, who had distinguished himself in the wars in Brazil, was among the poets who wrote elegies in honor of the martyrdom of Abraham Nuñez Bernal.

The breadth of the literature of the Marranos, and the versatility of the environment in which it flourished, is illustrated by nothing so well as by the career and the writings of Joseph Penso de la Vega. His father, Isaac Penso Felix, a native of Espejo, was arrested by the Inquisition early in the second half of the seventeenth century. While in prison, in danger of his life, he made a vow that, if he escaped, he would embrace Judaism openly within one year. After much suffering, he was released. He took the first opportunity to flee to Antwerp, whence he made his way to Amsterdam. On the day of his arrival on the free soil of Holland, at Middleburg, he was received into the Abrahamic covenant. His wife, Esther de la Vega, had accompanied him in his flight, together with other members of the family. Their eldest son, Joseph Penso de la Vega, who had been born at Espejo in 1650, displayed extraordinary literary ability. At the age of seventeen, he composed a play, *Assire ha-Tikvah*, which is among the earliest specimens of the Hebrew drama. He was a prominent member of the various literary academies of the time, and a favorite speaker at their meetings. He was interested in politics, composing more than two hundred epistles addressed to various statesmen all over Europe. In his *Triumphos del Aguila*, he celebrated the relief of Vienna by John Sobieski. In his *Retrato de la Prudencia*, he eulogized the wisdom and valor displayed by William of Orange in mounting the throne of England. His *Rumbos Peligrosos* are reckoned by critics among the finest examples of the Spanish short story of the period. Particularly outstanding is his *Confusion de Confusiones*, published at Amsterdam in 1688. This is the first work to treat of the business and methods of the Stock Exchange in all its branches, and has been characterized as being still, to the present day, the best description, both in form and substance, of dealings in stocks and shares. Joseph Penso de la Vega died in 1692, when he was little more than forty years of age. The measure of the loss caused to Spanish literature by his forced expatriation is not easily to be estimated.

Intellectual life in the Marrano Diaspora was centered to some extent about the literary academies, so characteristic of the period, which flourished in Holland and in Italy as they did on their native soil of Spain. In these, cultured men and women came together to read and to discuss their poetical effusions; and the stranger might have imagined himself transported back into the most polished literary circles of Madrid. The first of these societies, the Academy of the Thirsty, or *Academia de los Sitibundos*, was founded by the Baron Manuel de Belmonte in 1676. Among its members were the poetesses Isabella Enriquez and Isabella (Rebecca) Correa — the translator of Guarini's *Pastor Fido* into Spanish, and wife of the gallant historian, Nicolas de Oliver y Fullana. One of the Arbiters was Doctor Isaac de Rocamora, the former Dominican friar; another was Isaac Gomez de Sossa, a distinguished poet both in Latin and in Spanish, whose father, Abraham Gomez de Sossa, had been body-physician to the Infant Ferdinand, Governor of the Low Countries. This association was outdone in brilliance as well as in fame by the *Academia de los Floridos*, founded in 1685, similarly under Belmonte's inspiration. Its President was that doughty polemist, Isaac Orobio de Castro; the *mantenedores*, or Champions of the Poetic Art, included the versatile Daniel Levi de Barrios and Don Manuel de Lara, of whom it was recounted that he brought more than three hundred souls back to Judaism; the Secretary was the poet and economist, Joseph Penso de la Vega, of whom we have just spoken; Moses Orobio de Castro, the son of the President, and an illustrious physician like him, was the Advocate; while among the members were men of eminence in every walk of life, such as Geronimo Nuñes da Costa, Portuguese representative in Holland; Joseph Jesurun Lobo, the Spanish Consul; Joseph Israel Alvarez, who enjoyed some reputation as an historian; and Moses Machado, the Purveyor-General to the Dutch forces, to whom William III wrote in appreciation of his services, that he had saved the State, "*Vous avez sauvé l'état.*" Another similar institution, named *Academia de los Sitibundos*, likewise existed contemporaneously at Leghorn, being founded by Joseph Penso de la Vega during his residence in that city, in imitation of the more famous body at Amsterdam. Other informal groups no doubt existed elsewhere. The "Discourses" delivered before these bodies were occasionally published, to the inevitable accompaniment of laudatory sonnets.

By now, the courtly environment in which this transplanted culture flourished with such extraordinary vigor has entirely decayed. A whole literature consisting of many hundreds of volumes, however, remains; eagerly sought after by bibliophiles, and a standing record of the damage which a suicidal intolerance inflicted upon the intellectual life of the Iberian Peninsula.

CHAPTER XIV

THE DECLINE OF THE INQUISITION

In the middle of the seventeenth century, both in Spain and in Portugal, the Inquisition appeared to be at the height of its power. It was one of the wealthiest and most influential corporations in the land. The tribunals were housed in magnificent palaces, constructed with the wealth that a long series of confiscations had amassed. Ceremonious autos-da-fè were held at frequent intervals in all the principal cities of the Peninsula, vying with bull-fights in popularity, and frequently graced by the presence of royalty. For all that, it is obvious in retrospect that the first traces of decline were already to be discerned. If the autos had gained in pomp, they had lost ground as far as numbers were concerned. The importance of the Judaizers was appreciably diminished. In Spain, as we have seen, Moslems had also been subject to the Holy Office from 1525; and in the subsequent period an increasing number of Protestants and other heretics fell under its scope. The native Marrano tradition had by now almost entirely died out, so that the main attention for some time past had been devoted to immigrants from Portugal. Here, too, conditions had been altering. As in Spain, though to a minor degree, the exclusive preoccupation of the Holy Office with Judaizers had somewhat lessened in the course of time. The force of Marranism had been weakening — partly owing to ignorance, partly to assimilation, and partly

339

to the protracted emigration which had drained the country of its ablest brains.

The restoration of the House of Braganza, in which the New Christians had participated to a notable extent, marked the beginning of the decline of the Inquisition, which had attained its greatest influence under Spanish rule. The new King, João IV, was reported (probably unfoundedly) to be willing to allow freedom of conscience in the country, and certainly attempted to modify the rigor of the Inquisitional procedure. He was forced to forego this owing to the impossibility of obtaining confirmation from Rome; but he was able for a short time to suspend the sequestration of the property of persons accused. Meanwhile, the Inquisition had continued its activity with apparently unabated zeal; and, as a matter of policy, the King and his family had attended a series of autos held at Lisbon, in 1642 and 1645. In 1652 the poet-statesman, Manuel Fernandez Villareal, was relaxed, notwithstanding the favor which he enjoyed at Court. On June 23, 1663, an auto with one hundred and forty-two penitents was held at Evora, in spite or perhaps because of the fact that Don John of Austria was occupying the city with a hostile Spanish force. From 1651 to 1673, in the three tribunals of the kingdom, no fewer than 184 persons were relaxed in person and 59 in effigy, while 4793 were penanced.

In 1663, Duarte da Silva, who had been reconciled eleven years earlier, brought forward from his refuge in London proposals for the amelioration of the position of the New Christians (including, it was reported, though with obvious exaggeration, the establishment of an open synagogue) in return for which he promised the government considerable subsidies in men and ships. Dom Francisco de Mello, the eminent Portuguese statesman and man of letters (himself apparently of Marrano birth), threw the weight of his influence into the scales in favor of these concessions. They were viewed sympathetically by the Court; and the refugees, in London and elsewhere, were looking forward eagerly to hearing the good tidings of the release of their imprisoned kinsmen. Before long the rumor reached the ears of the Pope, who protested vigorously, and with complete success. On the death of João IV, in 1656, the Inquisition set about collecting the arrears of confiscations of which it had been deprived during the last half-dozen years. Within the next quarter of a century, the total reached twenty-five millions, of which not more than one-fiftieth found its way to the royal treasury. In 1671, a pyx with a consecrated host was stolen from the church of Orivellas in Lisbon. A great commotion was caused throughout the country. The Court put on mourning. An edict was actually signed banishing all New Christians (whose guilt was naturally assumed) from the country. Before this could be put into execution a common thief was arrested near Coimbra, with the stolen article in his possession. Fortunately, no Jewish blood was traceable in his veins; and, though he was burned, the New Christians were saved.

By this time, a ray of hope had burst through the clouds. An interregnum in the office of Grand Inquisitor from 1653 to 1672, though it did not bring about any decrease in the activity of the Tribunal, sensibly lessened its authority. Meanwhile, arms had been taken up on behalf of the New Christians by no less a person than Antonio Vieira, the distinguished Jesuit, who had earned

the name of the Apostle of Brazil. He had urged João IV
to abolish confiscations and to remove the differences
which still obtained between New and Old Christians.
His freedom of opinion brought upon him the enmity
of the Inquisition. After a three years' imprisonment
(1665–1667), his writings were condemned, and he was
formally penanced. His experience of the horrors of the
Holy Office increased his sympathy for the oppressed.
He transferred himself to Rome, where, at the citadel of
Christianity, he assailed the Portuguese Inquisition as an
unholy tribunal, inspired more by greed than by piety,
condemning the innocent as frequently as the guilty,
and inimical to all the best interests of Christianity.

The Society of Jesus, resenting the treatment which
one of the most distinguished of its members had received, espoused his cause. Heartened by the turn which
events were taking, the New Christians appealed to the
Crown for certain definite reforms, including the free
pardon of those persons then under trial and the modifi-
cation of the Inquisitional procedure by the adoption of
the more humane forms customary in Rome. In return
for these concessions, moderate though they appeared,
they offered to pay annually 20,000 *cruzados*, to maintain
4,000 troops in India, and to send out each year 1200
reinforcements, with an additional 300 in time of war.
The Inquisition protested strenuously against the consideration of this appeal. Nevertheless, it was supported
by many of the greatest magnates of the kingdom,
including the faculty of the University of Coimbra and
the Archbishop of Lisbon himself. It was accordingly
approved, and forwarded to Rome for authorization.
Here, Francisco de Azevedo, the representative of the

New Christians, prepared in conjunction with Vieira a scathing indictment, from which it appeared that the Portuguese Inquisition was nothing but an instrument of oppression, thriving upon blackmail, and preying upon any person of New Christian blood. The latter, it was alleged, were in truth nearly all fervent Catholics, who were either put to death as *negativos* for denying Judaism or reconciled as a result of confessing it falsely. After a prolonged struggle, the New Christians gained the day. On October 3, 1674, Pope Clement X suspended the action of the Portuguese tribunals, evoking all outstanding cases to Rome. Since the Inquisitors refused coöperation in the subsequent inquiry, on the ground that it would reveal the secrets of procedure, an interdict was pronounced upon them; and ultimately, on May 27, 1679, they were suspended from office.

The respite was only momentary. On August 22, 1681, the suspension was removed, after a few unimportant reforms had been ordered. The resumption of activity in Portugal was celebrated by triumphant processions and gala illuminations. In January of the following year, the first auto-da-fè since the Interdict was held at Coimbra. It was outdone a few months later at Lisbon, where, on May 10, four persons were burned — three of them alive, as impenitent. The latter included an advocate of Aviz, Miguel Henriques (Isaac) da Fonseca, who insisted that he should be called Misael Hisneque de Fungoça; Antonio de Aguiar, alias Aaron Cohen Faya, of Lamunilla near Madrid; and Gaspar (Abraham) Lopez Pereira, who were mourned by the litterateurs of Amsterdam as martyrs. All told, nearly three hundred persons appeared in the autos at Lisbon,

Evora, and Coimbra at this period. The resumption of
activity on the part of the last-named tribunal reached
its climax in the awful holocaust of November 25, 1696,
when fourteen men and women were relaxed in person
and five in effigy. The revival was signalized by an
order of September 1683, banishing from the realm,
within the impossible period of two months, all persons
who had been reconciled for Judaizing. They were,
however, to leave behind them all children up to seven
years old until it was proved that they were living the
lives of true Christians in their new homes. It was in
part to this measure, which was suspended only on the
outbreak of war with France in 1704, that the rapid
increase in the communities of the Marrano Diaspora
about this time was due.[1]

Notwithstanding superficial appearances, the power of
the Inquisition was not so great as it had previously
been. The number of its victims from year to year,
though still appalling, shows eloquently the change that
had come about. During the period 1651–1673, 184
persons had been burned in person by the three tribunals
of the country, while 59 had been relaxed in effigy and
4793 had been penanced. From 1682 to 1700, despite
the accumulations of the period of the interdict, only 59
suffered in person and 61 in effigy, while 1351 were
penanced. The yearly average was thus decreased by
two-thirds. During the War of Spanish Succession, there
seems to have been a recrudescence of violence, particularly at Lisbon — due, no doubt, to the prevalence
of war-time passions. The numbers that appeared were
reminiscent of the last century, the total rising on one
occasion, in September 1706, to as many as 111, and on

June 9, 1713, to 138. In spite of this, over the whole
period from 1701 to 1720 there was a further decrease
in the number of capital punishments, only 37 being
relaxed in person and 26 in effigy. Thus, in the course
of half a century, the average had gone down from more
than eight each year to less than two. The number of
penanced in the same period rose to 2126, indicating that
the change was in the temperament of the Inquisition,
not in the strength of crypto-Judaism. At Evora, for
many years after 1686, no relaxations in person took
place at all; while in Coimbra, the last burnings were
in 1718.

Subsequently, there was a recrudescence of activity,
and the figures again rose; but they never reached the
ghastly totals of the first half of the previous century.
Over a period of little more than forty years after 1721,
139 individuals were relaxed in person. Thus the yearly
average of victims was nearly quadrupled as compared
with the first two decades of the century, although the
total number of penitents was proportionately rather
less. The number of women who were punished was
surprisingly high, often far exceeding that of the men.[2]
But, as was subsequently to appear, this was a last
despairing outburst of ferocity, which preceded final
quiescence. By this time the offence of Judaizing had
apparently been almost crushed in the greater towns.
The center of activity was now the country districts,
where the New Christians were relatively more numerous
and where, it may be presumed, secrecy was more easy
to maintain. The vast proportion came from the northern
provinces of Beira and Tras-os-Montes, especially from
the towns of Covilhã, Fundão, Idanha, Guarda, Lamego,

and Braganza. There was a minor center farther south in the northern part of Alentejo. In this region, it was said, whole towns were deserted and prosperous industries destroyed by reason of the activities of the Holy Office. It was a systematic war of extermination. In 1718, over fifty natives of Braganza appeared at a single auto at Coimbra; and in succeeding years that city continued to provide nine-tenths of the total number of victims to the northern tribunal. In all, the names of no less than 805 persons from the city, and nearly 2000 from the district, figure in the records of those punished by the Holy Office; yet the lists are by no means complete. At an auto held on May 25, 1737, at Lisbon (whither at this period it became customary to send persons condemned by the other tribunals for punishment) all of the twelve persons who were relaxed, except one woman, were from Celorico and Lamego. Next, it was the turn of the district of Aviz; and, in 1744 and the following year, eight out of the ten persons burned were from that region. On October 16, 1746, the majority of those who appeared came from the same part of the country; all of the six persons relaxed — three in person and three in effigy — being natives of Beira or the northern part of Alentejo. However, from the middle of the century, the numbers decreased with the utmost rapidity. It almost seemed as though the intensification of the war against the Marranos had succeeded in its object, its adherents being at last exterminated.[3]

The reaction against the Inquisition, outside the Peninsula, had meanwhile been growing. The Protestants of northern Europe, whose compatriots and sympathizers were subject to its attentions fully as much as the Jews,

regarded it as the instrument of anti-Christ. Philosophical France thought of it with horror. Antagonistic books
and pamphlets poured from the press in a never-ending
stream. As early as the middle of the sixteenth century,
works began to appear in England and elsewhere, giving
details of the Protestant martyrdoms in Spain. In 1688,
there appeared in Paris Dellon's *Relation de l'Inquisition
de Goa*, giving an account of his protracted sufferings.
Contemporaneously, the Dutchman, Philip van Limborch, published his bitterly antagonistic history of the
Inquisition. Both of these books were widely translated
and exercised great influence among thinking persons in
all countries. A refugee Spaniard, Reginaldo Gonsalves
Montano, wrote a whole series of anti-Inquisitional works.
Dr. Michael Geddes, a Scottish divine, took up the
cudgels in London, where he published a couple of striking tracts laying bare the iniquity of the system.[4] Bayle,
Montesquieu, Voltaire, and Sterne joined in the fray, in
caustic comments.

The Jews were not behindhand. On September 6,
1705, a solemn auto-da-fè at which sixty-six penitents
figured was held on the great square of the Rocio at
Lisbon. The sermon was preached by Diogo da Anun-
ciação Justiniano, Archbishop of Cranganor, in India.
He opened it with a brutal series of insults directed
against the poor victims: —"Miserable relics of Judaism!
Unhappy fragments of the synagogue! Last remains of
Judea! Scandal of the Catholics and detestable objects
of scorn even to the Jews themselves!... You are the
detestable objects of scorn to the Jews, for you are so
ignorant that you cannot even observe the very law
under which you live." This savage address was naturally

deemed worthy of perpetuation in print. A copy reached
the hands of David Nieto—himself of Marrano descent—
who was then rabbi of the congregation established
by the refugees in London. He replied to it in a vigorous
but dignified pamphlet, in Portuguese, in which he
exposed simultaneously both the ignorance and the
brutality of the Archbishop. This was published anony-
mously in 1709 with the imprint Turin, but probably at
London. So sure was the author of his ground that he
had the courage, unusual in a controversialist, of reissuing
with his pamphlet the sermon to which it was intended
as a reply. A similar work, in Spanish, appeared some
years later (probably in 1722 or 1723), purporting to be
printed in Villa Franca ("The City of Freedom," obviously London) by Carlos Vero ("Charles Truth").[5] In
the meantime, in 1722, he followed up this initial encounter by publishing, similarly in "Villa Franca," the
Recondite Notices of the Inquisitions of Spain and Portugal,
in two parts, Spanish and Portuguese. This work comprised the memoranda prepared by Antonio Vieira, for
his onslaught upon the institution half a century before,
which the Marranos then settled in London had already
prepared for publication.[6] The abuses of the system
were once more laid bare in a damning fashion. In
1750, the work appeared again in Venice under a slightly
different title, this time under Vieira's own name. All
this adroit propaganda assisted in undermining the
position of the Holy Office; and it was inevitable that
ultimately repercussions should reach those parts of
southern Europe where it still held undisputed sway.

The spirit of humanity abroad in Europe at last began
to penetrate into the Peninsula, though by very slow

degrees. Antonio Ribeiro Sanchez, the eminent Marrano physician, who had become reconciled to Catholicism, submitted a striking memorandum suggesting in the interest of the State the abolition of distinctions between Old and New Christians and the restriction of the power of the Inquisition. Don Luiz da Cunha, the famous diplomat, went even further, suggesting that Jewish worship should be tolerated in the country. Alexandre de Guzmão, another personage of importance at the Court of João V, poured ridicule on the pretensions of certain families to complete purity of blood, pointing out that over a period of centuries the total number of ancestors of any person ran into hundreds, concerning the antecedents of all of whom it was impossible to be absolutely sure. Finally, this point of view was adopted by the reforming statesman, Sebastian Joseph de Carvalho e Mello, Marquis of Pombal, under whose competent rule Portugal was transformed from a medieval into a modern state.

The year of his accession to power, 1751, saw the first step, it being forbidden for any auto-da-fè to be held without the permission of the civil authorities, by whom all sentences were henceforth to be confirmed. Thus, the subordination of the Inquisition to the state was accentuated. This did not by any means put an immediate end to activity. In Lisbon, on September 24, 1752, 30 men and 27 women appeared, all but twelve for Judaizing. Besides these, three — all *negativos* — were condemned to relaxation in person, and one in effigy. All told, eighteen victims were relaxed in the first ten years of the enlightened new regime — an eloquent testimony to the hold which the Holy Office had established upon the country. After the great Earthquake of 1755, which laid the palace of the Inquisition in ruins, and according to legend facilitated the escape of many prisoners, no further Judaizers suffered in Lisbon. In Evora, on the other hand, there was a sudden resumption, after a complete cessation which had lasted since 1686. In four successive autos from the year 1756 to 1760, eight New Christians were relaxed there. In the year following the last of these, on September 20, 1761, the inoffensive Jesuit father, Gabriel Malagrida, was burned at Lisbon, for having dared to assert that the recent earthquake was a punishment from heaven for the sins of the country. He was the last of the many hundreds of persons to suffer capitally at the hands of the Portuguese Inquisition, and one of the comparatively few during the whole series whose crime was not that of Judaizing.[7]

The next move was against the old and by now ridiculous differentiation between Old and New Christians, which had been introduced by Manoel I in direct contravention of his promise at the time of the General Conversion, and had caused untold suffering to those of Jewish blood ever since. Antonio Ribeiro Sanches, who was himself in this category, has left a graphic description of the slights and disabilities which a child of New Christian parentage had to face at every stage of his life, from his school-days upwards. It was now an antiquated as well as a pernicious system. Pombal dealt with it with characteristic vigor. On May 2, 1768, he ordered the destruction of all registers containing the names of the New Christian families. Next, he gave instructions to the heads of all the so-called "puritan" houses (who had hitherto prided themselves on contracting no outside alliances) that within four months they must arrange matches for all their daughters of marriageable age with members of families hitherto excluded from their circle, as being contaminated with Jewish blood. This order, worthy of any Oriental despot, and communicated in private so as to avoid ridicule abroad, was to be enforced by depriving of all their dignities those who refused compliance. Finally, on May 23, 1773, all legal distinctions between Old and New Christians were removed. Thus, Marranism was officially abolished in Portugal; and the seal was set on the long process of assimilation which the Forced Conversion of nearly three hundred years before had begun.[8]

For the past few years, the Inquisition had been almost entirely inactive, Pombal having ensured its subservience by appointing his own brother to preside over it as Grand Inquisitor. It was now made powerless. On April 8, 1768, it was deprived of the power of censorship. On November 15, 1771, orders were given forbidding the celebration of autos-da-fè in public and the printing of *listas* of those who figured in them. Thus it was clearly indicated that, in the eyes of the government, this was entirely an ecclesiastical concern, which should not be allowed to interfere with the civil life of the country. Three years later, in 1774, there was issued a new code, or *Regimento*, for the Inquisition. This removed the worst of the old abuses, now naively attributed to the machinations of the Jesuits, and received the royal approval on September 21, 1774. (The last public auto-da-fè, with its invariable accompaniment of New Christian penitents, had been held on October 27, 1765.)[9] In succeeding years, the various tribunals continued to hold in private occasional autos, at which minor punishments were inflicted for technical offences, though the populace was deprived of the pleasure of participation. (The last recorded ceremony of the sort was in 1778.) Henceforth the dreaded Inquisition of Portugal was almost powerless. The three long centuries of martyrdom were ended.

In Spain, meanwhile, the first blow had been dealt at the power of the Inquisition at the beginning of the eighteenth century, when Philip V, the first king of the House of Bourbon, true to his French upbringing, had refused to grace with his presence an auto arranged (in accordance with precedent) to celebrate his accession. Under less august auspices, similar ceremonies continued with little intermission. As far as Judaism was concerned, indeed, it appeared for the moment as though the victory had been won. The native New Christians had long since been assimilated or else exterminated; and it seemed that the menace offered to orthodoxy by the Portuguese immigrants had finally been overcome. There was however to be one final outburst. At Madrid, a secret synagogue was discovered where for some years twenty families had been accustomed to meet for service, under the auspices of a spiritual guide whose name had been sent to Leghorn for confirmation. Five of those implicated in the affair were relaxed in an auto on April 7, 1720. This discovery aroused the other tribunals to renewed activity. There was a general recrudescence of persecution throughout the country.[10] Within the short period 1721–1727, there were held at least 64 autos. Of the 868 cases dealt with in these, no less than 820 were for Judaizing; 75 persons being relaxed in person and 74 in effigy.

The climax was reached in 1722–3, after which date there was a gradual diminution. At Cordova, autos were held in 1728, 1730, and 1731, 26 cases of Judaizing being punished in them; but thereafter there was none for a period of fourteen years. At Toledo, there was an intermission from 1726 to 1738 when fourteen cases were taken into consideration; but afterwards, down to the close of the series in 1794, there was only one more.[11] At Valladolid, a Judaizer was relaxed in person in 1745, and six in effigy, together with the bones of one dead woman, at Llerena, in 1752. These are the last recorded cases of the sort. Owing perhaps to the suspension of immigration from Portugal, crypto-Judaism in Spain seems suddenly to have collapsed. Out of a total of 4,000 cases tried by all of the tribunals of the country from 1780 to 1820, only sixteen were for Judaism. Of these, ten were in connection with foreign Jews who had been found in the kingdom without authorization, four were discovered to be groundless, and only two were really serious. In the Spanish colonies, similarly, cases concerned with Judaizers had been rare since the beginning of the century.

Thus, in its last days, the connection between the Spanish Inquisition and the Marranos was slight. Nevertheless, it continued its career, with undiminished authority though with no more than a fraction of its old vitality, down to the period of the Napoleonic wars — long after the sister-tribunal of Portugal had been rendered powerless. It was formally abolished by Joseph Bonaparte during his brief reign, in 1808, this action being confirmed after his fall by the liberal Cortes of 1813. The reactionary Ferdinand VII, however, reinstated it in all its previous power and authority by a decree of July 21, 1814. Its activity during the succeeding period was not great and it was abolished again during the constitutional revolution by a royal edict of March 9, 1820. With the counter-revolutionary movement of 1825, its powers automatically revived. As late as July 26, 1826, a Deist schoolmaster (not a Jew, as is commonly stated) was garroted at Valencia by an episcopal *junta de fé*. He was the last victim of the Inquisition in the Peninsula; for, on July 15, 1834, the Queen Mother, Maria Christina, finally and definitely abolished the Inquisition and all its powers, direct or indirect. Thus, the career of blood which had lasted for three and a half centuries was closed.[12]

For some years more, the discrimination between the Old and New Christians survived in Spain, proof of *limpieza*, or purity of blood "from any admixture of Jew or Moor," being required for entry into certain professions. This gradually disappeared. The last stronghold was the Corps of Cadets, where it hung on tenaciously. At length, in 1860, the need for this qualification was abolished by the Cortes. Socially, the differentiation still to some extent survived;[13] and, in the Balearic Islands, the prejudice against the descendants of the local crypto-Jews, or *Chuetas*, remained extraordinarily virulent and effective. This survival was beyond the power of legislation to control. Officially, the record of the Marranos in the Peninsula was ended by that trivial decree of 1860, by which the efforts of the past five centuries were crowned and the descendants of the Jewish converts were admitted finally and without qualification into the body politic.

EPILOGUE

THE MARRANOS OF TODAY

HAD the present work been written fifty, or even ten, years earlier it would have finished at this point. For, at that time it seemed as though at last, after all its efforts, the Inquisition had completed its task in the eighteenth century, and that crypto-Judaism in the Peninsula had been stamped out. Nothing, or barely nothing, is heard of Judaizers, whether in Spain or in Portugal, from the period of the French Revolution onwards. The tide of emigration, to Amsterdam or to London, had dwindled. A fresh, native-born generation had grown up, ignorant of Spanish and of Portuguese, for whose benefit the vernacular of the country had to be admitted, with lingering regrets, as the official language of the communities of the Marrano Diaspora. Not that the flow had altogether ceased. In the Lisbon auto of 1746, two boatmen had been punished for assisting fugitives to leave the realm. The great Earthquake of 1755 had caused great searchings of heart amongst the New Christians, numbers of whom had in consequence fled. Thus the parents of Abraham Furtado (the politician of the revolutionary era in France, a close friend of the Girondins and a leading figure in the Napoleonic *Sanhedrin*) had sought refuge in London in consequence of a vow which they had made when their lives seemed to be in danger. Simultaneously, quite a number of persons are said to have emigrated to America, joining the community of Newport, Rhode Island. As late as 1795, many members of the ancient Spanish and Portuguese congregation in London, in their Aliens Certificates, gave flight from the persecutions of the Inquisition as the reason for their coming to England; and one, Isaac Penha of Lisbon, added the tragic detail that his mother had been burned alive for Judaism. To Bordeaux, there had been a constant though decreasing influx during the whole of the eighteenth century. The last cases on record are those of Isaac Lopes Simões, of Lisbon, and David Pereira, of Lamego, aged 21 and 16 respectively, who were received into the Abrahamic Covenant there in 1791. There were the latest instances of the sort of whom any mention survived. Crypto-Judaism in the Peninsula seemed to be at an end. Many reasons were put forward to explain the phenomenon. It was generally assumed that persecution, after so many centuries, had at last succeeded in completing its work, or that the constant emigration had drained the country of the few who had been able to resist persecution on the one hand and assimilation on the other. Moralists took the phenomenon as proof that toleration could be more fatal than oppression, suggesting that the Marranos had required persecution as a condition of their existence, and that with its suspension they had melted away into nothingness.

Occasionally, suggestive pieces of information penetrated to the outside world. When the French invaded Portugal in 1807, it was said, they were hailed by twenty thousand "Jews;" and, in the following year, when war feeling was at its height, the cry "Death to the Jews and the Jacobins" was common in the pulpits of the northern provinces. A certain Jewish soldier who had fought under Napoleon in the Peninsula War, and was made prisoner near Gerona, used to recount how he was unexpectedly released by an innkeeper of Jewish descent, who happened to hear him recite the *Shema'*. When, after the resettlement of the Jews in Lisbon, a synagogue was first established, early in the nineteenth century, it is reported that descendants of the New Christians, many of them belonging to noble families, were present at its opening. A certain English Jew, who died in the United States in 1890, and had lived at Lisbon for a short time in his youth, left on record an interesting account of the condition of the Marranos in Portugal in the second decade of the nineteenth century: —

"The old families of private Jews, who outwardly professed Catholicism, but secretly kept to the fundamental belief of Judaism, received their co-religionists with open arms, aiding the poor traders as brethren . . . I have vividly remembered two gentlemen with decorated orders coming one Saturday evening to the *Minyan* held in the house of Simon Cohen and throw themselves down before the ark, containing the scrolls of the law, and on their knees fervently praying. They had come to Lisbon from the Tras-os-Montes, and there in Lisbon wished to know, when the *kippur* was held, and returned to the country, bearers of the date for the year 1819.

"Although (he continues) the Jews were allowed to reside freely in Portugal, the prejudices and laws against apostates prevented private Jews and their families, who had always outwardly professed Christianity, from being publicly known as Jews. A fashionable hatter in Lisbon was called 'Brandon the Jew,' although outwardly ostentatiously a Christian. On Sunday morning I have seen him go in Portuguese fashion with his family to mass — first himself, then his wife, daughters and servant girls, one after the other in line . . .

"My departed friend, Samuel the Pole, who lived with me for some time, was invited to spend the summer months in the country with private Jewish families, one of whom was a Justice of the Peace, and they assured Samuel that they never divulged to their children the secret of their religion until they had attained the age of reason. Many houses, including domestics, were Jewish, and in some districts the Jewish families were numerous, and a young man would often become a monk, so that he might pretend to be the confessor to families in the circuit . . . An old friend, named Periera, used to tell me that from a mixed marriage all trace of his being descended from a Jewish family were lost . . . and he was not at all a Catholic in belief, but was liable like all Catholics to fine or imprisonment, which was the consequence if any Portuguese did not annually show that he had confessed at least once a year; so a well known monk for a *Crusado* (a Portuguese coin of gold or silver) gave certificates of confessions to such persons as Pereira."[1]

George Borrow, the imaginative purveyor of the Bible in Spain, gives an extraordinary account of personal encounter in 1835, during his visit to the Peninsula.

Having regard for the exuberant fancy of the author, this was universally regarded as a characteristic piece of romancing. There is perhaps more in it than was at one time thought; and it is worth while to cite it at length: —

> "There was something peculiarly strange about the figure: . . . I see him standing in the moonshine, staring me in the face with his deep calm eyes. At last he said —
>
> 'Are you then *one of us*?'
>
> . . . . .
>
> *Myself*: You say you are wealthy. In what does your wealth consist?
>
> *Abarbenel*: In gold and silver, and stones of price; for I have inherited all the hoards of my forefathers. The greater part is buried underground; indeed, I have never examined the tenth part of it. I have coins of silver and gold older than the times of Ferdinand the Accursed and Jezebel; I have also large sums employed in usury. We keep ourselves close, however, and pretend to be poor, miserably so; but, on certain occasions, at our festivals, when our gates are barred, and our savage dogs are let loose in the court, we eat our food off services such as the Queen of Spain cannot boast of, and wash our feet in ewers of silver, fashioned and wrought before the Americas were discovered, though our garments are at all times course, and our food for the most part of the plainest description . . .
>
> *Myself*: Are you known for what you are? Do the authorities molest you?

Abarbenel: People of course suspect me to be what I am; but as I conform outwardly in most respects to their ways, they do not interfere with me. True it is that sometimes, when I enter the church to hear the mass, they glare at me over the left shoulder, as much as to say —'What do you here?' And sometimes they cross themselves as I pass by; but as they go no further, I do not trouble myself on that account . . .

Myself: Do the priests interfere with you?

Abarbenel: They let me alone, especially in our own neighbourhood. Shortly after the death of my father one hot-headed individual endeavoured to do me an evil turn; but I soon requited him causing him to be imprisoned on a charge of blasphemy, and in prison he remained a long time, till he went mad and died.

Myself: Have you a head in Spain, in whom is vested the chief authority?

Abarbenel: Not exactly. There are, however, certain holy families who enjoy much consideration; my own is one of these — the chiefest, I may say My grandsire was a particularly holy man; and I have heard my father say, that one night an archbishop came to his house secretly, merely to have the satisfaction of kissing his head.

Myself: How can that be? What reverence could an archbishop entertain for one like yourself or your grandsire?

Abarbenel: More than you imagine. He was one of us, at least his father was, and he could never forget what he had learned with reverence in his infancy . . . he then returned to his diocese, where he shortly afterwards died, in much renown for sanctity.

Myself: What you say surprises me. Have you reason to suppose that many of you are to be found amongst the priesthood?

Abarbenel: Not to suppose, but to know it. There are many such as I amongst the priesthood, and not amongst the inferior priesthood either; some of the most learned and famed of them in Spain have been of us, or of our blood at least, and many of them at this day think as I do. There is one particular festival of the year at which four dignified ecclesiastics are sure to visit me; and then, when all is made close and secure, and the fitting ceremonies have been gone through, they sit down upon the floor and curse.

Myself: Are you numerous in the large towns?

Abarbenel: By no means; our places of abode are seldom the large towns; we prefer the villages and rarely enter the large towns but on business. Indeed, we are not a nùmerous people, and there are few provinces of Spain which contain more than twenty families. None of us are poor, and those among us who serve, do so more from choice than necessity, for by serving each other we acquire different trades. Not unfrequently the time of service is that of court-ship also, and the servants eventually marry the daughters of the house . . ."[2]

In spite of these and similar revelations, nothing reached the outside world which made it appear that any trace of the Marranos had survived beyond the first decades of the nineteenth century, at the latest. In 1867, Kayserling, the eminent historian, who made a life-long study of the subject, closed his classical monograph on the Jews in Portugal with a pathetic reference to the complete oblivion of Judaism among the descendants of the New Christians of former years. When about 1885 the Portuguese consul at Holyhead died, leaving instructions that he should be buried among Jews, it hardly occurred to contemporaries that this request should be associated with the romantic history which, officially, had ended a century before. An article published in a learned periodical, the *Jewish Quarterly Review* in 1903, records a few prayers and customs current amongst the Marranos, but not in such a way as to make it appear that anything survived beyond the bare recollection of Jewish descent, in some isolated cases, coupled with a few meaningless and moribund traditions. The *Jewish Encyclopedia*, which summed up the state of Jewish knowledge at the beginning of the present century, mentions casually the existence of Marranos at Covilhã, but without further details. Even the well-informed historian of the New Christians in Portugal, J. Lucio d'Azevedo, writing on the spot as recently as 1921, declared, judicially, that the heavy hand of Pombal had solved the problem of nearly three centuries. An eminent American anthropologist, in a work published in 1911, went so far as to indicate the psychological cause for the disappearance. "It is evident," he wrote, "that the so-called Crypto-Jews are the product of social conditions, having no ethnic basis. With a change in social conditions, especially as soon as they are no more persecuted by the majority around them, they cease to be peculiar and are lost in the multitude."[3]

In 1917, a Polish Jewish mining engineer established at Lisbon, M. Samuel Schwarz, was on a business visit to Belmonte, a somewhat inaccessible spot in the hill-country in the north of Portugal, not far from the Spanish frontier. One of the inhabitants, desirous of obtaining his patronage, warned him pointedly against having anything to do with one of his competitors. "It is enough for me to tell you," he said, "that the man is a *judeu* — a Jew." The information naturally stirred M. Schwarz, a passionate student of things Jewish, to further inquiries. The person indicated by his informant could not help him much; he had married an "Old" Christian, and was thus out of touch with his former brethren in faith. However, he did his best to introduce the inquirer to them. *"E dos nossos"*—"He is one of us," he whispered to them, confidentially. With some difficulty, M. Schwarz began to gain their confidence. They were dubious as to the stranger's claims. They had not heard of any Jews different from themselves. They had no knowledge of the greater Jewish community living outside the bounds of Portugal. Their conceptions were limited to an exiguous body in their own township and the immediate neighborhood, for whom secrecy was a primary condition of religious existence. The stranger moreover could not recite any of the traditional Portuguese prayers current amongst that and the sister communities. It was in vain that he tried to point out that the universal Jewish language of prayer was Hebrew, in which the Jews throughout the world carried on their devotions. They had not heard of the language, and doubted its existence. At last an old woman, whom the rest treated with particular deference, asked him sceptically to repeat some prayer in the tongue for which he claimed such sanctity. His choice was an obvious one.

He recited the Jewish confession of faith — the same which Isaac de Castro Tartas had on his lips when he perished at the stake: "Hear, O Israel! The Lord our God, the Lord is One." As he pronounced the name of God — *Adonai* — the woman covered her eyes with her hands — the traditional formality, intended to shut out all outside distractions during the recital of this verse. When he had finished, she turned to the bystanders. He is indeed a Jew," she said, authoritatively, "for he knows the name of *Adonai.*" Thus this solitary survival of the old Hebrew tongue, which had been preserved orally throughout the long centuries of subterfuge and persecution, at last brought the remnant of the Marranos into touch with a representative of the outside Jewish world.

Now that he was recognized as a coreligionist, M. Schwarz had no difficulty in being admitted to full confidence. What he discovered was nothing less than amazing. Throughout the period subsequent to the fall of the Inquisition, there had continued to exist in the remoter parts of the northern provinces of Portugal whole colonies of crypto-Jews, absolutely isolated from the general Jewish world, and not even suspecting its existence. Long centuries of persecution had left its mark on their outlook. They could not conceive any form of Judaism except that stunted and furtive one which they followed. They were not conscious of any short-comings or lapses on their part. But, at the same time, their religion in its essentials was unmistakably Jewish — a natural development of that which their ancestors had practiced at the time of the Inquisitional persecutions, an account of which has been given above. They steadfastly denied the Messiahship of Jesus and

withheld recognition from the saints of the Roman
Catholic Church. They recognized themselves as Jews,
or as New Christians. They met together at regular
intervals for prayer. They married only among themselves. They observed with the utmost possible fidelity
the Sabbath and the major solemnities of Passover and
the Day of Atonement, together with the Fast of Esther.
True, the persecution of centuries had left its trace. On
Friday night, many of them placed the Sabbath light,
which they so religiously kindled, inside a pitcher, safe
from prying eyes. The Day of Atonement and Passover
were both observed a day or two after their proper date,
when the vigilance of their persecutors might be assumed
to have been relaxed.

Their prayers, though sadly altered and diminished,
were recognizably Jewish in inspiration and in origin.
They were in Portuguese — a large number of them in
verse. Nevertheless, the ancient archetypes are in many
cases recognizable. One or two words of Hebrew, even,
survived — notably, the name *Adonai*. The formula of
benediction, before performing any religious function,
was strikingly similar to the traditional one. It ran thus:
"Blessed art Thou, my Lord, my *Adonai*, who hast
commanded us with His blessed and holy commandments that we do . . . as our brethren do in the land of
Promise." Only the concluding phrase, with its striking
testimony to the unity of Israel and the living influence
of Palestine, is not to be found in the traditional Hebrew
formula.[4] The prayers were scanty in number, and were
seldom written down, being transmitted from generation
to generation by word of mouth. The principal reposi-
tories of these as of other traditions were the mothers

and the wives. Indeed, on those occasions when meetings were held for prayer, it was generally an old woman who acted as *sacerdotisa* ("priestess") or spiritual guide of · the community. Among themselves, they continued to maintain feelings of the utmost solidarity, expressed in mutual charity and characteristically generous help at times of stress.[5] All of this had continued for the past century and a half, absolutely unknown to the Jews of the outside world, who were meanwhile endeavoring to understand how it was that the Marranos had died away with such dramatic suddenness after Pombal's reforms.

What had happened was as a matter of fact by no means difficult to explain. In the principal towns, the main centers of the Inquisitional activity, where surveillance was continual and whence departure from the country was comparatively easy, the persecution had been more or less effective. Almost all the Marrano population had been driven to emigrate, exterminated, or else forced to conform. Indeed, in the last days of the period of the autos-da-fè, as has been seen, only a small proportion of those who figured had been natives of the capital or the greater cities in the western part of the country. But, in the rural centers, matters were different. The maintenance of some sort of communal life was simpler, and traditions could thus be perpetuated with greater ease. On the other hand, emigration from the country (for the poorer classes especially) was difficult in the extreme. Hence, crypto-Judaism had here a greater vitality than in the capital or the other great cities.

The Inquisition was deprived of its power by Pombal, at the close of the eighteenth century. But the fact that active persecution had finally ended, though obvious to us today, was by no means clear to contemporaries. Even when the institution was abolished entirely in 1821, the apparent change was by no means revolutionary. The Apostolic and Roman Catholic religion continued to be the only creed recognized by law. Its public renunciation remained a crime, punishable by heavy penalties. Even if the state were inactive, public opinion was not likely to be indifferent, so that apostasy was certain to be requited in some way. In the rural centers, above all, the power of the parish priest continued supreme. More- over, in their remote homes, often far removed from the railroads and highways of communication, many of the Marranos hardly realized the progress of civilization, and feared that, even in the nineteenth or twentieth century, they might be burned like their ancestors if they had the temerity to come out into the open.[6] By this time, more- over, the tradition of secrecy implanted during centuries of persecution had affected their whole outlook. They imagined that their God could not properly be worshiped except by stealth, and regarded a public profession of faith as little less than a profanation.

They were hence little affected by the alteration of circumstances. They continued to attend Church, though on a minimum number of occasions. They resorted auto- matically to the parish priest for baptism, marriage, and burial; inevitably so, since no civil form of registration had as yet been introduced. Though they continued to meet together for the purpose of worship, and retained their own secretive traditions amongst themselves, they remained Catholics in form. With the revolution of 1910, the public institutions of the country were secularized.

Henceforth, some of them took advantage of the new opportunities which offered themselves, abandoning the practice of getting their children baptized and no longer troubling to have their marriages solemnized in Church as well as by the civil authorities. It remained necessary for them only to have recourse to the priest for the purpose of burial, since none but the Catholic graveyard existed.

By this time, all touch with the main current of Judaism had been absolutely lost. Their own attenuated practices and orations appeared to them to be the whole of the Jewish religion. Even those who were sufficiently independent to neglect public opinion, and sufficiently enlightened to realize that the Inquisition and its horrors indeed belonged to the past, had no knowledge of any shortcoming in their traditional religious practice. Thus, the crypto-Jewish communities continued their strange, furtive existence, absolutely unaffected by the progress of time and the change of circumstances.

The number of persons and the extent of territory involved was far from negligible. In southern Portugal, so far as is known, the case is identical with that in Spain, where all traces of crypto-Judaism appear to have died out, save for the consciousness of Jewish descent in a few persons here and there.[7] In the northern provinces of the country, on the other hand — in the hill-country towards the Spanish border, Tras-os-Montes and Beira — the Marranos are still very numerous. Some villages, such as Villarinho, appear to be full of them. In all, they are to be found in some numbers in at least thirty-four places. At Covilhã, the Manchester of Portugal, there is a considerable colony. Other important centers are Belmonte, Fundão, Castello Branco, Idanha, Pernamacor, Guarda, Braganza, and Monsanto. It is a striking fact that it was precisely these townships which provided so large a proportion of the victims of the Inquisition in its last years, and that from there came many of the founders of the communities of the Marrano Diaspora in the seventeenth and eighteenth centuries. For the most part, the Marranos of today belong to the lower middle class, though they count among them also many prosperous merchants and professional men. As with the bulk of the population of Portugal, the proportion of illiteracy among them is high; this accounting to a large extent for their credulity and slight knowledge of conditions in the outside world.

As for their actual numbers, it is difficult to speak with any degree of certainty. Beyond doubt, the families who still follow their own conception of Judaism with more or less fidelity and refuse resolutely to conform to the dominant religion, are to be numbered by many hundreds — perhaps by thousands. In addition to these, there are many more, now professing Catholics, or attached to no religion, who still remember with pride the fact of their Jewish descent, and are in some cases designated by their neighbors as Jews. Throughout the northern provinces, indeed, traces of New Christian blood are extremely strong, in some localities almost predominating over the other elements of the population. Thus places like Pinhel, where the professing Marrano element is not large, are generally spoken of throughout the neighborhood as "Jewish" towns.

Contemporaneously with these sensational disclosures, a certain degree of Jewish consciousness had been stirring spontaneously amongst the Marranos. The lead was taken by a striking personality who irresistibly recalls the great figures of the sixteenth and seventeenth centuries. Arthur Carlos de Barros Basto was born in 1887 at Amarante, a little place near Oporto. He was a member of one of the old New Christian families, which remained true to their ancestral ideals. His grandfather in particular was meticulous in his attachment to the traditions which he had received from his fathers. It was the latter who instilled into his grandson his Jewish enthusiasm. Barros Basto's racial origin was perhaps betrayed by the phenomenally many-sided activity which he began to manifest as soon as he reached manhood. Like Daniel Levi de Barrios or Antonio Enriquez Gomez, three centuries before, he sought his career in the army, becoming a professional soldier. Like them, his passion was in writing. He made himself known as an author, and was a prominent member of the literary coterie which had its center in Oporto. He was responsible for the introduction into Portugal of the Boy-Scout organization. He took a prominent share in politics, becoming one of the first adherents of the revolutionary movement of 1910, to which modern Portugal owes its birth. It was he who, on one memorable day in that year, hoisted the Republican flag on the town hall of Oporto, at the risk of his life, being subsequently carried through the streets on the shoulders of the delirious populace. During the War of 1914–1918, he served on the British front with the Expeditionary Force in France, with exceptional distinction, being repeatedly decorated and mentioned in despatches for valor.

Throughout this profusion of activity, there was

surging up in Barros Basto a Jewish sentiment which could not be gainsaid; an overwhelming sense of the compelling force of the Jewish religion and of his personal identity with the body of the Jewish people. Already before the War, he had begun to frequent the synagogue of Lisbon and to study the Hebrew language, of which he attained an unusually good knowledge for a self-educated man. But the official community of the capital, brought up in the timorous traditions of the last century, gave him no encouragement. (It must be remembered that, before the Revolution, professing Jews lived in Portugal only on sufferance.) After the War, Barros Basto's Jewish sentiment became too strong to be further suppressed. Going across to Tangiers, he formally entered the Jewish fold. Some time after, he married a charming lady belonging to one of the most prominent families of the Lisbon community, and his ambition of setting up a truly Jewish household was realized. At Oporto, where his official duties called him, he organized the heterogeneous Jewish elements into a proper congregation, and established a synagogue. At the same time, he set about a systematic propaganda among his fellow Marranos to overcome their inherent timorousness, their ignorant prejudices and their curious attachment to secrecy, and to bring them back to the faith which their fathers had been forced to abandon over four centuries before. Thus his activities and those of M. Schwarz came to coincide.

The Jews of Lisbon, perplexed by the new situation which was arising, applied in 1924 to the Rabbinate of Jerusalem for advice concerning the attitude which they should adopt. The reply was encouraging. Early in the following year, students of Jewish matters throughout the world were astounded to read in the Anglo-Jewish press a communication from the Secretary of the Lisbon community, revealing the extraordinary fact that the Marranos, who had disappeared from view so strangely and so completely a century and a half before, still existed, and requesting assistance in bringing them back to the Jewish fold. It would have been extraordinary had such an appeal fallen upon deaf ears. Mr. Wilfred Samuel, of London, an eager student of everything connected with the Jewish past, generously defrayed the expenses of a mission of inquiry to Portugal on the part of the veteran diplomat, Mr. Lucien Wolf, who had long made a special study of Marrano history.[8] The latter returned full of enthusiasm. Thanks to his recommendations, a Portuguese Marranos Committee was formed in London under the joint auspices of the Alliance Israélite Universelle, the Anglo-Jewish Association and the Spanish and Portuguese community. This set itself to arouse interest in the object and to collect funds on its behalf. Thanks to the subsidies which it transmitted, Captain Barros Basto was able to extend very considerably the scale and radius of his activity. The congregation of Oporto was consolidated. Largely through the liberality of Baron Edmond de Rothschild, of Paris, and, later on, the munificence of the Kadoorie family of Shanghai, a handsome new synagogue was built on the outskirts of the city — a tangible sign of the revival. Attached to it, there was created a Seminary, in which boys might learn the tenets of their ancestral faith, which they might subsequently spread amongst their kinsfolk in the remoter centers. A newspaper was founded for the purpose of propaganda in the less

accessible spots. In it regularly appeared the rudiments
of traditional practice (especially with regard to any
forthcoming holiday), generally taken from the *Thesouro
dos Dinim* which Menasseh ben Israel had compiled for
the Marranos of Amsterdam three centuries before. The
main portions of the Jewish liturgy were translated for
the first time into Portuguese and published in convenient editions, which were circulated far and wide.
Pastoral journeys were undertaken throughout the region
where the Marranos were to be found, for the purpose
of propaganda. In one place after another, formerly
memorable in history, public services were conducted in
accordance with Jewish tradition for the first time in
four hundred years. It is not surprising that many of
those present shed tears — tears of joy, at the marvelous
consummation which had come to pass; tears of appre-
hension, lest the abandonment of the age-long tradition
of secrecy might after all bring disaster in its train.

The results of all this activity, though slow (for the
prejudices and habits of centuries are not easily to be
shaken off), were not negligible. Numbers of Marranos,
throughout the northern provinces of the country
declared openly their adherence to official Judaism; not
all simple country folk, but in some cases civil servants,
bankers, army officers, and professional men. Little,
quasi-open Jewish communities were established at
Covilhã, Belmonte, Pinhel, and Braganza — in the last
case, generously supported by the Central Conference
of American Rabbis.[9] Provisional Jewish centers were
moreover formed at smaller places, such as Argozêlo,
Escalhão, Villa Real, Vilarinho, and elsewhere. In various places in northern Portugal, services began to be

held at intervals, in increasingly close fidelity to the traditional Jewish forms, and attended by congregations numbering up to one hundred souls.

As to the ultimate outcome of this amazing movement, it is as yet too early to judge. It is not to be imagined that the prejudices, and the habits, and the fears, and the ignorance which have accumulated in the course of ages can be entirely eradicated in so short a time. Moreover, other difficulties hardly less serious are not absent. With the decline of the former prejudice against the New Christians, the forces of assimilation are beginning to make themselves felt to a degree hardly paralleled even in the age of persecution. Since the beginning of the present century, secularism and the modern pseudo-rationalistic tendencies have made considerable headway here, as in every other part of the world's surface. On the other hand, the forces of reaction are not by any means defeated, and, in country districts, the return to Judaism is by no means an easy task. It is not impossible that the Marrano Renaissance has set in too late to be effective amongst the great mass of the people. If, in the end, it appears that the revival has been left too long, the catastrophe will have been due to the slow, inexorable pressure of circumstance, and not to Inquisitional persecution. That protracted martyrdom, unexampled in history, proved powerless to vanquish the indomitable Jewish spirit. In spite of all its horrors, the Marranos were able to preserve their identity and the essentials of their faith down to the present day. In their own history, they exemplify the adage which the great Marrano poet prefixed as title to his elegy on the three Marrano martyrs in 1665: *Contra la verdad no ay fuerça* —"Against Truth, Force does not avail."

NOTES TO INTRODUCTORY CHAPTER

[1] Jewish Folk-Lore has preserved many stories illustrating the secret fidelity to Judaism of persons baptized under such circumstances. The most striking is the legend of Elhanan, the legendary Jewish Pope, kidnapped son of a learned Rhineland rabbi.

[2] See *Critique du nobilaire de Provence composé par M. l'Abbé Robbert de Briançon, contenant l'epurement de la noblesse du pays ... l'abrégé de l'histoire des Juifs en Provence, le catalogue des nouveaux chrétiens de race judaique de ce pays, etc.*, by Abbé Barcilon de Mouvans (British Museum, Ms. Add. 15653: John Rylands' Library, Manchester, Mss. Crawford 26 and 48).

[3] After the Greek occupation and the systematic Hellenization of Salonica, the Donmeh migrated, particularly to Smyrna, Adrianople, etc. It is difficult therefore to give exact details of their condition and distribution at the present day. It may be mentioned that the Young Turk movement of 1913 was to a large extent led by members of this sect (Djavid Bey, etc.).

[4] According to one theory, the famous ceremony of the Annulment of Vows on the eve of the Day of Atonement, the *Kol Nidre* service, was instituted for the benefit of these Spanish crypto-Jews, in order to absolve them from any undertaking for the observance of Christianity in the following year. According to this view, the congregation cover their heads with the *Tallit* at this point, so that any crypto-Jew amongst them should avoid recognition; while the initial reference to the '*Abaryanim* (i. e. "the transgressors") is taken as a cryptic allusion to the Iberians!

[5] Almoravides derives from the same root as the English *marabout*, with the Arabic definite article prefixed: Almohades is from the same root as the Hebrew *Ehad* ("One"), its followers vaunting their devotion to strict monotheism.

[6] A close parallel to these secret Jews was provided by the *Mavali*, or secret Christians of Moslem Spain.

[7] It is only right to add that the temporary apostasy of Maimonides, and even his authorship of the treatise here under discussion, are strenuously denied by many scholars.

377

NOTES TO CHAPTER I

[1] The story is told of one Marrano who ate unleavened bread throughout the year, on the pretext of ill health, so as to ensure having it on Passover!

[2] Jerome Munzer, a German traveler who visited Spain in 1494–5, recounts how there had existed up to a few years previous at Valencia, on the site subsequently occupied by the Convent of St. Catherine of Sienna, a church dedicated to St. Christopher. "Here the Marranos (that is false Christians, inwardly Jews) had their sepulchers. When one of them died, they feigned conformity to the rites of the Christian religion, going in procession, with the coffin covered with cloth of gold and bearing an image of St. Christopher in front of them. However, in secret they washed the bodies of the dead and buried them in accordance with their own rites . . ." He indicates that the same was the case at Barcelona, where it was understood that if a Marrano was heard to say: "Let us go today to the Church of the Holy Cross," he meant the secret synagogue, which was thus called. The classical account of Marrano conditions and subterfuges at this period may be read in Bernaldez, *Historia de los Reyes Católicos*, ch. XLIII.

[3] I use this term in a loose sense; scientifically it is meaningless no less with Jews than with other sections of humanity.

[4] There is extant an extraordinary letter of recommendation in Hebrew written by the community of Saragossa early in the fifteenth century to recommend a certain friar of Jewish birth, who was to preach a Holy War against the Moors. Their coreligionists were begged to believe that, notwithstanding appearances, he was favorable to them at heart!

[5] Out of the whole of Spain, it was only in Catalonia that the process was to some extent restrained, though the boast that the Catalan blood was never polluted by intermixture is unfounded. In Valencia, on the other hand, intermarriage took place mainly in the rural districts.

A similar work to the *Libro Verde de Aragon* was the *Tizon de la Nobleza de España*, drawn up about 1560 by the Cardinal Mendoza y Bobadilla for presentation to Philip II, and showing that virtually all the nobility both of Castile and of Aragon had Jewish blood in their veins.

⁶ A typical satire of the period was that directed by a penurious poet against the wealthy Alfonso Fernandez, previously known as Samuel, who had actually dared to refuse him alms. The other revenged himself by circulating a fictitious will, in which Fernandez is represented as leaving one penny to the Church and a hundred ducats to poor Jews, to enable them to rest on the Sabbath. He bequeaths his shirt to a Synagogue-beadle at Salamanca to recite psalms for the repose of his soul. He orders a crucifix to be placed in his coffin at his feet, a copy of the Koran on his breast, and a scroll of the Law of Moses at his head!

⁷ Another New-Christian painter, named Just, was an early victim of the Inquisition at Valencia, in 1490.

⁸ A famous anti-Jewish work of the fifteenth century was entitled *Libro del Alborayque.*

⁹ Not entirely; the Jewish grammarian and polemist, Ephodi, was familiar with the term, which he derived (in his *Kelimat ha-Goyim,* X, I) from the Hebrew *hamir,* apostatize.

¹⁰ As a matter of fact, the word *Maranatha,* found in the New Testament, I Corinthians 16.22, is simply a transliteration of the Judeo-Aramaic *Maran Ata* —"The Lord cometh." An alternative derivation is from *Muranita,* the rod with which those put under the ban were chastised.

NOTES TO CHAPTER II

¹ There is extant an amusing satire written to celebrate the marriage of one of his family with a relative of the eminent Churchman, Pedro Gonzalez de Mendoza, in which the descent of the bridegroom, from the Jewish families of Ibn Sason, Ibn Nahmias, and Saboca is vividly compared with that of the bride from the grandees of Castile.

² The attack here was instigated by Don Juan Pacheco — himself a member of a Marrano family.

³ A proposal was made at this period to hand over the fortress of Gibraltar to the *conversos* as a city of refuge.

4 Sometimes, similar powers were assumed by other authorities; for example, in England, precedent in common law for the burning of heretics had been provided by the condemnation at Oxford in 1222 of a certain Deacon who had become converted to Judaism for the love of a Jewess.

5 i. e. The Beautiful Woman.

6 For a full explanation of this and other technical terms, see infra, ch. V.

7 According to another account, Calle del Ataud (Street of the Coffin).

8 A record has recently been published which illustrates the extraordinary delicacy of the Jewish consciousness in such matters. In consequence of the governmental action, a certain rabbi at Saragossa had to order his coreligionists publicly, to obey the Inquisitors and to tell them under penalty of excommunication all they knew concerning any Marrano who followed Jewish practices. Subsequently, one of his flock privately implored for exemption from this, since, if he told all he knew about Alfonso de la Caballeria, the whole community would be placed in jeopardy. The rabbi complied: but after the publication of the edict of expulsion, in 1492, he considered it his duty to go to the authorities and inform them of the episode, since the plea of danger no longer applied.

9 One of the charges against Dávila was that, on the introduction of the Inquisition into Segovia, he had the remains of his ancestors exhumed, in order to destroy proof of the fact that they had been interred in accordance with Jewish tradition.

NOTES TO CHAPTER III

1 Not, as is usually assumed by historical writers, the island of St. Thomas in the West Indies which (a) had not been discovered at that time (b) was never in Portuguese possession and (c) is a Garden of Eden in comparison with the other island, which actually lies on the Equator.

2 That all were packed into this building at the same time, as some contemporary records imply, is a physical impossibility. The building was subsequently used as the Palace of the Inquisition, being radically reconstructed at a later date. Thus the Marranos

were tried for Judaizing on precisely the same spot where they had been forcibly made into Christians. The site is now occupied by the National Theater (formerly the Theater of Donna Maria II) which pious Lisbon Jews even now refuse to enter.

[3] In the above account, an attempt has been made to summarize in a few pages the long and wearisome negotiations spread over many years, which form the subject-matter of Herculano's classical *History of the Origin and Establishment of the Inquisition in Portugal.* For fuller information, reference should be made to this massive work, now available in English.

NOTES TO CHAPTER IV

[1] Mention may perhaps be made in this connection of the family of Manoel Pereira Coutinho, all of whose five daughters were nuns in the convent of *La Esperança* at Lisbon, while his sons were living as Jews at Hamburg, under the name of Abendana!

Among noteworthy ecclesiastical figures of the seventeenth century in Spain, who were of Jewish extraction, were the famous dramatist and novelist, Juan Perez de Montalvan, a close friend of Lope de Vega, who was priest and notary of the Holy Office; and Felipe Godinez, a famous preacher and playwright, who was reconciled by the Inquisition in 1624 at Seville as a Judaizer, but was afterwards allowed to continue his career.

[2] Mariana de Macedo, a Dominican nun burned at Lisbon for Judaizing, in 1647, is worthy of record as another case in point. For other instances, cf. the cases of Frei Diogo da Assumpção (infra, p. 149) and Father Manuel Lopes de Carvalho (ch. XI, note 9). At the earlier period of Inquisitional activity in Spain, there were some cases which were if anything even more striking. Thus on his trial at Toledo, in 1486, Andrés González, parish priest of San Martin de Talavera, confessed that for the past fourteen years he had been a Jew at heart and had failed to take his sacerdotal functions seriously. More extraordinary still were the stories circulated about Fray Garcia de Zapata, prior of the Geronimite monastery of Toledo.

[3] *Ganephe*: the characteristic Jewish garb in northern Africa.

[4] *Progging*: Industrious.

⁵ The person in question is probably to be identified with Dr. Jacob Israel Belgara, a Spanish Marrano who had graduated at Saragossa and was circumcised in Barbary (at Tangiers?) in 1667, in his fortieth year. Addison mentions him repeatedly (pp. 63, 226). It is not impossible, however, that we have here one of the native Barbary Jews who, according to the same authority (p. 83), concealed their religion and went to the Spanish and Portuguese Universities to study medicine.

⁶ The prophetess and her companions are said to have recounted to their adherents how they were taken up to heaven and there had a vision of the Marranos who had been martyred, installed on thrones of gold. They foretold the speedy advent of Elijah and of the Messiah, who would lead them all to the Promised Land.

⁷ It was added that the image, besides shedding blood, actually spoke to them in reproof; after which they consumed it in fire! Continued stubbornness in the face of so extraordinary a manifestation is a phenomenon deserving of more than passing note.

It may be added that a certain woman who was discovered to have been responsible for these denunciations was put to death by order of the local New Christians, the assassin subsequently escaping to Holland.

⁸ See p. 124 for an explanation of these terms.

⁹ So Adler in *Auto de Fé and Jew*, pp. 36–8; but cf. the correction in D'Azevedo, *Historia dos Christãos Novos Portugueses*, p. 217.

¹⁰ Such activity as there was centered about immigrants from the mainland. Thus, at an auto on January 13, 1675, the effigies of six fugitive Portuguese Judaizers were solemnly, but innocuously, committed to the flames; and one refugee from Madrid was burned alive.

¹¹ The word is a contemptuous dialectical form of *judio* (Jew). According to another theory, it is a diminutive of *chuya*, a Majorcan term for pig, or pork — perhaps a contemptuous reference to these unfortunates' antipathy to the flesh of the pig. Another derivation is from the local equivalent of the Spanish *chuco* or French *chouette* — a cry used when calling a dog.

¹² As recently as 1904, the Prime Minister of Spain, Miguel Maura, was publicly taunted in the Cortes with being a *Chueta*! Even this is

not perhaps quite so surprising as the fact that in 1877 a student for the priesthood named Terongi (like two of the martyrs of two centuries earlier) was actually disqualified from taking Holy Orders by reason of his ancestry.

The famous novel of Ibañez, *The Dead Speak* (*Los Muertos Mandán*), is inspired by the pitiable condition of the *Chuetas* in our own time. (See now also Sylvette de Lamar's somewhat insubstantial *Jews with the Cross*, 1932). The most recent reports however indicate that the condition of the Chuetas has very greatly ameliorated recently. It is said that there are a couple of local families who still hold secret Friday evening services.

¹³ To the Canary Islands, also under Spanish rule, numerous New Christians had penetrated at an early date after discovery. An Episcopal Inquisition was set up to deal with them as early as 1499. As a result of its inquiries, there was discovered to be in the group a number of secret Jews, who went so far as to maintain a synagogue for their services. A branch of the Inquisition of Andalusia was accordingly set up at Las Palmas in 1504. Autos, at which a few persons were penanced or reconciled, were held in 1507 and 1510. In 1526, however, the tribunal was very active, eight individuals being relaxed in person, ten reconciled, and two penanced. Of these, over one half, including six out of the eight *relaxados* (persons relaxed; see ch. V, p. 124), were condemned for Judaizing. Further autos, at which however no persons suffered capitally, were held in 1530 and 1534. This outburst of activity seems to have temporarily eradicated crypto-Judaism in the islands. Only four New Christians figured in the sporadic prosecutions which continued until 1581, and none at all thenceforth until 1597, when all activity was temporarily suspended. The immigration of Marranos from the mainland — principally from Portugal — at the beginning of the seventeenth century stimulated fresh activity. In 1625, an Edict of Faith against Judaism was issued. The information which this elicited revealed the presence of a whole colony of secret Jews. A considerable proportion of them had however fled. Owing partly to this and partly to political considerations, no prosecutions ensued; and crypto-Judaism in the islands was henceforth virtually unknown.

NOTES TO CHAPTER V

[1] The description which follows is based principally upon the system of the Spanish Inquisition. With a slight change of vocabulary, it applies equally well to Portugal.

[2] = *Zom Kippur* (Fast of Atonement).

[3] The foregoing is a composite text, based mainly upon that given in Wolf, *Jews in the Canary Islands*, pp. 26–9, but including a few characteristic passages from other Edicts which happen to be omitted there. The original belongs to the early part of the sixteenth century. At a later period, naturally, the Inquisition was even less well-informed. The disproportionate prominence given to unimportant customs and mere superstitions is worthy of note.

[4] It is pertinent to remember, in this connection, that even in enlightened England, it has only been since 1836 that persons accused of felony have been able to avail themselves of the assistance of Counsel or to see copies of the depositions made against them.

[5] It appears that, owing to some confusion, another physician settled in London as a Jew, Dr. Jacob de Castro Sarmento (whose father's name was Francisco and his mother's Mesquita: see infra, pp. 105, 268) was accused by his coreligionists of having been responsible for these denunciations. After a formal inquiry by the Synagogue authorities he was absolved.

[6] Menasseh ben Israel (*Vindiciae Judaeorum*, p. 11) recounts an amusing tale of a Portuguese nobleman, who in order to secure the release of his body-physician, who had confessed to the crime of Judaizing under torture, seized the Inquisitor himself and extracted a precisely similar confession out of him by the same means!

[7] This account is taken from Lea, *A History of the Inquisition of Spain*, III, 23–6, who derived it from the original Inquisitional process in the National Archives at Madrid. It is right to add that the Inquisition of Portugal was less ferocious in this respect than that of Spain, the methods of torture being restricted.

[8] In those rare cases where the Holy Office felt inclined to exercise clemency in the case of a second condemnation, the culprit would be sentenced to the physical penalties of imprisonment, etc., without the formal act of abjuration, which could only be admitted on one occasion.

[9] "House of Penitence" or "House of Mercy"

[10] In Portugal, the term was fixed in 1640 at three to five years.

[11] Cases are on record of persons who made confessions implicating hundreds of others, including the whole of their own families, but were nevertheless condemned to the flames on the pretext that their admissions were incomplete.

[12] E. g. Rabbi Judah ibn Verga (supra, p. 46): Abraham Bibajo, the philosopher, accused in 1489 with other notables of the community of Huesca of converting certain Marranos and assisting them to escape to Palestine (he, however, died in prison): and a couple of the ancestors of the famous Rabbi Moses Almosnino.

[13] The opponents of the Inquisition, on the other hand, maintained that out of one hundred *negativos* punished, hardly a single one was guilty. They pointed above all to the case of two nuns who were burned at Evora in 1673. One of them had lived an unblemished life in her convent for forty years and died invoking Jesus with her last breath. It is difficult to know whether she is to be reckoned a martyr to Judaism or to Christianity. In the same category is a distinguished New Christian soldier, the Quartermaster João Alvares de Barbuda, who went to his death at Lisbon in the auto of April 4, 1666, and who took with him into prison a book of hours and a little image of Saint Antony. In the Lisbon auto of May 10, 1682, eight victims who had perished in prison were pronounced innocent. In the following year, the acquittal was ordered at Coimbra of a woman who had died in prison after seventeen years of incarceration, under a false accusation, and was now discovered to be after all an Old Christian of unblemished family and reputation. Such cases were, however, rare.

[14] "Sacred Sack."

[15] The horror which the *sambenito* inspired was extreme. Ribeiro Sanchez, the famous Marrano physician and reformer, records an amusing story connected with this. In Lisbon, those New Christians who had been penanced at an auto had to present themselves at Church every Sunday to learn Christian doctrine. Once, the press of people who were waiting to see the "Jews" (as they called them) was so great that they were unable to leave the building. One of them therefore took off his *sambenito* and advanced, waving it about in front of him. So great was the popular fear of being contaminated with its touch that there was a general stampede, and the path

was completely and immediately cleared. Sanchez was told this story by the hero of the occasion, then living as a Jew in London.

[16] Also known as *brasero* ("brazier"). The function of mounting guard at the autos and furnishing wood for the pyre was relegated in some cities to a body, known as the *compañia de la Zarza*.

[17] Orobio de Castro, and Antonio Enriques Gomez. See infra, chapter XII, p. 299 and XIII, p. 333.

[18] *Elogios que zelosos dedicaron á la felice memoria de Abraham Nuñez Bernal, que fue quemado vivo, sanctificando el nombre de su Criador, en Cordova a 3. de Mayo anno 5415.* Others similarly commemorated include the seventy-five year old Abraham Athias (alias Jorge Mendes de Castro), Jacob Rodriguez Casseres and Raquel Nuñez Fernandez, who "sanctified the Name" in the same place in the great Auto of June 1665.

[19] The translation here given is in accordance with the Old Spanish version rather than the exact grammatical meaning, so as to convey the idea in the mind of those who recited the prayer. It is to be found in more than one edition of the prayer-books printed in Amsterdam in the seventeenth and eighteenth centuries. It is interesting to note that, in his introduction to the first full edition of the Hebrew ritual printed in America, the editor, Solomon Jackson, says in reference to this: "Martyrdom having ceased, and the liberality of mankind assuring us it will no more be revived, it was thought best to omit the prayer." This was in 1826. In the same year, the Inquisition claimed a human victim!

[20] See *Publications of the Jewish Historical Society of America*, XXIII, 132, 134. One would gladly assume a misprint. However, since apparently a son of Maria Carillo was "relaxed" on the same occasion at the age of 56, the possible margin of error is not great.

Beauty, apparently, made no more impression on the Inquisitors than did age. Gracia d'Alarçon, wife of Pedro Montero, who was reconciled at Granada in 1593, was described in the official record as the most beautiful woman in the kingdom!

[21] I now have reason to doubt the Portuguese figures. Details for the period 1651–1750 indicate that 419 culprits were relaxed in person — and this was the period of comparative mildness.

NOTES TO CHAPTER VI

[1] The only complete account of the trial of a Marrano available in English is that of Gabriel de Granada, who was sentenced by the Mexican Tribunal in 1645. A complete translation of the official record, extending over 127 printed pages, was edited by David Fergusson and Cyrus Adler as volume VII of the *Publications of the American Jewish Historical Society* (1899). The persons concerned in it are of no great importance; but it gives a remarkably graphic impression of a typical Inquisitional case. A somewhat more important trial, that of Jorge d'Almeida, was edited in less detail by Cyrus Adler, ibid., vol. IV, pp. 29–79.

[2] Or, "of the Shoe." Perhaps there is some confusion with Luis Dias, the cobbler; or else *Sapato* refers to the mythical river Sambation which rested on the Sabbath — a piece of Jewish folk-lore which is known to have retained its hold amongst the Marranos for a considerable time later. [See now my article in *Revue des Etudes Juives* 116: 93–5.]

[3] "Long live the Law of Moses."

[4] The stateman's son, José da Villareal, became Professor of Greek at Marseilles towards the close of the century, and was the author of the work *Escada de Jacob* (Jacob's Ladder), still in manuscript.

[5] The reputed "miracle" could, of course, equally conveniently be interpreted in a diametrically opposite sense.

[6] Lea, *Inquisition in the Spanish Dependencies*, p. 425, adds to the martyr's gifts that of miracle-working, asserting that he used pens cut out of egg-shells. He has obviously confused *huevos* (eggs) and *huesos* (bones)!

[7] It is remarkable that the report of these two martyrs in the New World, like that of some of those in the old, reached the Jewish communities of Europe, where they were duly celebrated in prose and verse.

NOTES TO CHAPTER VII

[1] The following account applies most faithfully to the Marranos of Portugal, reflecting their more organized religious life. It is difficult to say how far any active proselytization was carried on among the Marranos of the Peninsula by their coreligionists abroad. We

occasionally hear of professing Jews, or else returned fugivites, who were arrested by the Inquisition; but their presence in Portugal appears in every case to have been due to private business only. Contemporary Catholic writers inform us that Fernando Gomez, alias Daniel Franco, who was relaxed at Evora in 1608, was a rabbi sent from Salonica to initiate his kinsmen into the elements of their ancestral faith. An examination of the original record of his trial, however (Archives of Torre do Tombo, Lisbon: *Inquisição de Evora*, processo 8424), makes it plain that he was in fact nothing more than a talkative and not over-courageous youth, who had come to the country about his own affairs. The only piece of definite evidence in the reverse direction is a statement contained in a Denunciation of 1639, and emanating indirectly from Menasseh ben Israel, that "every year there went certain Jews from Holland to the capital of Madrid to circumcise the New Christians."

² The case is on record of an ignorant Marrano who knew no prayers, and learned to recite Psalms without the orthodox conclusion on hearing the sentence on a New Christian burned at Lisbon. One sees thus how the Inquisitional severity defeated its own ends.

³ The custom has, of course, a parallel in traditional practice; but the Marranos attached a disproportionate importance to it.

NOTES TO CHAPTER VIII

¹ Above all, the capture of Constantinople by the Turks in 1453 had caused some searching of heart amongst the Marranos, who imagined that it was a portent of the close of the rule of the Cross. In the subsequent period, many of them set out for the Levant. In 1464, for example, no less than seventy families embarked at Valencia for Valona, in Albania, though one was intercepted on the journey. The depositions made by the latter indicate the strength of the mystical expectations amongst the Marranos, who believed that the Messiah had actually been born near Constantinople, invisible to all but true Jews.

² See above, p. 5.

³ At Venice, Daniel Bomberg, the famous Christian printer of Hebrew books, assisted in transmitting the property of the Marranos;

while his rival, Jeronimo Soncino, boasted that he was instrumental in the reconversion of many of them to Judaism.

⁴ See above, ch. IV, p. 81.

⁵ Another eminent Marrano who settled in Turkey at the close of the sixteenth century was João Lopes, who, after administering the business affairs of Pope Sixtus V for some years, in the guise of an earnest Christian, fled to Constantinople or Salonica, where he settled down as a Jew!

⁶ This was not always the case in Italy. Thus in 1640 Fernando Alvarez, alias Abraham da Porto, was martyred at Rome; while in 1602 Emmanuel Mocato of Scandiano, who had saved himself by flight, was burned in effigy at Reggio.

⁷ One point of especial interest may here be noted. It is to be presumed that the original Marrano settlers began by attending the Levantine synagogue, forming among themselves only a society for the purpose of studying the Law — *Talmud Torah*. When they set up their own congregation, they transferred the same name to it, so that it became known as the *K. K.* (*Kahal Kadosh*, or Holy Congregation) *Talmud Torah*. Hence it became the fashion in the Marrano diaspora for each congregation to have its own distinctive title; as, for example, the *K. K. Talmud Torah* of Amsterdam, or the *K. K. Sha'ar ha-Shamayim* ("Gate of Heaven") in London. The fashion was imitated in the New World, with the congregations *Shearith Israel* ("Remnant of Israel") in New York, *Yeshuath Israel* ("Salvation of Israel") in Newport, etc. When at the beginning of the nineteenth century Ashkenazic congregations began to be established by the German settlers in the United States, they very naturally followed this example, adopting a specific, picturesque title for each one. It would appear therefore that the characteristic practice prevalent throughout America today is directly traceable to the Marrano community of Venice.

⁸ The story is told of a certain priest in Rome, who could not find anybody to tell him the way to the Ghetto, it being assumed that, as a Portuguese, he must necessarily know it! Somewhat similarly a preacher at a Portuguese auto-da-fé repeated the jocular statement of a certain Venetian rabbi who, when challenged to state whether the Jews anywhere had a kingdom of their own, replied that they certainly had — in Portugal.

[9] At Bordeaux, a stream of immigrants from other parts — notably from the Papal States in southern France — took advantage of the toleration won by the Marrano element; much, indeed, to the disdain of the latter, who did not hesitate to give drastic expression to their opposition. Paradoxically enough, these also, notwithstanding their different antecedents, had to submit to the surreptitious designation locally applied, becoming known similarly as "Avignonese New Christians." Avignon itself, like Rome, attracted a few Marranos from the Peninsula, who joined the ancient community which had continued to exist there, under the papal aegis, even after the expulsion of the Jews from the rest of France.

[10] The Inquisition always did its best to obtain details of the commercial pseudonym of any Marrano fugitive, as well as the identity of his business correspondents in the Peninsula. Thus, for example, Abraham Isaac Pereira of Amsterdam traded as Gerard Carl Bangardel.

[11] For an elaboration of these points, see my article in *The Menorah Journal* for April, 1929.

NOTES TO CHAPTER IX

[1] Above, p. 200.

[2] In August, 1598, a Maria Nuñez, aged 19, married one Duarte Saraiva at Amsterdam; in the following November, another person of the same name, aged 23, married Manuel Lopez Homem. It is not easy to see which of the two is the heroine of this romantic story.

[3] It may be mentioned, however, that the story of their being largely instrumental in its foundation is untrue. At the outset they owned only $1/10$ of 1% of the shares.

[4] This traditional story can be reconciled with a little ingenuity with the official documents in the *Hatfield Papers*, VI, 536.

NOTES TO CHAPTER X

[1] See below, p. 325.

[2] Dormido is generally stated, though on insufficient authority, to have been Menasseh's brother-in-law. For this and other points in which the present account differs from the generally accepted story, see my *History of the Jews in England*, Oxford, 1941, etc.

NOTES TO CHAPTER XI

[1] In the above sketch no account has been taken of the by no means negligible share in the discovery of America which may be ascribed to professing Jews, both scientists (such as Abraham Zacuto, the astronomer, and the "Map-Jew" Crescas) and financiers (like Abraham Senior).

[2] See above, p. 164.

[3] So far was the family looked up to by their fellow-Marranos that (as we have seen) their son, Gaspar Vaez Sevilla, born in 1624, was said to be hoped to be their Messiah.

[4] See above, p. 162.

[5] On this occasion the executioner began to garrot one of the victims by mistake, under the impression that he had received this preliminary act of mercy by a profession of repentance. The error was however discovered in time, and the unfortunate person was dragged half-dead to the *brasero*; thus (as the chronicler triumphantly puts it) "tasting the agony of both deaths."

[6] As late however as 1754 a zealous Jesuit proposed the establishment of an independent Inquisitional tribunal at Buenos Aires, where he alleged that there were residing from four to six thousand Portuguese Judaizers.

[7] When at a later stage in the campaign Rio de S. Francisco was recovered, five Judaizers of Portuguese birth were captured with the Dutch and sent back to Portugal for trial. They all appeared as penitents in the auto-da-fè held at Lisbon on December 15, 1647 — the same in which Isaac de Castro Tartas, who had been arrested at Bahia, perished as a martyr. In 1649 another batch of five captured in Brazil were relaxed at Lisbon.

[8] Recife = Rock: a play upon words.

[9] The Portuguese reconquest did not of course close the association of the Marranos with Brazil. Transportation to that country continued to be a common sentence against condemned Judaizers until well on in the eighteenth century; while voluntary emigration remained frequent. The Marranos of Brazil were at this period very important in the diamond trade as well as other branches of commerce. The Inquisition continued its activities. On one occasion, the arrests were so wide-spread as to create a crisis in the sugar industry at Rio de Janeiro. When, in 1702, the Bishop of Coimbra

was appointed Governor of the Colony, there was a recrudescence of persecution. Over one hundred persons from Rio de Janeiro alone were committed to prison in 1712. In the following year, seventy-two of these — thirty-two men and forty women — figured at an auto in Lisbon. In the following year, there was a further batch. Among the prominent Brazilian victims were Antonio José da Silva, the dramatist; and the visionary Father Manuel Lopes de Carvalho was burned alive as a Judaizer.

[10] The founder of the Bridgetown community was Joseph Jessurun Mendes (1616–1699), whose Marrano origin is proved by the alias Lewis Dias, which — highly exceptionally — was also inscribed on his tombstone, still to be read in the local cemetery.

[11] Even in the remotest parts of the Old World, Marranos were to be found. The Portuguese Inquisition maintained a branch at Goa, in India, whither the New Christians had penetrated at an early date. Here, as early as 1543, a certain Dr. Jeronimo Diaz had been burned for maintaining heretical opinions. The Holy Office was formally introduced some years later. In 1546, "St." Francis Xavier petitioned for its establishment, but his wishes were complied with only in 1561. From that date to 1623, no less than 3,800 persons were tried — many of them native "St. Thomas" Christians. The first auto took place on September 27, 1563, two Judaizers figuring amongst the four victims. The subsequent activities became greater and greater. Autos of peculiar virulence took place in 1575 and 1578 under the zealous Inquisitor Bartholomeu da Fonseca. In each of these, seventeen Judaizers lost their lives. With the return of Fonseca to Portugal, the fury abated, so that from 1590 to 1597 no death sentences were pronounced. Simultaneously, the number of Judaizers diminished, only two figuring among the twenty victims from 1597 to 1623. Elsewhere in India, outside the Portuguese sphere of influence, considerations of caution did not obtain. A few individuals made their way to Cochin, where they joined the ancient and romantic native community which had existed there from time immemorial. Thus there was in the sixteenth century a local Hebrew poet who had apparently lived previously as a Marrano in the Peninsula; and early in the seventeenth century a New Christian physician from Oporto, named Manuel Lopes, fled thither to return to his ancestral faith. At Madras, under English rule, a small open

Jewish community was formed later in the century with one of the Nieto family as its minister. Its components were all of Portuguese origin, some of them having no doubt come directly from the Peninsula, and others by way of the free countries of northern Europe. Thus Domingo, alias Abraham Israel da Porto, who had been one of the leading spirits of the London community at the time of the Resettlement, and had settled in India in 1691, was one of the first freemen of the city. As in Brazil, the diamond industry was almost entirely in their hands. At a later period, there were a few Portuguese Jews at Fort St. George, as Calcutta was then called.

A few New Christians also found their way to the Portuguese colony of Angola in West Africa, where there was an Inquisitorial visitation to hunt them out in 1626.

NOTES TO CHAPTER XII

[1] Cf. the testimony of an erudite contemporary: "What can I say of Spain and Portugal, where nearly all the princes, and nobility, and commoners are descended from apostatized Jews? This fact is there so well known that nobody doubts it ... The monasteries and convents are all full of Jews, while many even of the canons, Inquisitors, and Bishops themselves are of Jewish descent. There are many of them who are convinced Jews at heart, though for the sake of the goods of this world they pretend to believe in Christianity. Some subsequently suffer from pangs of conscience and, if they find an opportunity, escape. In Amsterdam and elsewhere there are Augustinians, Franciscans, Jesuits and Dominicans who are Jews. In Spain, on the other hand, there are Bishops and observant friars whose parents and relatives live here and in other towns in order to be able to practice the Jewish religion" (Limborch, *Amica Collatio*, pp. 102, 209, 276. The authority for this statement is Isaac Orobio de Castro, for whom see below).

If one include men of partly Marrano extraction, the roll would be greater and more distinguished by far: Cf. the case of Luis de Leòn, the very distinguished Spanish poet and theologian who when arrested and investigated by the Inquisition was found to be one-eighth New Christian. The background of Sᵗᵃ Teresa de Avila was similar.

[1a] See the dedication to the Spanish translation of the *Contra*

Apionem (Amsterdam, 1687); the statement that he taught at Salamanca or at Alcalá de Henares has apparently no foundation.

2 See above, ch. IV, p. 77.

3 Two brothers of this prelate, Abraham and Jacob Curiel, died in the Levant as Jews, in Tripoli and Safed respectively.

4 Above, p. 288.

5 Diogo Nuñes Ribeiro had been reconciled for Judaizing at Lisbon at the auto of October 19, 1704.

6 It may be mentioned that Ribeiro Sanchez was not the only Marrano representative at the court of Russia. The court jester under Peter the Great and the Empress Anna was João d'Acosta ("Lyacosta"), who had previously been in business as a broker in Hamburg, and had heated arguments with the fiery Czar on theological topics.

7 The last prominent member of the family was Erskine Childers, the Irish author and patriot, who was executed for his share in the Irish Rebellion of 1922; while in the female line, a descendant of Rachel de Payba, Rowland Gideon's daughter, became Duchess of Norfolk.

8 It is perhaps worth while to mention, in this connection, that a Mathias Mendes Seixas, of Covilhã, merchant, was reconciled and condemned to perpetual imprisonment at the auto-da-fè held at Lisbon on October 16, 1746.

NOTES TO CHAPTER XIII

1 Similarly further East, we find Judeo-Greek, Judeo-Arabic and Judeo-Persian. There was a considerable amount of literature written in the vernacular by the Jews of Spain before the expulsion, but this was largely intended for the gentile world.

2 There were earlier translations in manuscript from the beginning of the eighteenth century. In print, however, Pinto's was preceded only by *The Book of Religion, Ceremonies and Prayers of the Jews*, published in London by an apostate in 1738.

3 Some circumspection had of course to be exercised so as not to arouse feeling in gentile circles. In consequence a considerable number of these works were never published, and are extant only in manuscript.

⁴ Besides this there was a considerable amount of internal apologetic and polemical literature, intended to confute unbelievers like Uriel Acosta or Samuel Prado.

⁵ The version is that of Dean Milman, who has placed it on record that Melo's translation "is one of the finest in any European language" (*History of the Jews*, Book XXX). The view of Menendez Pelayo (*Heterodoxos Españoles*, II, 608–9) is obviously motivated by religious prejudice.

⁶ The Spanish epic *David* by Jacob Uziel, which appeared at Venice in 1630, dedicated to the Duke of Urbino, should be mentioned in this connection, though on the one hand the author was a professing Jew at the time of its publication, and on the other it is not certain that he was of Marrano origin. A further very distinguished Marrano writer who chose biblical subjects was Felipe Godinez, a fashionable preacher as well as dramatist, who was reconciled by the Inquisition at Seville in 1624, though afterwards reinstated in his clerical functions. His case, with those of Antonio Enriques Gomez and Isaac Orobio de Castro, shows the unfairness of Menendez Pelayo in belittling the importance of the Spanish Judaizers at this period.

NOTES TO CHAPTER XIV

¹ This law may be responsible for the curious phenomenon that persons, who afterwards became loyal Jews, lived for some time in London or Amsterdam without joining the community, subsequently visited Portugal and embraced Judaism only several years later.

² Perhaps the most characteristic auto in this respect was that held at Coimbra on May 23, 1660, with 176 penitents. Of these, eighteen were relaxed, including five men and no less than thirteen women.

³ The extent to which the original purity of blood of the Portuguese Marranos had been modified by this period may be realized by the fact that, out of 625 persons convicted in various autos between 1683 and 1746, only 364 were classified as "New Christians," 207 as "partly New Christians," 22 as "Half New Christians," 6 as "Quarter New Christians." 2 as "Old Christians," and the few

remaining by various other gradations (Wolf, *Jews in the Canary Islands*, p. xxvii).

4 In one of these, republished in his *Miscellaneous Tracts*, there is a complete translation of the *Lista* of the persons who appeared in the great Lisbon auto of May 10, 1682. Geddes gives a first-hand account of a certain "New Christian" acquaintance of his whose Catholicism was unimpeachable until he was arrested by the Inquisition, but whose sufferings at its hands turned him into a convinced Judaizer.

5 It may be mentioned that this little work is so able that it was thought worthy of republication in English at London, in 1845, and at Philadelphia in 1860.

6 David Machado de Sequeira, a well-known litterateur of the period and the leading spirit of the little community of Dublin, had come over to London in 1708 for the purpose. He had prepared a letter to send to the King of Portugal to accompany the book; but it was not despatched for fear that it might prejudice the position of the native New Christians. Even before this time, the *Noticias* had been in circulation in London in manuscript.

7 The last person to be burned at Lisbon for Judaizing was the New Christian merchant, Jeronimo José Ramos, of Braganza, who suffered the extreme penalty immediately before the great Earthquake, on January 15, 1755. He had managed to escape, by some means which it has been impossible to trace, in the auto of September 24, 1752, when he had been condemned to be relaxed.

It may be mentioned, for the purposes of comparison, that as late as 1786 the body of a woman condemned and executed for the crime of coining was burned at the Old Bailey in London; while in enlightened France, in 1761, a Jew and a Christian were burned at Nancy, after strangulation, for an alleged offence against the consecrated Sacrament.

8 This measure did not receive anything like unanimous approval in the country. It was actually rumored that Pombal had received in return for it a bribe of half-a-million *cruzados* from the "Jews," as those who benefited by its provisions were still called.

A well-known but apocryphal story recounts how the king was by no means satisfied with the policy of his minister, and intimated that if he had his own way he would make all of the descendants of New Christians wear yellow hats, like their unconverted ancestors. On the next day, Pombal turned up at Court with three of the articles in question: — one for His Majesty, one for himself, and the other for the Inquisitor General.

⁹ The last auto at Lisbon had been held on September 20, 1767, being the 227th anniversary of the first. The last private auto recorded in Portugal was in 1778, but there may have been later instances.

¹⁰ In all, during the reign of Philip V (1700–1746), 1564 heretics are said to have been relaxed and 11,730 otherwise punished — an appalling total, in the century of enlightenment, when the Encyclopedists were flourishing in France and the breath of religious liberty was sweeping throughout Europe. The figures are however gravely suspect. Lea (*History of the Inquisition*, III, 310) speaks of a final recrudescence at Madrid in 1732, when several New Christians were relaxed on the fantastic charge of having scoured and burned an image of Jesus in a house in the Calle de las Infantas. It is obvious that this is the result of some confusion with the events of precisely a hundred years previous, when a number of persons were punished for having performed an identical outrage at Madrid, at a house situated in a road of a similar name. Perhaps the last recorded punishment for Judaizing in Spain was that of Lorenzo Beltran, who appeared at an auto in Seville on March 31, 1799. It is symptomatic that, notwithstanding the heinousness of his offense, his punishment was comparatively slight.

¹¹ See Lea, *History of the Inquisition in Spain*, III, 310. However, as late as 1801, an accusation of Judaizing was made before that tribunal. See Vignau, *Catálogo . . . de la Inquisición de Toledo*, p. 164.

¹² To complete the picture, it should be added that the Portuguese Inquisition, which had survived Pombal's reforms in an emasculated form, was finally abolished on March 31, 1821. That of Goa had been abolished in 1774, was reinstated in 1778, and finally disappeared in 1812. The American Tribunals ended their existence at the same period — Peru and Mexico in 1820, etc.

¹³ Until the nineteenth century was well advanced, notices were displayed in many parish churches indicating which were the *converso* families and warning the faithful not to intermarry with them.

NOTES TO EPILOGUE

[1] Schechter, "An Unfamiliar Aspect of Anglo-Jewish History," in *Publications of the American Jewish Historical Society*, XXV, 72–3.

[2] George Borrow, *The Bible in Spain*, ch. XI.

[3] Fishberg, *The Jews*, p. 161.

[4] The traditional counterpart reads: Blessed art Thou, O Lord, our God, King of the Universe, who has sanctified us with His commandments and commanded us to do . . .

[5] An interesting piece of folk-etymology current amongst the Marranos illustrates this fact in a striking manner, as well as indicating the utter decay of Jewish knowledge amongst them: "*A denominação de judeu vem do facto de nos ajudarmos mutuamente*" (The name *Jew* is derived from the fact that we *assist* one another).

[6] It is significant that a prayer on behalf of their brethren in the dungeons of the Inquisition has remained in their liturgy for the Day of Atonement down to the present day. By a curious coincidence, the Spanish and Portuguese congregations in London, etc. preserve a similar petition for the service on the Eve of Atonement, which was recited down to a few years ago in Portuguese.

[7] This statement does not apply to the Balearic Islands, where the *Chuetas* (as the descendants of the Jews are still called) continue to maintain their own separate, and somewhat despised, existence although they have apparently lost all traces of their ancestral faith. (Some very recent reports contradict this. See above, ch. IV, note 11.)

In the rest of Spain, where after the sixteenth century the crypto-Jewish tradition was never really strong, there are a number of persons who are conscious of Jewish origin, and possibly even a few very vague recollections of Jewish practice; but nothing more. Thus the present writer has been informed of a Spanish country gentleman who kindles a lamp in his cellar every Friday night, without knowing the reason: of families which abstain from pork, etc.

As far as the former Spanish colonies are concerned, the recollections seem to be no stronger. In Mexico, there was published in 1889 a curious periodical named *El Sabado Secreto* (The Secret Sabbath), which appears to have been intended mainly to appeal to persons of Marrano blood. In Southern Chile, near Temuku (according to an article published in *The New Judaea* in 1928), there is still a semi-secret community of "Sabbathist Cabanists," who observe the Sabbath and the Feast of Tabernacles. It is difficult to tell what credence is to be placed in this report. The small group of autochthonous "Mexican" Jews, notwithstanding their romantic legends concerning their origin, are apparently descended from recent converts.

[8] It is a source of gratification to the present writer, which he would like to put on record here, that he was the first person outside Portugal to express himself publicly in favor of a movement to help the Marranos.

[9] The funds for this were provided by the veteran philanthropist, Lucius N. Littauer.

BIBLIOGRAPHY[1]

of some of the more important works used

(i) *General*

H. C. Lea, A History of the Inquisition in Spain, 4 vols., 1906–7.

J. Lucio d'Azevedo, Historia dos Christãos Novos Portugueses, 1921.

J. Mendes dos Remedios, Os Judeus em Portugal, 2 vols., 1895–1928.

H. Graetz, History of the Jews.

M. Kayserling,[2] Geschichte der Juden in Portugal, 1867; Die Juden in Navarra, den Baskenländern und auf den Balearen, 1861.

---

[1] Use has also been made throughout of various manuscripts and pamphlet sources, especially anti-Jewish tracts, records of Inquisitional trials at the State Archives in Lisbon, etc., and "Relations" of the autos-da-fè, as well as the invaluable Hebrew "Responsa" Literature. Recourse should be made to the standard works of reference, particularly *The Jewish Encyclopedia*, for further information about the various persons and places mentioned. Separate mention of various monographs will be made with reference to the chapters in which they are first of special utility, and will not be repeated in connection with other sections on which they may contain equally valuable information.

[2] It is impossible to mention here individually all of Kayserling's very numerous contributions to this subject, some in volume form and some scattered about in various periodicals. But it would be churlish not to pay a tribute to his valuable researches, but for which this work could never have been written. It is my duty to point out, in addition, that my debt to Lea's classical writings is immeasurably greater than the small space which they occupy in this bibliography might lead the reader to suppose.

J. A. Llorente, Historia Critica de la Inquisición de España (frequently translated and re-issued).

M. Menendez y Pelayo, Historia de los Heterodoxos Españoles, 3 vols., 2nd ed., 1929.

S. Asaf, The Marranos of Spain and Portugal in the Responsa Literature (Hebrew), in Zion, Part 5, 1932.

H. J. Zimmels, Die Marranen in der rabbinischen Literatur, Berlin, 1932.

(ii) *Detailed Monographs*

INTRODUCTORY

A. Emanuelson, The Remnant of the Jews, 1929: for the crypto-Jews of Persia, etc.

U. Cassuto, Un' ignoto capitolo di storia ebraica, in Herman Cohen Festschrift, Judaica, Berlin, 1912: for the *Neofiti* of Apulia.
See also L. V. Vitale, Un particolare ignorato di storia pugliese: neofiti e mercanti, Naples, 1926.

I. Abrahams and D. Yellin, Maimonides, Philadelphia, 1903: for the Almohadan persecution.

S. Katz, The Jews in the Visigothic and Frankish Kingdoms of Spain and Gaul, Cambridge, 1937.

CHAPTER I

J. Amador de los Rios, Historia de los Judios de España, vol. II, 1876.

F. Baer, Die Juden im christlichen Spanien, vol. I pt. 1, 1929; pt. 2, 1936.

A. Farinelli, Marrano: storia di un vituperio (for the derivation of the word).

N. Lopez Martinez. Los judaizantes y la Inquisición, 1954.

Chapter II

J. Amador de los Rios, Historia de los Judios de España, vol. III, 1876.

M. Serrano y Sanz, Origenes de la dominación española en America, vol. I, 1918.

W. T. Walsh, Isabella of Spain, 1931.[3]

Chapter III

A. Herculano, Historia da origem e estabelecimento da Inquisição em Portugal, English translation, 1926.

A. Baião, A Inquisição em Portugal e no Brasil, 1921.

Chapter IV

E. N. Adler, Auto de Fé and Jew, 1908.

Idem, Documents sur les Marranes d'Espagne et de Portugal sous Philippe IV (in Revue des Études Juives, vol. XLVIII, et seq.).

(V. Vignau), Catalogo...de la Inquisición de Toledo, 1903.

L. Wolf, Jews in the Canary Islands, 1926.

J. de la Puerta Vizcaino, La sinagoga balear, 1857.

A. Lionel Isaacs, The Jews of Majorca, 1936.

B. Braunstein, The Chuetas of Majorca, 1936.

Chapter V

M. Kayserling, Ein Feiertag in Madrid, 1859.

J. del Olmo, Relacion Historica de Auto General de Fee que se celebró en Madrid este Ano de 1689 con assistenci del Rey, 1680. (The most famous of the

---

[3] This work is important, psychologically if not historically, as a twentieth-century restatement of the standards and prejudices of the fifteenth.

"relations" of the various great Autos which were periodically printed, and cited as characteristic. Kayserling's little work mentioned above is based upon this).

D. Fergusson and C. Adler, Trial of Gabriel de Granada by the Inquisition in Mexico, 1642–1645 (Publications of the Jewish Historical Society of America, vol. VII, 1899: The only complete Inquisitional trial available in English).

A. J. Moreira, Historia dos principaes actos e procedimentos da Inquisição em Portugal.

Chapter VI

J. Lucio d'Azevedo, A Evolução do Sebastianismo: in Arquivo Historico Portugueses, X (1916). On Luis Dias and his companions.

A. J. Teixeira, Antonio Homem e a Inquisição, 1895–1902.

Ramos Coelho, Manuel Fernandes Villareal e o seu processo, 1894.

A. Baião, Episodios Dramaticos da Inquisição Portuguesa, 3 vols., 1919–1937.

Chapter VII

C. Roth, The Religion of the Marranos, in Jewish Quarterly Review, new series, 1931. (The only study devoted to this subject containing full documentation. I am indebted to the Editor for his kind permission to reproduce here substantial portions of it).

Chapter VIII

G. Rosanes, History of the Jews in Turkey (Hebrew).

M. A. Levy, Don Joseph Nasi, 1859.

D. Kaufmann, Gesammelte Schriften, vol. II (1910) (for the Marranos of Ancona, etc., cf. also Revue des Études Juives, vols. XVI, XXXI, LXXXIX).

C. Roth, Ibid., LXXXVIII, LXXXIX, XC (on the Marranos in Venice, Leghorn and Rouen).

C. Roth, The House of Nasi: Dona Gracia, 1947; The Duke of Naxos, 1948.

T. Malvezin, Histoire des Juifs à Bordeaux, 1875; also important subsidiary studies by Cirot, 1909–1920.

M. Léon, Histoire des Juifs de Bayonne, 1893.

M. Grünwald, Portugiesengräber auf deutcher Erde.

U. Cassuto, Elementos para a historia dos judeus portugueses de Hamburgo (and other studies).

Chapter IX

S. Ullman, Histoire des Juifs en Belgique.

J. A. Goris, Études sur les marchands méridionales à Anvers, 1925.

J. S. da Silva Rosa, Geschiednis der Portugeesche Joden te Amsterdam, 1925.

S. Seeligman, Bibliographie en Historie, 1927; and other writings by the same.

I. Prins, De Vestiging der Marranen in Noord-Nederland in de XVIe eeuw, 1927.

C. Gebhardt, Uriel Acosta, 1922.

J. Zwarts, Hoofdstukken uit de geschiednis der Joden in Nederland, 1929, and other studies.

J. Hillesum, Uri-ha-Levi 1904, from the Centraal Blad
v. Isr. in Nederland; and other studies.

H. I. Bloom, Economic Activities of the Jews of Amsterdam in the 17th and 18th centuries, 1937.

Chapter X

L. Wolf, Menasseh ben Israel's Mission to Oliver Cromwell, 1901.

M. Gaster, History of the Ancient Synagogue of the
Spanish and Portuguese Jews, 1901.

Transactions of the Jewish Historical Society of England
18 vols., 1894 et seq.

C. Roth, Menasseh ben Israel, Philadelphia, 1934. History of the Jews in England, Oxford, 1941.

A. M. Hyamson, The Sephardim of England, London,
1952.

Chapter XI

H. C. Lea, The Inquisition in the Spanish Dependencies,
1908.

M. Kayserling, Christopher Columbus and the Participation of the Jews in the Spanish and Portuguese
Discoveries, 1894 (from the German).

J. T. Medina, Historia de la Inquisición de Lima; de
Chile; de la Plata; de Cartagena de las Indias; en
las Islas Filipinas, 6 vols., 1887–1899.

Publications of the American Jewish Historical Society,
48 vols., 1893, et seq.

G. Garcia, La Inquisición de Mexico (Reprint of original
"Relations"), 1906.

Leite, S., Os Judeus no Brasil, 1923.

Los Judios en la Nueva España, Publicaciones del
archivo general de la nacion, XX, 1932.

A. Toro, La familia Carvajal, 2 vols., 1944.

B. Lewin, Martires e conquistadores judíos en la America hispana, c. 1950, and numerous other studies.

CHAPTER XII

I. da Costa, Israel and the Gentiles (from the Dutch), 1850. [Now available in Noble Families among the Sephardic Jews . . . with some account of the Cafadose Family, by G. B. Brewster and C. Roth, London, 1936.]

M. Lemos, Ribeiro Sanches, 1911, and other studies by the same author on other Marrano physicians, such as Amato Lusitano, J. de Castro Sarmento, etc.

A. da Silva Carvalho, Um celebre medico Portugues (João Baptista Silva), 1928; Garcia d'Orta, 1934; and other studies on Marrano physicians by the same author.

CHAPTER XIII

M. Kayserling, Sephardim: Romanische Poesien der Juden in Spanien, 1859.

Idem: Biblioteca Española-Portugueza-Judaica, 1890.

M. B. Amzalak, As operações de bólsa segundo Iosseph de la Vega, 1926.[4]

CHAPTER XIV

J. Lucio d'Azevedo, Historia de Antonio Vieira, 2 vols., 1918–20.

Jordão de Freitas, O Marques de Pombal e o Santo Oficio da Inquisição.

[4] I cite this as an example of the very numerous contributions to the subject of the literature of the Marranos by this scholar.

Epilogue

S. Schwarz, Os Christãos-Novos em Portugal no século XX, 1925 (an English abstract in the Menorah Journal, XII (1926), pp. 138–149, 283–297).

L. Wolf, Report on the Marranos or Crypto-Jews of Portugal, 1925.

C. Roth, L'Apôtre des Marranes, Paris, 1929 (impressions of a personal visit).

N. Slouschz, The Marranos in Portugal (Hebrew), 1932.

[P. Goodman] Marranos in Portugal; survey by the Portuguese Marrano Committee, London, 1938.

INDEX

409